the Louisiana new Garde©

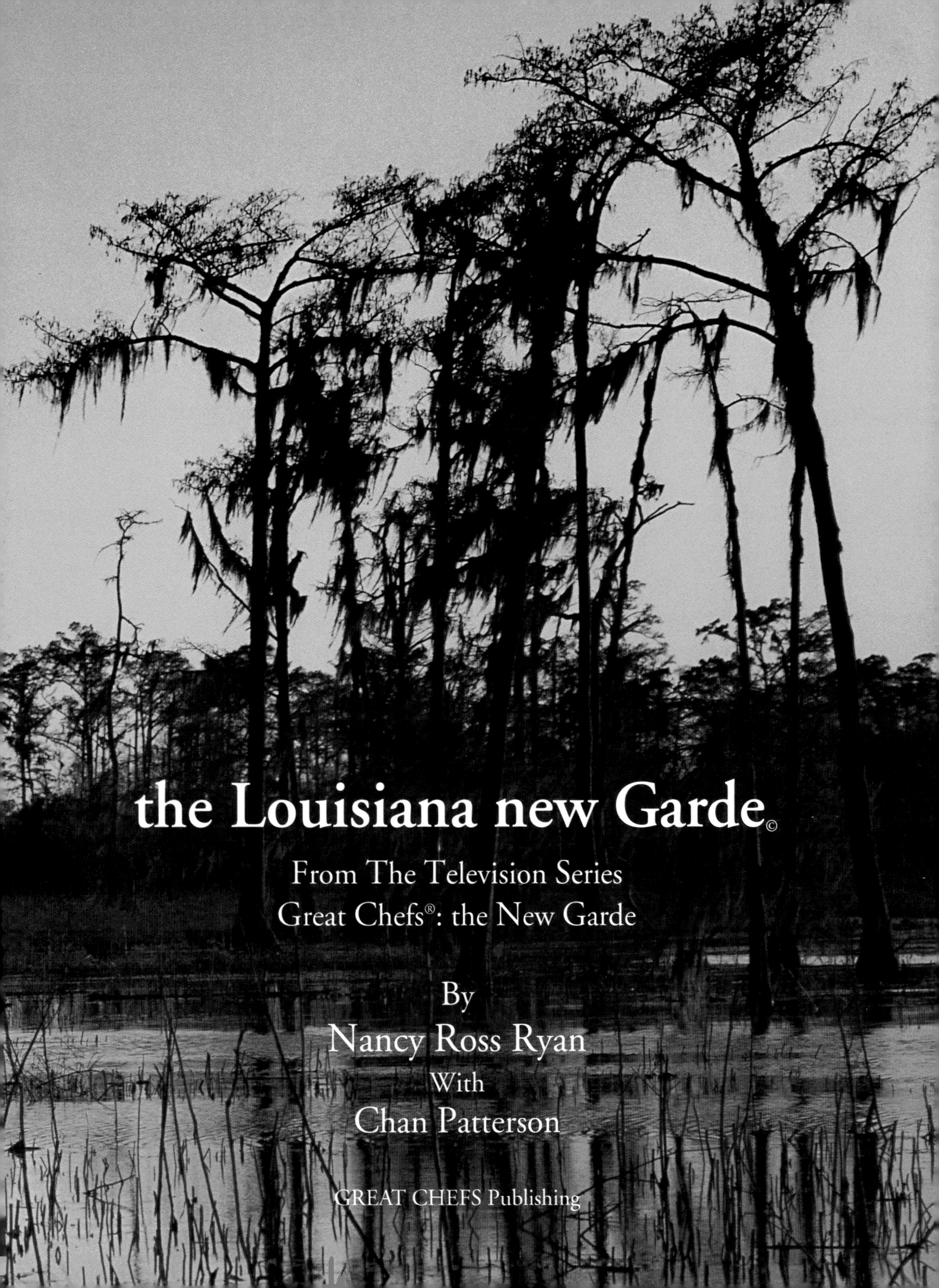

the Louisiana new Garde©

From The Television Series
Great Chefs®: the New Garde

By
Nancy Ross Ryan
With
Chan Patterson

GREAT CHEFS Publishing

Other Great Chefs
Companion Cookbooks
are available

Great Chefs of New Orleans I & II
Great Chefs of San Francisco
Great Chefs of Chicago
Southwest Tastes
Great Chefs of the East

Cover: Caramelized Salmon with Mirliton Slaw, NOLA,
New Orleans
Back cover: Roasted Chicken Stuffed with Crawfish Country
Rice, Gabrielle, New Orleans (top), and
Twists of Sorbet, Windsor Court Hotel,
New Orleans (bottom)

Published by Great Chefs Publishing
G.S.I., Inc.
For Information:
P.O. Box 56757
New Orleans LA. 70156
1-800-321-1499
Printed in China
1st printing

**Library of Congress Cataloging in
Publication Date**

Nancy Ross Ryan
with Chan Patterson
Great Chefs: the Louisiana new Garde

Library of Congress Catalogue Card Number 94-76410
Includes index:
     1. Cookery in American
        I. Great Chefs: the Louisiana new Garde
        II. title
ISBN   Hardbound 0-929-714-63-6
         Softbound 0-929-714-64-4

Notice: The information contained in this book
is true and complete to the best of our
knowledge. All recommendations are made
without any guarantees on the part of the
author or Great Chefs Publishing. The author
and publisher disclaim all liability in connection with use of this
information.

Great Chefs Trademark
Reg. U.S. Pat. Off. and in
other Countries

TABLE OF CONTENTS

APPETIZERS

ENTRÉES

L ouisiana's New Garde represents not so much a passing of the torch as the lighting of several new ones. The young chefs whose recipes grace this book are the next wave behind those who appeared in the first Great Chefs television series. Indeed, Susan Spicer and Dennis Hutley assisted as sous-chefs on those tapings shot more than ten years ago.

It makes me feel (in the words of a popular forties song) that I'm my own grandpa. Aside from the melancholy reminder of time's relentless march, it shows that although the Great Chefs TV format is more or less unchanged, the chefs who are in it are not.

As Julia Child has pointed out, most of the best of the new generation of chefs are still grounded in the classical French culinary rubric. But a dozen years and hundreds of chefs later there are some subtle changes. For example, one is far more likely to encounter women now, and not only as sous-chefs or at the pastry station, but running the show. Also, a good many of today's young chefs come out of the formal programs of the Culinary Institute of America in Hyde Park, New York; the New England Culinary Institute in Montpelier, Vermont; Johnson & Wales University in Providence, Rhode Island, and the French Culinary Institute in Manhattan, to name a few. Perhaps as a result of this, young American chefs often exhibit considerable business acumen, not to mention media savvy. After all, starting and keeping a restaurant afloat is not a walk in the park. When the young Philadelphia chef Jack MacDavid was asked why he got into the restaurant business, he deadpanned, "Ignorance."

Finally, current young American chefs actively seek and utilize high-quality fresh local products, often going directly to farms to find them. Furthermore, they have no compunction about using a rainbow of ethnic gestures in their cooking.

Having offered these general observations that really apply to all regions of the country, I now turn to Louisiana. Media-fueled food fads are a dime a dozen in the states today. About the time a Montana housewife discovers that arugula is a salad green, she's got to scare up some miso. But Louisiana cookery is not particularly trendy (unless a fad can take more than two hundred years to develop). Its deep culinary roots are today a tangle of Creole and Cajun cooking which, in turn, grew out of several ethnic heritages. Thanks to years of isolation, Louisiana's food was (and to a large degree still is) unique.

Although this is reflected in the cooking of the chefs in this book, they are not enslaved to the Cajun-Creole tradition. Sometimes they use it as a point of departure, as with David McCelvey's Mirliton Slaw, Emeril Lagasse's Andouille Cheesecake and André Begnaud's Wild Mushroom Bread Pudding. Then a Cajun favorite is faithfully executed by Gigi Patout: Cajun Smothered Duck and Maque Choux. In other instances, the traditions are ignored, as in Susan Spicer's Lamb with Couscous or John Neal's Summer Soup.

In short, the dishes in this book are as diverse as the chefs themselves, but they can all be pulled off in the home kitchen. As for me, when I go into a restaurant kitchen these days, I watch the sous-chefs, whom I will, no doubt, be working with around the turn of the century.

JOHN BEYER
Producer/Director
GREAT CHEFS TELEVISION PRODUCTIONS

No editor is an island—to paraphrase John Donne—and when I think about all the people who made this book possible, and without whom it would have been impossible, I think with thanks of the following:

The young Louisiana chefs who gave so generously of their time, their talent, and their recipes.

Chan Patterson, director of Everyday Gourmet cooking school, who transcribed and tested their all of recipes for the home kitchen.

John Shoup, executive producer of *Great Chefs, the New Garde*, for having the vision to see that Louisiana's regional cuisine is evolving and redefining itself, and for having the dedication to explore it.

John Beyer, Great Chefs producer-director, who has fearlessly filmed two successive generations of Louisiana chefs—and will undoubtedly be focusing in on the third.

Bill Rice and Daniel Mann, the first for his food for thought, the second for his thoughts on food and wine.

Eric Futran, photographer *sine qua non*, whose photographs bring Lousiana's food to life.

Larry Escudier, who created the grand design for the book—and executed it down to the smallest detail.

Mimi Luebbermann, whose unswerving editorial guidance piloted the project—through all kinds of weather—safely to shore.

Cybil Curtis, assistant to the executive producer, and Linda Nix, director of publicity, "Great Chefs," who tracked down and kept track of chefs, menus, and photographs, and tied up a thousand loose ends.

NANCY ROSS RYAN
Chicago, Illinois

By William Rice

There are, for me, only three cities in the world that a food-lover can approach with singleness of purpose and unrestrained joy. They are Hong Kong, Lyon, and New Orleans. My sole reason for visiting each of them is to eat, and my joy is caused by the certainty that I will do so with considerable pleasure and satisfaction.

There are other great—perhaps greater—eating cities, but one cannot be so single-minded in Paris or New York or even Tokyo. There are too many distractions, too many other reasons to be there. But in my favorite dining destinations no one questions the obsessive quest for a great restaurant, a memorable market, or even a spontaneous streetside snack, because the local population is totally captivated by food, too. Ask a native for directions to a restaurant, and you are likely to walk away with a recommended menu as well.

I revisit the monuments to dining in each of these cities for solace and continuity, but also scramble like a child on his first Easter egg hunt to find the food shop or neighborhood family restaurant someone has mentioned or written about.

Happily, Nancy Ross Ryan has provided the impetus to scramble once again to taste the food of Louisiana's new garde from the Great Chefs television series. Thanks to the innovative skills and creative energy of this talented and personable group of chefs, flocks of food-lovers will be making pilgrimages to the Crescent City and the rest of the Bayou State well into the new century.

Why? Because, as you will discover for yourselves when you re-create the recipes presented in this book, it is never enough for a Louisiana chef to make a dish that is merely proper or even passably pleasing. As in Lyon, and Hong Kong, there is more at stake. He or she is no mere craftsman, but an alchemist, happiest working with fresh, local ingredients and shaping them into something that imparts joy as well as sustenance. The new garde chef cooks for his customers, but also cooks with momma and generations of chefs who have gone before in mind. And like those who have gone before them, the new garde is making food alive with flavor that stays in your taste memory long after the meal has ended.

Ryan, one of the best and most perceptive observers of the national restaurant scene, vividly brings the culinary history of Louisiana up to date and adroitly unravels the diverse influences of this country's most distinctive regional cuisine.

The new garde chefs are reaching farther afield for technique and even ingredients (note Mike Fennelly's Asian Napoleon and Michelle Nugent's Tuna with Japanese Noodles and Soy Dipping Sauce), but the core of Louisiana cooking remains rooted in home-grown Creole and Cajun traditions.

I would be unfaithful to history, however, if not to myth and legend, if I did not point back to a period in the 1960s and seventies when culinary Louisiana appeared trapped in amber. The restless creativity and hunger for change that were igniting the new American cuisine movement in California were missing in the Crescent City.

Complacency reigned, and its Krewe was made up of journeymen chefs, smug owners, and local diners who, despite obvious political and social changes, were all too happy to have yesterday, today and tomorrow blur together on the unchanging menus of their favorite restaurants.

Ryan recognizes the seminal role played by chef Paul Prudhomme in changing the status quo. He surely deserves such recognition, but would, I am sure, insist it be shared with Ella Brennan, who was his mentor during the period in the mid-seventies when they worked together at Commander's Palace. They formulated a fresher, lighter approach to Louisiana cooking that inspired others to innovate. When Prudhomme moved on, Miz Ella recruited the irrepressible Emeril Lagasse, a Rhode Island Yankee with a college degree in cooking. When Lagasse, in his turn, left to found Emeril's and, more recently, NOLA, Jamie Shannon stepped in to keep Commander's at the top of the heap. Meanwhile, Miz Ella and a slew of Brennan relatives have continued to break new ground there, at Mr. B's, the Palace Café and Bacco.

In recent years, I've crisscrossed Cajun country with my friend, chef Pat Mould of the Hub City Diner in Lafayette, a worthy member of the new garde team, to watch local craftspeople produce Louisiana's unique boudin and andouille sausages. I've been served oysters so fresh they wriggle, especially when you anoint them with a drop or two of Tabasco sauce. I've heard chefs talk with increasing commitment about the need to obtain the freshest of local vegetables as well as seafood and to protect the taste and texture of these ingredients by shorter and more careful cooking.

I've also found Louisiana diners increasingly responsive to the cooking of this new garde. Meanwhile, the economic downturn became a force for change as well. Instead of large, costly landmark restaurants, investors began to finance small, distinctive, frequently chef-owned operations such as Brigsten's, Bayona, and Gabrielle.

A memorable passage in *The Picayune Original Cookbook*, first published in 1900 by the New Orleans newspaper, discusses the contributions of immigrant French and Spanish chefs to the local cuisine in the last century: "After awhile they borrowed ideas from one another. After a still longer while the people of the New World, who learned from them, adapted what they learned to their needs and to the materials they had at hand.

"The result was beyond speech."

It is still.

Louisiana Chefs: The New Garde

Louisiana cooking! In all the world, there's nothing even remotely like it. It's sophisticated but not formal, complex but not complicated, richly traditional but not hidebound. Above all else, it is the embodiment of lagniappe (pronounced "lah-nyahp"), a Southern Louisiana word meaning "a little something extra." In Louisiana cooking that little something extra is flavor: big, bold, sensational.

Louisiana made culinary history in 1979, first by waking up America to a long-neglected heritage of great regional food and, second, by jump-starting American tastebuds with high-voltage Cajun seasoning. Once again, Louisiana is making food history with a new generation of Louisiana chefs, whose innovative but accessible cookery and signature recipes are featured on the following pages. These new garde chefs are taking Louisiana cookery beyond Cajun and Creole, to a new dimension.

THE OLD GARDE

Old garde Louisiana chefs were hardly stuffy, if Paul Prudhomme is any example. A charismatic missionary with a thousand-watt smile, chef Prudhomme carried the Cajun-Creole gospel throughout the land and put Louisiana on America's culinary map. Before he and his wife (the late K Hinrichs) opened K-Paul's Louisiana Kitchen in New Orleans in 1979, Louisiana's Creole-Cajun cookery was familiar only to Louisiana natives, who took it for granted, and to tourists, who tasted it only during their Louisiana trips. Natives grew up with the bounty of land and sea, and cooked Louisiana's distinctive regional fare according to their custom—Creole or Cajun, country- or city-dweller—and their means—rich or poor.

When it comes to cities, although Baton Rouge is the state capital, the port city of New Orleans is the culinary capital where tourists have always come to celebrate Mardi Gras, listen to Dixieland, and to eat and drink in the city's great French Quarter and Garden District restaurants. Until recently, they left with great memories but without taking anything—except perhaps pralines, cans of coffee with chickory and boxes of beignet mix—back home to enrich their own tables.

Although interest in Louisiana-style cookery was undoubtedly growing, it was Prudhomme who captured the imagination of the nation and focused attention on Cajun-Creole food. K-Paul's, his unpretentious, no-reservations restaurant with communal seating, soon sprouted around-the-block waiting lines and was featured in magazines and newspapers, and on television both here and abroad. In May of 1983, Prudhomme cooked Louisiana food for the historic Economic Summit Meeting in Williamsburg, Virginia. Later that year, he took K-Paul's on the road and operated the restaurant in San Francisco for two months, causing a national sensation. (That same year the first Great Chefs television series, *Great Chefs of New Orleans*, took viewers into the kitchens of thirteen other great chefs of New Orleans.)

With the publication of his first cookbook, *Chef Paul Prudhomme's Louisiana Kitchen* in 1984 (New York: William Morrow), Americans realized they no longer had to wait for a trip to New Orleans; they could cook jambalaya, etouffée and gumbo at home. Suddenly crawfish (called "crayfish" outside Louisiana), red beans, dirty rice, and bread pudding appeared on restaurant menus from coast to coast.

So did blackened redfish, soon joined by blackened tuna, blackened shrimp, blackened sea scallops, blackened chicken breast, blackened pork chops, blackened steak and blackened anything-the-chef-could-lay-hands-on. Blackening (cooking butter-dipped, spice-coated food in a white-hot cast iron skillet) became a bona fide fad. During its heyday in the mid- to late-1980s, it was responsible for smoking up kitchens from Maine to California and charring beyond recognition tons of seafood, poultry, and meat.

Like most fads, it is hard to explain. For a while, blackened redfish was the most popular dish at K-Paul's Louisiana Kitchen. But there is only one recipe in Prudhomme's cookbook for blackened redfish among more than two hundred for traditional Louisiana dishes and new variations, all of which are based on Prudhomme's personal history as a Cajun, and his knowledge of the cultural history of Creole cooking. Fortunately, fascination with blackening faded. Just as fortunately, interest in the roots of Louisiana cookery grew.

REGIONAL ROOTS

It is a useful simplification to say that traditional Louisiana cooking has two great branches: Cajun and Creole.

Cajun is the more rustic, heartier, spicier of the two. It is the cooking of the French refugees from Acadia (Nova Scotia), who settled in southern Louisiana in 1755 after the British conquest drove them from Canada. These Acadians had originally come from southern France to Canada (in the 1600s), bringing with them the flavorful country cooking styles of southern France. When the Acadians (some say Cajun is a corruption of Acadian) migrated to Louisiana, they settled not in cities but in the country, where they returned to their traditions of fishing, hunting, and farming.

Louisiana's natural resources amplified their cooking, turning up the decibels on seasonings and increasing the number of ingredients. The native American Choctaws made filé powder from ground dried sassafras leaves, and the Cajuns used it to flavor and thicken stews. Bay laurel leaves and fiery hot peppers grew wild. Louisiana's location, on the Gulf of Mexico and at the mouth of the Mississippi river, provides a combination of fish and shellfish—from saltwater, fresh-water lakes and streams, and brackish coastal waters—that is staggering. Add to that a subtropical climate with a long growing season for fruits and vegetables, and marshlands teeming with game birds, and the result is an abundant natural larder. Cajuns also smoked and cured meats, creating the popular andouille sausage and tasso ham.

Creole cooking, on the other hand, is closer to French classical cuisine, more restrained in seasoning, more refined in presentation, more reliant on sauces and French cooking techniques. However, Creole cooking was also influenced by the Spaniards, Africans and Native Americans, so its flavors are every bit as vibrant, if not as explosive, as those of Cajun cookery. Italian immigrants added southern European flavors to New Orleans's cookery, and Yugoslavians from Dalmatia on the Adriatic Sea became great oyster cultivators and harvesters. Because New Orleans was a port city, trade with the West Indies, Cuba and Mexico added sugarcane, tropical fruits, vegetables and spices to the Creole pantry.

The city was settled by the French in 1718, became Spanish in 1762, French again around 1800, and American in 1803 with the Louisiana Purchase. Louisiana was admitted into the Union in 1812. At the outbreak of the Civil War, half the state's population was black. Before the Civil War, African-American cooks contributed their methods of slow-cookery, and such crucial ingredients as okra—called *gombo* in Africa—to the rich stew of New Orleans cookery.

After the Civil War, the contribution of black cooks to Creole cuisine was even greater. In 1885, there was a Creole cultural revival in New Orleans, the first two Creole cookbooks were published (*The Christian Women's Exchange Creole Cookery Book*, and *La Cuisine Creole*, by Lafcadio Hearn), and Creole cuisine became all the rage. According to Rima and Richard Collin in *The New Orleans Cookbook* (New York: Alfred A. Knopf, 1975), "In wealthy New Orleans homes, most of the older cooks were blacks, whose ancestors had contributed some of the earliest important Creole dishes, such as gumbo. These blacks had inherited a love of spicy food and were adept at preparing the old dishes; now they were encouraged by their employers to follow the 'new' fashion. Frequently, when wealthy New Orleanians dined out, they would taste a dish they liked and then transmit it to their black cooks at home. Black cooks moved freely from job to job, in homes, boardinghouses, and cafes, cooking vigorous versions of favorite local specialties; their skill was the most important thread of continuity in the fabric of Creole cuisine."

Creole cuisine was served forth in splendor in elegant hotels and restaurants, some of which still operate today. (The Monteleone Hotel was founded in 1886 and still operates under the fourth generation of the same family. Antoine's restaurant was founded in 1840, Galatoire's in 1905, and both are still family-owned and operated. And although Arnaud's is no longer under family ownership, it is entering its seventy-sixth year of fine dining.)

Some of the great traditional dishes of Creole fine dining are also the richest, sending shudders up our nutritionally-correct spines. Ponder the calories in:

- Oysters Rockefeller (named for the richness of the sauce, containing 1/2 pound of butter per four servings)
- Eggs Sardou (poached eggs with creamed spinach, artichoke hearts, and hollandaise)
- Shrimp rémoulade (bathed in a highly seasoned, paprika-pink mayonnaise)
- Pompano en papillote (fish cooked in parchment in a double-bound sauce of cream, egg yolk, flour, and butter)
- Trout meunière (deep-fried or pan-fried trout with a brown butter sauce)
- Brabant potatoes (twice-fried potatoes that are then oven-baked in butter)
- Desserts such as Bananas Foster (bananas sautéed in sugar and butter, flambéed in rum and liqueur, then topped with ice cream); flaming crêpes, pecan pie, and bread pudding.

But fine dining was not alone in its tradition of richness. Cajun cookery developed its own specialties, including:

- Cochon du lait (roast suckling pig larded with garlic, seasoned with black and hot red peppers, and anointed with oil)
- Andouille (hot, garlicky pork sausage)
- Fried catfish (peppery, cornmeal-crusted, and deep-fried)
- Chicken maque choux (smothered pan-fried chicken, fresh corn, ripe tomatoes, celery, and onions in a concentrated chicken stock)
- Couche-couche (cornmeal-and-water batter that is either pan-fried slowly in a cast iron skillet and served with cane syrup as a breakfast cereal, or else deep-fried as fritters)
- Chicken and sausage filé gumbo (sausage, ham, and chicken cooked with a flour-fat roux) Traditionally, Cajun roux (the browned fat-flour mixture used to thicken and flavor stews) was made not with oil but with lard.

The boundaries between Cajun and Creole cookery blurred in boardinghouses, cafes, and home kitchens where pots were simmering with jambalayas, gumbos, and etouffées, and, every Monday, red beans and rice. (Some say this dish grew out of a need to use up Sunday dinner's ham bone; others that the rice helped absorb the alcohol left over in the bloodstream from weekend revelry; still others insist that it was a convenient slow-cooking dish that tended itself on washday: Monday.)

New Orleans street food is in a category all its own:

- Calas (deep-fried, raised rice cakes)
- Beignets (powdered sugar-dusted rectangular doughnuts still served in the French Market with cafe au lait)
- Muffuletta, an Italian sandwich created in the first part of the twentieth century from a round Italian bread loaf, split and filled with cured meats, cheese, and an inimitable olive "salad" mixture of chopped green and black olives, pickled Italian vegetables, olive oil, garlic, oregano, and parsley.
- The po' boy sandwich, which comes with its own choice of legends. This ubiquitous South Louisiana sandwich is made (always!) with French bread and stuffed with roast beef and gravy, or fried seafood, andouille or other sausages, meatballs and even potatoes. According to one version of its origins, it was created at a New Orleans bar as a Depression sandwich big enough to fill the stomachs of hungry longshoremen, but cheap enough for the poor to afford. A more colorful legend claims it was a pourboire ("for drinking," the French word for a tip) sandwich that husbands and lovers picked up on their way home after a long night of imbibing to appease the wrath of their waiting women.

REGIONAL RENAISSANCE IN THE EIGHTIES

The new American cuisine movement, which was spearheaded in the mid-seventies by such then-young American chefs as Larry Forgione, Bradley Ogden and Jeremiah Tower—to name a very few—preceded by a few years the renaissance in American regional cuisine. Both culinary movements emphasized American chefs cooking American (as opposed to French) dishes, using primarily American ingredients. But there were subtle differences. The new American cuisine used French culinary techniques, even as it declared its independence from the tyranny of French cuisine.

The new American regional cuisine often incorporated local, homespun cooking techniques—such as iron-pot cookery, barbecuing, and stewing—adapting them to the professional kitchen. New American cuisine favored fine dining. For example, Jeremiah Tower was inspired by reading *The Epicurean* written by Charles Ranhofer, who, in the late 1800s was chef of Delmonico's New York. (This encyclopedic 1,183-page fine-dining cookbook was completed in 1893, and published in 1920 by *The Hotel Monthly Press*, Evanston, Illinois.) The new American regional cuisine was more likely to update hand-written "receipts" for biscuits, cornbread, pot pie, and stews from somebody's grandmother.

Louisiana was the epicenter of the renaissance in American regional cuisine. In rediscovering and reviving its own regional food, Louisiana launched a renaissance of regional cookery across the country in the 1980s, paving the way and setting the stage for chefs in other regions who were already exploring their culinary roots. Soon, new Southwestern cookery began taking its show on the road, and America's tastebuds began to sizzle with fiery chilies. And once again, a regional culinary technique became fad as American restaurant and home grills caught fire—sometimes quite literally—from the red-hot burning Mesquite wood indigenous to the Southwest. (In 1987, the TV series *Great Chefs of the West*, featuring traditional and new Southwestern cookery and chefs, was produced, and the companion cookbook, *Southwest Tastes* by Ellen Brown, was published [New Orleans, Great Chefs Publishing, 1987].)

The decade of the eighties was an American regional renaissance where innovative chefs in the Southwest, Midwest, Northeast and other regions began to research recipes, explore culinary roots, revive traditonal regional dishes and update them by making them lighter.

BEYOND CAJUN AND CREOLE

Heavy fats and roux are scarce in the cooking of the new garde Louisiana chefs. But lightness is neither the only nor the main change taking place in Louisiana cookery today.

If the eighties saw a renaissance in regional cookery, the nineties are witnessing a revolution: cooking without boundaries. Louisiana cookery has traveled beyond its state borders to cities in other regions and established itself in successful restaurants. (In 1993, for example, New York City alone had nine Cajun-Creole restaurants.) It is also expanding its menu boundaries beyond Cajun and Creole food to dishes from other regions, dishes inspired by ethnic cuisines, and—perhaps most exciting—innovative, eclectic dishes created by young chefs.

Some chefs reinterpret traditional dishes creatively, for example, Gigi Patout's Cajun Smothered Duck, Jamie Shannon's Creole Bouillabaisse, and Frank Brigtsen's Blackened Yellowfin Tuna with a Roasted Vegetable Salsa, and Smoked Corn Sauce. Some chefs create new dishes using traditional ingredients, for example, Emeril Lagasse's Shrimp and Andouille Cheesecake with Creole Mustard-Tomato Coulis, and Daphne Macias' Pecan Profiteroles. And some of the new garde chefs invent eclectic dishes using cooking techniques or seasonings from other ethnic cuisines, for example, Mike Fennelley's Asian-inspired Crawfish Spring Rolls with Three-chili Dipping Sauce, and Susan Spicer's Crêpes with Walnut-Cream Cheese Filling.

Whatever their differences in style, the new garde chefs are united in their commitment to seasonal, fresh, top-quality ingredients. Says Jamie Shannon, "About seventy-five percent of our products come from within a one hundred-mile radius. And for American cuisine to grow, we're going to have to support local producers. And be flexible as chefs and customers—and not demand what's not available. The best cuisine is to cook and to eat what's in our own back yard."

That commitment to the integrity of ingredients can be carried into the home kitchen, by using the easy-to-follow recipes in this book. All the recipes have been tested for the home kitchen by Chan Patterson in the kitchens of her cooking school, the Everyday Gourmet, in Jackson, Mississippi.

Once you invite Louisiana's new garde into your kitchen—we guarantee—it will never be the same. Their food has the power to change the way you cook, taste, and above all—a lagniappe—enjoy food and entertaining.

—Nancy Ross Ryan

Note: Although most chefs featured in this book are still to be found in the restaurants listed, a few have changed kitchens. To avoid confusion, their names remain associated with the restaurants where they were filmed for the television series Great Chefs: the New Garde.

Techniques

Professional kitchens differ from home kitchens in two basic ways: equipment and manpower. The professional chef has at his or her command, a battery of specialized equipment and a staff of cooks. The recipes in this book, however, were written with the home cook in mind. All can be prepared easily in the home kitchen, with the help of a few techniques. Following are explanations of some of the special techniques called for in the recipes.

PREPARING ARTICHOKE HEARTS: Soak the artichokes in cool water for ten minutes. Drain, then remove any tough, discolored outer leaves, usually found around the base of the stem end. Cut off the stem. Working in circular fashion around the artichoke, cut off all of the leaf tips with a pair of scissors. With a large, sharp knife cut off the top quarter of the artichoke and discard.

Cook the trimmed artichokes in boiling water to cover, to which 1 or 2 tablespoons of lemon juice or vinegar and $\frac{1}{2}$ to 1 teaspoon of salt have been added. Cook until a knife inserted in the base of an artichoke goes in easily, about 30 minutes. Drain the artichokes, upside down, in colander. When cool enough to handle, peel off all of the artichoke leaves and pull out small purple-tinged core of thin leaves. Use a spoon to scrape out the hairy choke in the center and discard. Trim the edges of the heart.

CLARIFYING BUTTER OR MARGARINE: Always use unsalted butter or stick margarine. Melt the butter or margarine in a saucepan over low heat. Remove from heat and let stand. The milk solids will drop to the bottom, and the clear golden liquid will rise to the top. Pour clear liquids from top into separate container, being careful to leave the milk solids in the pan. Always melt more butter or margarine than the amount of clarified butter or margarine the recipe calls for because the milk solids reduce the yield. Melt $\frac{1}{2}$ cup butter or margarine for a yield of $\frac{1}{3}$ cup clarified.

MAKING CRÈME FRAÎCHE: In a small saucepan, stir 2 tablespoons buttermilk into 1 cup heavy (whipping) cream. Over very low heat, bring to about 80°F, or just enough to take the chill off. Pour into a clean glass container and cover. Let sit at room temperature until the cream is thickened, between 6 to 24 hours, depending on the temperature. Stir well; cover and refrigerate.

MAKING YOGURT CHEESE: Place plain, unflavored yogurt in cheesecloth-lined colander or sieve set over a bowl and let drain for six to eight hours or overnight. When yogurt is thick, place in covered glass container and refrigerate until use.

ROASTING GARLIC: With sharp knife, cut top quarter off head of unpeeled garlic. Rub head with olive oil. Place in baking dish in 350°F oven and roast for 1 hour. Remove from oven. When cool enough to handle, separate cloves from head and squeeze roasted garlic pulp from each.

TOASTING NUTS: Place shelled nuts in large dry skillet on stovetop over low to moderate heat. Cook, while stirring and turning constantly with spoon or spatula, until the nuts are heated through and just beginning to change color. Do not let nuts turn brown. Remove pan from heat immediately and spread the nuts on a large plate or tray lined with paper toweling to cool.

ROASTING AND PEELING PEPPERS AND CHILIES: When handling hot chilies, wear gloves. Place a pepper or chili directly in the gas flame of a stove or under a broiler. Turn with tongs until the pepper or chilies are evenly charred on all sides. Remove from flame or broiler and place in a closed brown paper bag for about 15

Artichoke and Hearts of Palm Salad,
André Poirot, Begue's

Abita Saffron Crêpes with Wild Mushroom and Crab Meat Filling and Caviar Sauce, Christiane Engeran Fisher, Chez Daniel

Sea Scallops with Roasted Red Pepper Sauce,
Robert Krol, Crozier's

minutes, or until cool enough to handle. Remove them from bag one at a time and peel or scrape off skin. After most of the blackened skin is removed, core and seed the peppers or chilies.

PEELING AND DEVEINING SHRIMP: To peel raw or cooked shrimp, with small sharp knife slit through shell between legs from front to back. With fingers, remove shell by peeling off body from slit. The tail shell may be removed as well or left attached.

To devein raw or cooked, peeled shrimp, with small knife, make a shallow slit along the back curve, then pull out the black vein that runs from head to tail section and discard. Rinse deveined shrimp quickly under cold water. Pat dry.

To butterfly raw, peeled shrimp, slice from top or dorsal (curved) side of shrimp down to but not all the way through the ventral (leg) side of shrimp. Spread shrimp open and flatten gently with flat side of knife. Tail shell may be left on or discarded depending on recipe.

STOCKS AND BROTHS: Any home cook who has the desire and the time can make homemade stocks. Recipes for easy chicken, beef, fish, and vegetable stock follow.

An easier way to have a ready supply of all manner of stocks is to purchase condensed frozen stock bases at a quality meat or fish market, store them in the freezer, and reconstitute them as needed according to package directions. Low-sodium stock bases are preferred. When using stock bases, don't salt the dish until it is finished, because the bases, even low-sodium, will add salt to the recipe.

Another alternative is canned low-salt beef, chicken and vegetable broths, which may be diluted with half red or white wine. A convenient substitute for fish or shrimp stock is half bottled clam juice and half white wine. Again, the "don't add salt until the end of cooking warning" applies. Half undiluted beef consommé and half dry red wine is another substitute for demi-glace.

To reduce stocks or broth for a recipe calling for rich or reduced stock or as a substitute for demi-glace, cook over medium heat until the liquid is reduced by half.

EASY CHICKEN BROTH
(Makes approximately 2 quarts)

4 pounds chicken parts (wings, backs, necks, or combination)
1 carrot, peeled, halved
1 medium yellow onion, peeled, halved
1 stalk celery, halved
2 parsley sprigs
4 to 6 white peppercorns
2 quarts water
1 cup dry white wine
1 teaspoon salt

Combine all ingredients in a 6-quart stockpot. Bring to boil. Lower heat. Simmer for 1 to 2 hours, skimming top of fat and foam. Add water if necessary. Remove from heat. Strain stock through fine-meshed sieve lined with cheesecloth into 3-quart bowl. Discard solids. Place bowl with the stock into larger bowl of ice cubes. Stir stock to quicken cooling. When stock is cool, transfer into clean covered containers. Refrigerate or freeze.

EASY BEEF BROTH
(Makes approximately 2 quarts)

5 pounds beef soup bones (shin and marrow)
2 carrots, peeled, halved
2 stalks of celery, halved
1 large yellow onion, peeled, halved
1 clove garlic, unpeeled
1 bay leaf

Tournedos Louis Armstrong,
Armand Jonté, Armand's

2 sprigs parsley
6 black peppercorns
3 quarts water
2 cups dry red wine
2 teaspoons salt

In 8-quart stockpot, combine all ingredients. Bring to boil. Lower heat. Simmer for
3 to 5 hours, skimming top of fat and foam. Add water if necessary. Remove from heat.
Strain stock through cheesecloth-lined fine-mesh sieve into large bowl. Discard solids.
Place bowl with the stock into larger bowl filled with ice cubes or into sink filled with
ice cubes. Stir to hasten cooling. When stock is cool, transfer to clean containers with
lids. Refrigerate or freeze.

EASY FISH STOCK
(Makes approximately 2 quarts)

1 pound bones, heads, tails, and trimmings from white-fleshed, non-oily fish (cod,
    halibut, sole, catfish, etc.)
1 bay leaf
6 white peppercorns
1 medium yellow onion, peeled, halved
2 sprigs parsley
1 stalk celery, halved
2 quarts water
1 cup dry white wine

Combine all ingredients in a 6-quart stockpot. Bring to boil. Reduce heat. Simmer for
1 hour, skimming foam from top. Add water if necessary. Remove from heat. Strain
stock through cheesecloth-lined fine-meshed sieve into large bowl. Place bowl with the
stock into larger bowl filled with ice cubes. Stir to hasten cooling. When stock is cooled,
transfer to clean containers with lids. Refrigerate or freeze.
Note: Avoid using oily fish such as mackerel, bluefish, etc.

EASY VEGETABLE BROTH
(Makes approximately 2 quarts)

2 large carrots, peeled, coarsely chopped
2 celery stalks, coarsely chopped
2 large onions, peeled, quartered
1 lb. mushrooms, stems included, cleaned, chopped
3 garlic cloves, unpeeled
1/2 small head of cabbage, cleaned, chopped
2 parsley sprigs
3 quarts water
2 teaspoons salt

Combine all ingredients in 8-quart stockpot. Bring to boil. Reduce heat. Simmer for
1 to 2 hours, skimming top of foam. Add water if necesary. Strain stock through
cheesecloth-lined fine-mesh sieve into 3-quart bowl. Set bowl with the stock into larger
bowl filled with ice cubes. Stir stock to hasten cooling. Transfer cooled stock into clean
containers with lids. Refrigerate or freeze.

PEELING TOMATOES: With a sharp knife, cut an X on the blossom, not the stem,
end of tomatoes. Using a slotted spoon, place the tomatoes in rapidly boiling water
to cover for about 5 seconds. Lift out and plunge the tomatoes into bowl of ice water.
When the tomatoes are cool enough to handle, lift out with slotted spoon and core the
tomatoes, then slip off skins. Cut each tomato in half and hold upside down over the
sink, shaking the tomato and squeezing it slightly to discard the seeds.

*Filet Mignon with Shiitake Mushrooms and
Cabernet Sauce, and Garlic Mashed Potatoes
with Roasted Onion, Richard Hughes, Pelican
Club*

Flexible First Courses: *Appetizers*

The word grazing was coined in the eighties to describe a major change in the way America ate. From a country committed to three square meals a day, we had become a nation of nibblers and noshers. And instead of having a proper dinner at the proper time, Americans young and old began to eat their main evening meal whenever it suited them, either because of convenience or impulse. And instead of the prescribed number of courses—appetizer, soup or salad, entrée and dessert—Americans began sampling the restaurant menu as if it were a buffet, ordering two or three appetizers, then going straight for dessert, bypassing the entrée altogether.

Grazing encouraged sampling, and sampling encouraged sharing. And a behavior that was considered impolite in previous decades—the passing of plates and the sharing of food when dining out—became widespread restaurant behavior in the eighties and is standard procedure today.

Some of the reasons for our newfound gastronomic freedom are obvious: the increase in the number of women working outside the home and longer work days, and the subsequent decrease in cooking at home and the increase in incidence of eating out. But some of the reasons are less obvious, and foremost among them is the new approach that chefs have taken to the first course on the menu.

The character of first courses changed dramatically in the eighties. Appetizer pastas and pizzas were created in seemingly endless variety. Soups were transformed in the same creative culinary spirit, and *la soupe du jour* became the chef's signature. Chefs brought exciting new flavors and textures to first-course salads by varying the kinds of salad greens; adding poultry, meat, game, seafood and cheeses; creating "designer" salad dressings with top-quality oils and vinegars, and combining hot and cold foods.

The restaurant menu changed as a result: The appetizer section got longer and more interesting. And our happy legacy today is the first course reinvented. Not only is it possible for customers to order several appetizers and call it a meal, chefs actively encourage it, some of them showcasing their appetizer menus by creating sampler plates.

The starter courses that follow offer variety, individuality, and the inimitable flavors of new Louisiana cooking—along with enormous flexibility.

Many of these first courses can be transformed into entrées merely by doubling the recipe, such as Susan Spicer's Grilled Shrimp with Coriander Sauce, and Black Bean Cakes, or Horst Pfeifer's Pecan Wood-smoked Shrimp Quesadillas. And for comfort food at its best, turn Gigi Patout's appetizer Cabbage Rolls into the main course of a hearty dinner.

Many of the following appetizers are admirably suited for brunch, such as Greg Sonnier's Oysters Gabie, Tom Weaver's Shrimp Carrie, Dick Brennan's Crawfish Cakes with Lemon Butter Sauce, and Christiane Engeran Fisher's Abita Crêpes with Wild Mushroom and Crab Meat Filling and Caviar Sauce.

Other appetizers may be served with style at the cocktail hour: Keil Moshier's lovely little baked tomato-cheese French Bistro Tarts, André Poirot's Goat Cheese in Filo Provençal, and Gerard Maras' showstopping, easy-to-prepare, New Orleans Barbecued Shrimp.

And most of the first-course salads can do double duty as entrée salads, which are among today's most popular main courses. Some are simple to prepare, such as Joel Gourio de Bourgonnier's Asparagus with Tomato-Basil Coulis, and Michael Uddo's Prosciutto di Parma Salad. And some are more demanding of the cook—such as Richard Hughes's Quail Salad with Pâté, Baby Greens, Roquefort Cheese, and Caramelized Shallots and Sherry Vinaigrette—but worth every step of the preparation.

(For suggestions on how to combine appetizers and entrées, see "Menus for Entertaining.") ∎

Crawfish Spring Rolls with Three-chili Dipping Sauce, Michael Fennelly, Mike's on the Avenue

PATRICK MOULD
Hub City Diner, Lafayette

Born in Paris and bred in Crowley, Louisiana, at twenty-five Patrick Mould was an ironworker and not entirely happy with his job. "It gives you a decent tan," he says, "and the hours are regular." Then he heard that Lafayette Vocational Technical School was offering, for the first time, a culinary occupational course. "All men in Southern Louisiana know how to cook. We're notorious for that." So, to become a professional chef, he started going to school in the daytime and working in restaurants at night, completing two years of work in one year and graduating first in his class. By taking continuing-education courses from the American Culinary Federation (the largest professional chefs' organization in America), he became a certified executive chef.

After graduation he worked in restaurants in Lafayette, eventually becoming executive chef at Café Vermilionville. He moved to the Café owner's new restaurant, Charley G.'s Seafood Grill and Bar, as executive chef and culinary consultant before opening Hub City Diner in 1990, when he was barely thirty-six.

Mould's culinary talent has been showcased in magazines such as *Town & Country, Cook's, Food and Wine, Louisiana Life*, and *The Chicago Tribune Magazine*. He has cooked on "Good Morning America" for celebrities, and he hosted his own cooking radio show on Lafayette's KPEL, and served as chef-host of "Cajun Country USA" on CBS affiliate television.

But the people Mould most likes to cook for are not celebrities but the everyday folks who come into Hub City to chow down. "We'll do anything to accommodate our customers, be they vegetarians, on a diet—any way of cooking we'll do."

And how does life as a chef compare to life as an ironworker? "Well, being an ironworker was strenuous, but after forty hours I went home. I put a lot more hours into the restaurant, and it's a lot more demanding—but it's ever-changing and I never know what's going to happen next. That excitement is what satisfies me—that and meeting people in different situations."

Mould's recipes in this book are Louisiana Corn and Crab Bisque (first course), Catfish Louisiana (entrée), and Acadian Bread Pudding with Roasted Pecan Rum Sauce (dessert).

Louisiana Corn and Crab Bisque

From Pat Mould of Hub City Diner, Lafayette, LA

Serves 4

There are soups and there are supersoups, such as this corn and crab bisque, rich, unctuous, and unforgettable. Concentrated shrimp stock may be found in the freezer section of well-stocked fish markets. Bottled clam juice may also be substituted, but reduce the salt in the recipe. For an easy three-course lunch, serve this soup with a green salad, a loaf of French bread, and a glass of white wine.

2-1/2 cups (5 sticks) unsalted butter
1/2 cup all-purpose flour
4 ears of corn, shucked
1/4 large onion, chopped
1/4 red bell pepper, seeded, deribbed, and chopped
1/4 green bell pepper, seeded, deribbed, and chopped
1 celery stalk, chopped
1 tablespoon minced garlic
2 cups shrimp stock or bottled clam juice
1/2 cup dry white wine
1-1/2 teaspoons minced fresh thyme, or 1/4 teaspoon dried thyme
3-1/2 cups heavy (whipping) cream
1 tablespoon seasoned salt
1 teaspoon hot sauce
1 pound fresh cooked lump crab meat
16 jumbo crab claws (optional)
3 tablespoons minced fresh parsley
3 tablespoons chopped green onions

For the white roux: Melt 2 cups butter in a medium sauté pan. Add the all-purpose flour and cook over low heat, stirring constantly, for 4 to 6 minutes.

Cook corn in boiling, salted water to cover, until tender. Remove corn with slotted spoon and reserve half of the corn stock. Cut the kernels from the corn cobs.

Melt the butter in 4-quart saucepan. Add the onion, peppers, celery, and garlic, and sauté for 1 minute. Add the shrimp stock or bottled clam juice, white wine, and thyme, and bring to a boil. Add the roux and whisk until thickened. Add the cream and lower heat to a simmer while whisking. Add the seasoned salt, hot sauce, corn and corn stock. Simmer for 3 to 4 minutes. Add the crab meat, optional crab claws, parsley and green onions. Simmer until heated through. Divide among 4 large bowls and serve. ∎

Artichoke and Hearts of Palm Salad

From André Poirot of Begue's, New Orleans, LA

Serves 4

Easy does it in preparing this perfectly beautiful salad that looks a little bit like Mardi Gras confetti. Although the preparation is simple, the result is a show-stopping salad that makes a dramatic first course.

Citrus Vinaigrette
2 tablespoons fresh lemon juice
2 tablespoons fresh orange juice
4 tablespoons red wine vinegar
1/2 cup salad oil
1 tablespoon minced shallot
Salt and pepper to taste
1 teaspoon sugar

Salad
1 cup (3 ounces) quartered white
   mushrooms
6 to 8 cooked artichoke hearts
   (see Techniques)
1 cup sliced or julienned hearts of palm
   (1-16 ounce can)
1 cup julienned peeled carrots
   (about 4 carrots)
4 cups romaine lettuce, leaves separated
   and cut into shreds
16 cherry tomatoes, stemmed and
   quartered

To make the vinaigrette: Whisk all the ingredients together until emulsified.

To make the salad: In a salad bowl, combine the mushrooms, artichoke hearts, hearts of palm, carrots, and 3/4 cup of the citrus vinaigrette. Let sit for 1 hour.

Louisiana Corn and Crab Bisque, Pat Mould, Hub City Diner

Line the rims of 4 plates with the artichoke leaves. In the center of each plate place 1/2 cup of lettuce. Atop this, place one fourth of the marinated vegetable mixture. Garnish with cherry tomatoes and drizzle a little of the remaining vinaigrette over the artichoke leaves. ∎

Prosciutto di Parma Salad, Michael Uddo, G&E Courtyard Grill

Prosciutto di Parma Salad

From Michael Uddo of G&E Courtyard Grill, New Orleans, LA

Serves 4

Among Chef Michael Uddo's great food memories from visits to Italy is one of a large bowl of tender, fresh-from-the-garden greens with extra-virgin olive oil on the side, set out in a hotel lobby for guests to enjoy. He seems to have distilled this memory in the recipe that follows.

2 Belgian endives
1 cup frisée
2 cups mâche
1 head radicchio
3-1/2 ounces prosciutto di Parma, sliced paper thin
2-1/2 ounces Romano cheese
2 tablespoons coarsely ground black pepper
3/4 cup extra-virgin olive oil

Wash, drain, and chill all of the greens. Remove the core from the radicchio, cut into quarters, and chill. Cut the prosciutto into strips, and set aside. Shave the Romano into thin pieces and place in a large salad bowl. Add the greens, radicchio, prosciutto, black pepper, and extra-virgin olive oil. Toss and serve, or arrange on the plate in a radial design with the prosciutto in the center.■

Quail Salad with Pâté, Baby Greens, Roquefort Cheese, and Caramelized Shallots with Sherry Vinaigrette

From Richard Hughes of Pelican Club, New Orleans, LA

Serves 4

So you don't have any duck pâté in the fridge? Don't let that keep you from trying this fabulous dish. Just grill the quails without the pâté stuffing and proceed with the recipe.

Marinade
1/4 cup olive oil
1 tablespoon fresh lime juice
1 tablespoon red wine vinegar
1 tablespoon soy sauce
1 teaspoon minced garlic
1 teaspoon minced shallots
1 bay leaf
1 teaspoon brown sugar
1/2 teaspoon fresh chopped rosemary
1/2 teaspoon fresh chopped thyme
1/4 teaspoon ground nutmeg
1/4 teaspoon ground allspice

4 boned quail
4-1/2 ounces duck liver pâté (optional)

5 tablespoons caramelized shallots and
    Sherry Vinaigrette (recipe follows)
4 cups baby greens
3/4 cup (3 ounces) Roquefort cheese,
    crumbled
Fresh raspberries or blackberries for garnish

To make the marinade: Combine all of the marinade ingredients. Pour into a large non-aluminum container. Stuff each quail with one fourth of the optional pâté. Marinate the quail, covered, in the refrigerator for 4 to 6 hours. Remove from the refrigerator 30 minutes before cooking. Grill the quail on all sides over medium coals for a total of 8 to 10 minutes, or until medium rare. Cut each quail into quarters and set aside.

Caramelized Shallots and Sherry Vinaigrette

Makes 2 cups

4 ounces shallots, peeled (about four)
1/4 cup demi-glace (see Techniques)
1/8 teaspoon salt
1/8 teaspoon black pepper
1 tablespoon chopped fresh sage
1 tablespoon Dijon mustard

1/2 cup dry sherry
1 tablespoon red wine vinegar
1 tablespoon balsamic vinegar
1-1/2 cups extra-virgin olive oil

Preheat the oven to 350°F. Place the shallots in an ovenproof pot and bake until soft and brown, about 10 minutes. Add the demi-glace, salt, and pepper. Place the pot on the stove and cook over medium heat until the mixture is reduced by half, about 5 minutes. Purée in a blender or food processor with the rest of the ingredients (vinaigrette not used may be stored in refrigerator for up to one week).

To serve: Toss the greens with the vinaigrette. Place 1 cup greens in the center of each plate. Divide the crumbled cheese over the greens. Arrange 4 quail quarters on each plate of greens. Garnish with raspberries or blackberries. ∎

Asparagus with Tomato-Basil Coulis

From Joel Gourio de Bourgonnier of Honfleur, New Orleans, LA

Serves 4

Asparagus is one of life's virtuous indulgences: 4 cooked spears have about 15 calories and are packed with vitamins A and C. To ensure freshness, cut the ends from the stalks and stand the asparagus in a couple of inches of cool water until ready to clean and cook. Recipes for asparagus too often fall into one of two extremes: painfully plain (blanched) or fatteningly fancy (with hollandaise sauce, cream, or cheese). This recipe strikes a perfect balance: simply sautéed green asparagus atop a fragrant tomato coulis.

4 minced shallots
10 minced garlic cloves
1/2 cup plus 1 tablespoon olive oil
5 peeled tomatoes (see Techniques)
3/4 cup V8 juice
1 tablespoon chopped fresh parsley
2 tablespoons chopped fresh basil
Salt and freshly ground pepper to taste
1 cup dry white wine
2 tablespoons butter
1 bunch (1-1/2 pounds), asparagus, blanched
Chives cut into 1-inch lengths, minced
    green onions and whole basil leaves for
    garnish

In a skillet, sauté the shallots and garlic in 1 tablespoon of the olive oil for 2 minutes or until soft. Quarter 3 of the tomatoes and add to the garlic and shallots. Add the V8 juice, parsley, and basil. Season with salt and freshly ground pepper. Cook for 5 to 7 minutes over medium heat or until heated through.

Pour the mixture into a food processor or blender. Pour the wine into the pan and cook and stir over medium heat to remove any cooked juices from bottom of the pan. Add this wine to the blender or processor and purée the mixture. With the motor running, add the remaining 1/2 cup olive oil in a slow, steady stream and process for 2 minutes. In a large 10-inch sauté pan, melt the butter and sauté the asparagus for 4 to 5 minutes, or until tender-crisp.

To serve: Cover four plates with coulis. Arrange 5 asparagus in a fan over the coulis. Mince the remaining 2 tomatoes and arrange equal portions at base of the asparagus. Garnish with chives, green onions and fresh whole basil. ∎

Beer-fried Asparagus with Crab Meat and Crawfish in Creole Mustard-Honey Butter

From Kim Kringlie of The Dakota, Covington, LA

Serves 4

Chef Kim Kringlie of The Dakota knows how to make asparagus with a few added calories worth our while. Flavorfully battered and crisply fried asparagus spears are accompanied with an out-of-this-world crab meat and crawfish sauce. This dish could easily be the main course for lunch or brunch, served with a spicy rice pilaf and a glass of beer.

Crab Meat and Crawfish in Creole Mustard-Honey Butter

2 tablespoon olive oil
4 ounces cooked crawfish tail meat
4 ounces fresh jumbo crab meat
1 teaspoon minced garlic
1 tablespoon minced shallots
2 tablespoons diced red bell peppers
1 teaspoon minced fresh basil
1/4 cup dry white wine
1 tablespoon fresh lemon juice
1 tablespoon honey
3 tablespoons Creole mustard
1/4 cup heavy (whipping) cream
2 tablespoons chopped green onions
4 tablespoons cold unsalted butter
Salt, pepper, and cayenne to taste

Beer-fried Asparagus
16 asparagus spears trimmed and cut into
    4-inch lengths
1 egg
1 egg white
1-1/2 cups (12 ounces) beer
1-3/4 cups all-purpose flour
1 teaspoon baking powder
4 cups vegetable oil
Salt, pepper and cayenne to taste

To make the crab meat and crawfish:
Heat the olive oil in a large sauté pan or skillet. Add the crawfish meat, crab meat, garlic, shallots, red peppers, and basil; sauté for 1 minute. Add the white wine, lemon juice, honey, Creole mustard, and cream, and simmer until the sauce is reduced by half. Add the green onions and add the cold butter, 1 tablespoon at a time, stirring constantly until all the butter is dissolved. Season with salt, white pepper, and cayenne. Keep warm.

To make the asparagus: In a medium bowl, mix the egg and egg whites, beer, flour, baking powder, and seasonings. Heat the oil in heavy-bottomed pot to about 325°F. Dip the asparagus into the beer batter and fry in the hot oil until golden brown. Remove the asparagus with slotted spatula and drain on paper towels.

To serve: Place 4 asparagus on each of the 4 plates. Evenly divide the crab and crawfish mixture over the asparagus. ∎

Cabbage Rolls

From Gigi Patout of Patout's, New Orleans, LA

Serves 4 to 6

In Louisiana, when people sit down to eat, they *eat!* This recipe for cabbage rolls could easily serve four as a main dish. It's great for company, because all the preparation comes at the beginning and it tends itself while cooking. It's also a perfect dish to cook ahead and re-heat the following day.

1 large head white cabbage
1 pound ground beef
1 teaspoon salt
1 teaspoon cayenne pepper
1 teaspoon ground black pepper
1/2 teaspoon ground white pepper
4 minced garlic cloves
1/2 cup chopped green onions
1/2 cup chopped fresh parsley
2 cups raw rice
Two 8-ounce cans Rotel tomatoes or
    tomatoes with chili
Two 16-ounce cans tomato sauce
1 cup water

Bring a large kettle of water to a boil. Core the cabbage and place it in the boiling water base-side down. Remove each cabbage leaf with slotted spoon as it comes loose and set aside to drain on paper towel.

In a large bowl, mix together the ground beef, seasonings, garlic, green onions, and parsley. Add the rice and mix well. Form the mixture into cylinders about 2 inches long and 1 inch in diameter. Roll each cylinder in a cabbage leaf, tucking in the ends to seal the stuffing completely. Line the bottom of a Dutch oven or other large, heavy pot with a layer of the remaining cabbage leaves. Layer the cabbage rolls on top. Drain the tomatoes and place them in a large mixing bowl. Break them up with your fingers and stir in the tomato sauce and the water. Pour the tomato mixture over the cabbage rolls and cover with another layer of cabbage leaves. Bring to a simmer over medium-high heat, then reduce the heat to low, cover, and let cook for about 1 hour and 45 minutes. Check occasionally to be sure there is sufficient liquid in the pot. If not, add a little water. To test for doneness, remove a cabbage roll. Taste the rice; it should be tender. Transfer cabbage rolls to plates and serve with tomato sauce from cooking pan. ∎

Eggplant Eloise

From Armand Jonté of Armand's, Waveland, MS

Makes about 8 eggplant slices; serves 8

This is another dish that looks like Mardi Gras on a plate: fried eggplant stuffed with shrimp-crab meat filling, topped with a rosy Choron sauce and garnished with bright green snow peas, carrot and shreds of red cabbage. This dish could also serve as the main course at lunch or brunch.

Beer Batter
2 eggs
1-1/2 cup (12 ounces) beer
1 cup all-purpose flour
Pinch of baking powder
1 tablespoon seafood seasoning
    (see page 41)

Seafood Filling
3 stalks celery
1 small onion
1 small peeled carrot
1 small green bell pepper, seeded, and
    deribbed
2 cloves garlic
4 tablespoons butter
1 cup medium shrimp (30 count),
    shelled, and deveined
3 tablespoons dry white wine
6 ounces fresh cooked crab meat
2 green onions
4 dashes Worcestershire sauce
1 tablespoon seafood seasoning

Eggplant Eloise, Armand Jonté, Armand's

1 eggplant
Seafood seasoning to taste (see page 41)
Flour for coating
Beer batter
Two quarts vegetable oil

Choron Sauce
6 egg yolks
White wine
2 pounds butter, clarified (see Techniques)
Dash Worcestershire sauce
Salt to taste
Cayenne pepper to taste
Juice of 1/2 lemon

Tarragon Reduction:
4 tablespoons minced fresh tarragon leaves
2 tablespoons minced fresh chervil
2 tablespoons minced shallots
4 teaspoons dry white wine
1 teaspoon cracked pepper

In a small sauté pan combine all ingredients and reduce 3 to 4 minutes or until the wine evaporates.

Tomato Reduction:
2 medium tomatoes peeled , seeded, and diced
1 tablespoon dry white wine

Cook tomatoes in wine in a medium skillet for 5 minutes or until softened and most of the liquid is evaporated. Purée the tomatoes and pass through a fine sieve.

To make the beer batter: In a medium bowl, whisk together all of the ingredients until mixture is smooth.

To make the filling: Finely dice the celery, onion, carrot, bell pepper and garlic. Melt 2 tablespoons of the butter in a medium sauté pan or skillet and sauté until tender, about 5 minutes. Add the shrimp, and cook until pink, then add the wine. Add the crab meat, then the remaining butter and green onions. Season with Worcestershire sauce and seafood seasoning.

To make sauce: In a medium saucepan whisk egg yolks over medium heat until thickened, about 3 to 4 minutes. Gradually whisk the warm clarified butter into the egg yolks. Season with Worcestershire, salt, cayenne, and lemon juice. Add tarragon reduction and tomato reduction.

Peel the eggplant and cut into 1-1/4-inch thick crosswise slices. Using a spoon or melon baller, hollow out the center of each eggplant slice. Sprinkle with seafood seasoning and dip in flour, then beer batter. In a large, heavy pot or deep fryer, heat the oil to 375°F and deep fry the eggplant for 3 to 4 minutes, or until golden brown.

To serve: Fill the fried eggplant slices with the seafood mixture and top with the Choron sauce. Garnish with snow peas, shredded red cabbage and carrot.■

Pan-fried Eggplant with Crab Meat, Basil Hollandaise, and Creole Tomato Sauce, Dennis Hutley, The Versailles Restaurant

Pan-fried Eggplant with Crab Meat, Basil Hollandaise, and Creole Tomato Sauce

From Dennis Hutley of The Versailles Restaurant, New Orleans, LA

Serves 6

Here chef Dennis Hutley tops eggplant rounds with a meaty mixture of crab meat. Each plate is garnished with a Creole tomato sauce and basil hollandaise for color and flavor counterpoint. Like Eggplant Eloise, this makes a good centerpiece at lunch or brunch.

Creole Tomato Sauce
1 tablespoon olive oil
1/2 small onion, diced
1/4 green bell pepper, seeded, deribbed, and diced
1 teaspoon chopped garlic
3 tablespoons tomato paste
3 cups diced Creole tomatoes (about 3)
2 cups veal stock or chicken broth
1/2 cup Sauternes (or other sweet white wine)
Salt and white pepper to taste
1 tablespoon arrowroot, dissolved in 1 tablespoon wine or water

Basil Hollandaise
3 large egg yolks at room temperature
1/4 cup dry white wine
Dash of fresh lemon juice
3 large basil leaves, chopped
Salt and pepper to taste
1/2 cup warm clarified butter (see Techniques)

Eggplant
1 large eggplant, peeled and cut into six 1/2-inch thick crosswise slices
Salt and white pepper to taste
Flour for dredging
2 beaten eggs
Cornmeal for dredging
4 to 5 tablespoons olive oil

Crab Meat
2 tablespoons butter
2 tablespoons sliced green onions
1/2 teaspoon minced shallots
1/2 teaspoon minced garlic
1/2 cup brandy
12 ounce fresh cooked crab meat
Salt and pepper to taste
Dash of liquid crab boil

2 tablespoons butter
Fresh green and opal basil leaves for garnish

Maque Choux

From Gigi Patout of Patout's, New Orleans, LA

Serves 6 to 8

If there are vegetarians at the table, this sweetly savory vegetable stew - a traditional Cajun specialty - will melt their hearts. There is one problem: they won't leave any for the other guests.

2 dozen ears corn
1 cup (2 sticks) butter plus more as needed
2 finely chopped onions,
2 large bell peppers, seeded, deribbed, and finely chopped
6 large ripe tomatoes, peeled, seeded, and coarsely chopped
2 teaspoons salt
2 teaspoons ground black pepper
Milk as needed

Shuck the corn. Working with one cob at a time, hold it over a bowl and cut away the kernels, then scrape the cob to release the corn milk.

Melt the butter in a Dutch oven or other large heavy pot over medium-high heat. Add the onions, bell peppers, and tomatoes, and sauté until the onions are translucent, about 5 minutes. Stir in the salt and pepper, then add the corn kernels and corn milk and stir well. Reduce heat to medium and cook until the corn is tender, 20 to 30 minutes. If the mixture begins to thicken too much before the corn is tender, add a little milk.■

To make the tomato sauce: In a large saucepan, heat the olive oil and sauté the onion, pepper, and garlic until soft, about 5 minutes. Stir in the tomato paste and cook for 5 minutes. Add the tomatoes and stock or broth, bring to a boil and cook for 20 minutes. Strain through a fine-meshed sieve, pressing all the juice from the mixture, and return the liquid to the saucepan. Add the wine, bring to a low boil and reduce by half, about 5 minutes. Add salt and pepper, then stir in the arrowroot mixture and cook for 2 more minutes; remove from heat and keep warm.

To make the hollandaise: Combine the egg yolks, wine, lemon juice, basil and salt and pepper in a double boiler. Cook over simmering water until the mixture forms a heavy ribbon on the surface of the sauce when dropped from the whisk, about 2 to 3 minutes. Remove from heat. Whisk in the butter 1 teaspoon at a time. Add salt and pepper. Keep warm over hot water.

To prepare the eggplant: Sprinkle the eggplant with salt and pepper, dredge in flour and shake off the excess. Immerse in beaten eggs, then dredge in cornmeal. In a large sauté pan or skillet heat the olive oil and brown the eggplant on each side, for a total of 4 minutes. With a slotted metal spatula, transfer to paper towels or napkins to drain. Keep warm.

To prepare the crab meat: In a medium sauté pan or skillet, melt the butter and sauté onions, shallots and garlic until softened, about 3 to 4 minutes. Add the brandy and cook over medium heat to reduce slightly. Add the crab meat, sprinkle with salt and pepper, add dash of liquid crab boil and toss gently until well heated. Keep hot.

To serve: Place the tomato sauce over medium heat, bring to a boil and add the butter. Pool tomato sauce on each of six heated plates. Divide the eggplant evenly among six heated salad plates and top the eggplant with crab meat in a dome shape. Top the crab meat with basil hollandaise and garnish with fresh green and opal basil leaves and serve.

WILLIAM DENNIS HUTLEY
The Versailles Restaurant, New Orleans

"Cooking—I like everything about it," says Dennis Hutley, executive chef at The Versailles. And, he says, there is more than meets the eye: "The logistics of production, preparation, setup, purchasing, handling, the coordination of dishes and the menu—and the chemistry of cooking itself." Although Hutley was born in Sharon, Pennsylvania, he qualifies as a Louisiana native: he has lived in New Orleans since he was four years old.

After studying business administration in college, Hutley changed direction and began to study cooking under some of the city's best chefs: Claude Aubert, then at Romanoff's; Robert Finely, of Masson's; and Gunter Preuss, chef-proprietor of The Versailles where Hutley has spent thirteen years. "Gunter is very classical but very progressive," says Hutley, who credits Preuss for giving him the green light to bring a distinct New Orleans flavor to The Versailles Restaurant's French menu. "I'd call my style progressive Creole," he says.

Hutley has an affinity for sauces and makes no apologies. "I really like sauces. They enhance and round out the flavors of food." While he's not anti-salsa, and even makes some himself for appetizers, cold foods that need a pick-me-up, and dry foods that need moisture, he says that salsas aren't as elegant as sauces. "It's hard for me to violate the classical guidelines, but I'm always glad to innovate on classical cuisine."

Hutley's most recent innovation at The Versailles Restaurant is a menu written all in English (some French words and phrases excepted). "Although we preserve the European traditions of unpretentious good service, elegance, and fine food, we are here to serve Americans." His featured recipes are Pan-fried Eggplant with Crab Meat, Basil Hollandaise, and Creole Tomato Sauce (appetizer), Braised Pork Tenderloin with Sautéed Apples, Celery Julienne, and Louisiana Sweet Potato Pancake (entrée), and Terrine of White Chocolate and Praline, with Coconut Tile Cookies and Caramel Sauce (dessert).

David McCelvey and Michael Jordan
NOLA, New Orleans

Sometimes a slow start is prelude to a whirlwind career. Take Michael Jordan: His first job in high school was as a sauté cook in Bettendorf, Iowa. While Jordan was attending the University of Iowa he worked as kitchen manager at the Iowa River Power Company, and with his mother's encouragement, he enrolled in the Culinary Institute of America in Hyde Park, New York. There, he says, "I caught the cooking bug" (and met his future wife). Before graduating in 1989 he completed a culinary externship in the kitchens of Printers Row in Chicago, owned and operated by celebrity chef Michael Foley, a Midwest pioneer of regional cooking and the farm-restaurant connection.

After graduating, Jordan and his wife took two cooks' tours of Europe, sandwiched between two stints of working at an Iowa City restaurant called The Kitchen. "It was wonderful because the owner gave us freedom to be creative. We found out that Iowa City might not be ready for truffles and foie gras, but we were amazed at how receptive people there were to food."

In 1990, on a motor trip that took them to Alaska, the Pacific Northwest, Nevada, and Texas, they reached New Orleans. On impulse, Jordan said, "If we see a "For Rent' sign, let's move in." They saw one. They moved in. Emeril Lagasse's reputation had preceded him, so Jordan went to Emeril's and applied for a job. He was hired to work the dessert station, right across from David McCelvey, who was working salads.

Jordan had been just a class behind David McCelvey all the way through the Culinary Institute, and now McCelvey was a station ahead of him all the way through Emeril's to NOLA, where they both work now, McCelvey as day chef and Jordan as night chef.

McCelvey's first job was busboy in a little restaurant in his home town of Bowling Green, Kentucky, where "I watched them go out of business." He subsequently worked in other restaurants during college until graduating from Western Kentucky University in 1989 with a degree in philosophy. When he enrolled in the Culinary Institute. "I was pretty green," he says, "But I was determined to maximize the experience, and I was very aggressive about learning." Before graduating, McCelvey, like Jordan, externed in a trendsetting restaurant, Bistro Rôti in San Francisco.

McCelvey was among the top ten student chefs chosen as apprentice to celebrity chefs at the Aspen Food and Wine festival in 1989. There he first met Emeril Lagasse. "He brought Creole tomatoes and he sliced one and sprinkled it with kosher salt and gave it to me. "Just taste this!' he said." After graduation McCelvey studied French, traveled to France, apprenticed in a Michelin one-star restaurant, and cooked in a French West Indian restaurant in Paris where "the cooking was a distant cousin to Creole."

Back in the States McCelvey went for a weekend to New Orleans. "I ate at Emeril's for the first time. I was blown away!" The next day he gave Emeril his résumé, and was hired to work the dessert station, just a few months ahead of Jordan. When Lagasse opened NOLA, a restaurant "for locals" in the French Quarter that serves what Lagasse terms new New Orleans cooking, McCelvey and Jordan were appointed sous-chefs. The food and atmosphere at NOLA is more casual than at Emeril's, but, says McCelvey, "Necessity is the mother of invention. We may not have truffles and Beluga caviar at NOLA, but we make some great food that's also great fun." Jordan's recipe for NOLA Vegetable Terrine, an appetizer, appears in this chapter. McCelvey's recipe for Caramelized Salmon with Mirliton Slaw, an entrée, appears in the Entrées chapter.

Potato Cake with Creamed Leeks and Escargots

From John Neal of Peristyle,
New Orleans, LA

Serves 4

The most convenient way to purchase snails is canned. Snailophobes should follow chef John Neal's suggestion to substitute bits of cooked meat or poultry for snails.■

4 slices diced smoked bacon
2 leeks, white parts only, coarsely chopped
1/2 cup heavy (whipping) cream
3 baking potatoes
8 escargots or 8 small pieces of cooked meat or poultry
4 tablespoons peanut oil
Tomato Sauce (recipe follows)
Salt and pepper

In a medium sauté pan or skillet, cook the bacon for 3 to 4 minutes over medium-low heat. Add the leeks and cook until tender. Add the cream and cook until thickened, about 9 minutes. Let cool.

When ready to serve, peel and grate the potatoes. Place on kitchen towel; fold it up, twist and squeeze out the moisture. Place the grated potatoes on a work surface and season with salt and pepper. Divide the potatoes in half and divide one half into 4 piles. Place one fourth of the chopped leeks on top of each pile. Divide the escargots among the 4 piles and cover each with remaining potatoes. Pat each one down to make sure the filling is secure in each cake.

Over medium heat in a large non-stick skillet, heat the peanut oil. Carefully add potato cakes and cook until brown on one side (about 4 minutes). Carefully turn the cakes over and cook for another 4 to 5 minutes or until browned. Make a pool of tomato sauce on each serving plate. Place a potato cake on the sauce. Serve hot.

Tomato Sauce

3 tablespoons olive oil
1 medium onion, chopped
2 cans Progresso plum tomatoes (28 ounces)
1/2 cup tomato paste
1 tablespoon dried basil
1 teaspoon salt
Pinch of ground black pepper
1 teaspoon sugar

Heat the olive oil and sauté onions until soft. Add remaining ingredients and simmer for 40 minutes, stirring from time to time.■

NOLA Vegetable Terrine

From Michael Jordan of NOLA,
New Orleans, LA

Serves 12 to 15

This surprising and elegant first course looks like a mosaic of jewels on the plate. It can be made a day or two in advance, and it makes a stunning buffet platter.

12 heads of garlic, separated into cloves
1 tablespoon olive oil
1 teaspoon fresh cracked black pepper
1 globe eggplant, sliced lengthwise into 1/4-inch slices
1 yellow squash, sliced thin
1 zucchini, sliced thin
Extra-virgin olive oil for drizzling
Salt and pepper to taste
2 tablespoons vegetable oil
3 red onions, thinly sliced
1 pound spinach, stemmed
30 to 40 slices Provolone cheese
1 large red bell pepper, roasted, seeded and deribbed (see Techniques)
1 carrot, peeled, blanched and sliced
1 large yellow bell pepper, roasted, seeded and deribbed (see Techniques)

To roast garlic: Preheat the oven to 400°F. Peel garlic cloves. Toss with the olive oil and pepper and place on sheet of aluminum foil. Fold the foil around the garlic to form a bag and roast until tender, for about 40 to 45 minutes. Cool the roasted garlic slightly, press the pulp from the husks and purée.

Preheat the oven to 425°F. Place the eggplant, squash, and zucchini slices flat on a baking sheet and drizzle lightly with olive oil. Season with salt and pepper and bake for 4 to 5 minutes, or until just wilted. Set aside.

In a large sauté pan or skillet, sauté the red onions in oil until golden brown, about 6 to 8 minutes. Remove from the pan, cover, and chill. In the same pan sauté the spinach until just wilted and season with salt and pepper; set aside.

Preheat oven to 350°F. Thoroughly oil a small bread pan with extra-virgin olive oil. Line the pan with plastic wrap so that the plastic hangs over the edges of the pan. Oil the plastic wrap with extra-virgin olive oil. Line the bottom and the sides of the inside of the pan with slices of provolone cheese. Cover with overlapping slices of eggplant so that the eggplant is hanging over the edge of the pan by 1-1/2 to 2 inches. Rub the eggplant lightly with the roasted garlic purée. Place a layer of cheese over the garlic. Top with a thin layer of sautéed red onions. Top with a layer of cheese and press down firmly. Top with a layer of roasted red bell pepper and another layer of cheese. Then a layer of yellow squash and again cheese, Press down firmly. Add a thin layer of sautéed spinach and top with 1 layer of cheese, carrot, cheese, bell pepper and cheese. Press down firmly once again. Top with a layer of onions and a final layer of cheese and press firmly.

Fold the eggplant over the top of the mold to form a seal. Fold over and seal the plastic. Place the pan in a baking pan. Add warm water to a depth of 1 inch to the baking pan. Place in the oven and bake for 45 minutes. Chill overnight. Slice and serve cold or at room temperature.■

NOLA Vegetable Terrine, Michael Jordan, NOLA

Calamaretti in Zimino con Polenta alla Griglia

From Fernando Saracchi of Ristorante Bacco, New Orleans, LA

Serves 4

Grilled polenta triangles are the base for the topping of spinach and spicy baby squid. Squid may be purchased frozen but it is infinitely better fresh. Buy squid that has been cleaned, but make sure the purplish skin is pulled off and discarded. Check to see that the quill (a small, thick, plastic-like blade) is removed from the body. Rinse the squid under cold water to remove any sand and pat dry. If your guests are squeamish about tentacles, chop them finely and add to the pan. Squid should have sweet, mild flavor and no fishy smell. It is high in protein, extremely low in fat and very inexpensive.

Polenta
3 quarts water
3 tablespoons sea salt
2-2/3 cups (1 pound) polenta
  (a coarse-ground cornmeal)
6 tablespoons butter

Calamaretti
3 tablespoons extra-virgin olive oil
2 minced garlic cloves
6 ounces cleaned baby squid
Salt and black pepper
Pinch of dried red pepper flakes
1/3 cup dry white wine
2 tablespoons unsalted butter
4 to 5 spinach leaves

To make polenta: Bring the water to a boil in a very large saucepan. Add the salt. Pour in the polenta, stirring continuously with a whisk. Reduce heat to low and cook about 45 minutes. Stir in 4 tablespoons of the butter. With the remaining 2 tablespoons butter, grease a jelly-roll pan, and pour in the polenta when it is still very hot; let cool completely. When cold, cut polenta in triangles and grill it over medium-hot coals until browned on both sides, about 3 minutes.

To cook the calamaretti: In a medium sauté pan or skillet, heat the olive oil and sauté the garlic until golden. Remove the garlic from the pan. Season the squid with the salt, black pepper and red pepper, and

sauté it on both sides for 3 to 4 minutes or until crisp. Add the wine and cook until the wine has evaporated, about 4 minutes. Add 1 tablespoon butter and mix it in. In another medium sauté pan or skillet, melt the remaining 1 tablespoon butter and stir in the spinach leaves until wilted, about 5 minutes. ▪

To serve: place 1 triangle of polenta on each of 4 plates. Top each serving with an equal amount of wilted spinach and the calamari.

Grilled Shrimp with Polenta

From Randy Windham of Bistro at Maison de Ville, New Orleans, LA

Serves 4

Polenta, an Italian specialty now found on menus from coast to coast, is served either soft, or cooled, then sliced and fried or baked. Chef Randy Windham's recipe for soft polenta topped with pesto-marinated grilled shrimp is comfort food elevated to a new level of flavor. For a

Calamaretti in Zimino con Polenta alla Griglia, Fernando Saracchi, Ristorante Bacco

hearty lunch or simple dinner menu, double the portions and accompany with a green salad, Italian country bread and a dish of oil-cured black olives.

Pesto
1 bunch basil, stemmed
3 garlic cloves
1-1/2 tablespoons toasted pine nuts
    (see Techniques)
1-1/2 teaspoons salt
1 cup (4 ounces) grated Parmesan cheese
1 cup olive oil

20 large shrimp, peeled and deveined

Polenta
2 cups cold water
2 cups milk
1 cup polenta (coarse-ground cornmeal)
1/3 cup unsalted butter
1/2 cup freshly grated Parmesan cheese
Salt and pepper to taste

1 tablespoon balsamic vinegar
1 tablespoon basil-flavored olive oil
4 teaspoons freshly grated Parmesan cheese
1 tablespoon minced fresh chives

To make the pesto: In a food processor, purée basil leaves, garlic, pine nuts, salt, and Parmesan cheese until smooth. With the motor running, add oil in a slow steady stream. Pour into a medium bowl, add the shrimp, and marinate at room temperature for 30 minutes.

To make polenta: In a large, heavy saucepan, stir the water, milk, and cornmeal together. Cook over low heat until thick, stirring constantly, about 25 to 30 minutes. Stir in the butter and Parmesan cheese. Add salt and pepper.

Grill the shrimp over medium coals for about 2 to 3 minutes on each side. Divide the polenta among four large flat-rimmed soup dishes. Place shrimp on top and sprinkle with balsamic vinegar and flavored oil. Sprinkle with Parmesan cheese and chives. ∎

Fernando Saracchi
Ristorante Bacco, New Orleans

When it comes to Italian cuisine, Fernando Saracchi couldn't have picked a better place to call home. He was born in Parma, Italy, a city famous for its food. Parma is the birthplace of *prosciutto di Parma*, the pink, perfectly cured, sweet ham sliced paper thin for antipasto. Parma is also a source for prime pancetta (unsmoked bacon) and a producer of parmigiano-reggiano cheese, "a cheese so treasured," writes Sam Tanenhaus in Robert Freson's *Savoring Italy* (New York: Harper Collins Publishers, 1992), "that each of two cities—Parma and Reggio—lay unique claim to it."

Saracchi's affinity for food surfaced early, and after graduating from high school in Parma, he attended the State Culinary Institute in Salsamaggiore Terme.

After graduating from culinary school, he started working with his grandfather, who gave him his training in restaurant work.

In 1985, Saracchi moved to New York. He cooked in several restaurants, and while at Rosolio Restaurant, his talents and his menu caught the attention of *Gourmet* magazine, where he was favorably reviewed.

In July 1991, he came to New Orleans to join the Brennan family in their first Italian restaurant Bacco. And when it comes to translating Italian cuisine to the American menu, Saracchi couldn't have chosen a better place. He was the opening chef, bringing his experience with authentic Italian food and his culinary talents to a restaurant that combines authenticity and whimsy. For example, special restaurant features include traditional wood-fired ovens for baking pizza, as well as lessons in conversational Italian that play in the restrooms and over the phone when customers are put on hold.

Saracchi's featured recipes are Calamaretti in Zimino con Polenta alla Griglia (appetizer), Risotto Mille e Una Notte (entrée), and Crespella di Ricotta con Salsa al Caramello (dessert).

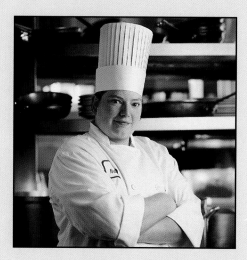

HALEY GABEL
Ristorante Bacco, New Orleans

At twenty-seven, Haley Gabel is the youngest chef—since Emeril Lagasse (formerly at Commander's Palace)—to head a kitchen in one of the Brennan family restaurants. And she is the first woman. She says, "What a wonderful opportunity to cook a food I love—Italian— in a city I love—New Orleans." (Other Brennan family restaurant chefs featured in this cookbook include Jamie Shannon at Commander's Palace, Gerard Maras at Mr. B's, and Dick Brennan, Jr., at Palace Café.)

Gabel began cooking in restaurants in 1985, and graduated in 1990 from the Culinary Arts Academy of Cincinnati, an affiliate of the Culinary Institute of America in Hyde Park, New York. During culinary school, as part of her curriculum, Gabel applied for an externship at Mr. B's Bistro in New Orleans. Ever since, brother and sister co-owners Ralph and Cindy Brennan have kept their eyes on this rising young star.

After graduation, Gabel returned to New Orleans to work as a line cook at Mr. B's. In 1991, she helped open Bacco, a restaurant in the French Quarter run by Ralph and Cindy Brennan that offers Creole Italian fare. At Bacco, Gabel was sous-chef and a guiding force in the kitchen. She left Bacco for a brief stint cooking at Tatou in Aspen, Colorado, but when Cindy and Ralph asked her to come back to Bacco as head chef, it was an offer she couldn't refuse.

Gabel's youth is belied by her grace under pressure and her culinary wisdom. She is able to preserve traditional Italian dishes (such as wood-fired pizzas and housemade pastas), while incorporating local Louisiana ingredients and innovative variations. For example, in her featured appetizer recipe, Oyster and Eggplant Ravioli, traditional Italian pasta is stuffed with local oysters and the sauce is flavored by a touch of Herbsaint, a licorice-flavored liqueur that is a favorite of New Orleanians. Her entrée, Veal Chops with Roasted New Potatoes and Escarole, pairs a veal chop, wood-roasted in the Tuscan style, with oven roasted potatoes, wilted greens and an innovative chicken liver-balsamic vinegar sauce.

Crawfish and Angel Hair Pasta Beignets with Garlic Mayonnaise

From Tom Weaver of Christian's Restaurant, New Orleans, LA

Makes about 18 beignets; Serves 6

Louisiana chefs can give anything a new twist. This example is Chef Tom Weaver's recipe for making beignets (deep-fried fritters) made from pasta.

12 ounces cooked angel hair pasta, cooked al dente
12 ounces cooked crawfish tails or shrimp, chopped
3 teaspoons dry mustard
1-1/2 teaspoon salt
1/2 teaspoon cayenne pepper
2 beaten eggs
3/4 cup all-purpose flour
1/2 cup chopped green onions
2 quarts vegetable oil
Garlic mayonnaise (recipe follows)

Place the pasta, crawfish or shrimp, mustard, salt, cayenne pepper, and eggs in a medium non-aluminum bowl and mix well. Add the flour and green onions and stir until blended. Roll into slightly firm balls about the size of golf balls. In a 4-quart deep-fryer or heavy pot, heat the oil to 350°F and cook the beignets in batches of 3 for about 3 minutes or until golden brown. Remove with slotted spoon and drain on paper towels.

To serve: Spread garlic mayonnaise on each of six plates. Place 3 beignets on each plate. ■

Garlic Mayonnaise

Makes 2 cups

3 egg yolks
1 cup olive oil
1 cup vegetable oil
6 teaspoons minced garlic
5 tablespoons ketchup
5 teaspoons chopped parsley
Salt and pepper to taste

Place the egg yolks in a large bowl and beat at medium speed, adding the oil in a thin stream until all the oil is incorporated. Whisk in all the remaining ingredients. Keeps two days.

Oyster and Eggplant Ravioli

*From Haley Gabel of Ristorante Bacco,
New Orleans, LA*

Serves 5 (4 ravioli per person)

The combination of minced oysters and
roasted eggplant in the ravioli filling is
captivating; the sauce is a reduction of
oyster liquor and cream, with a touch of
Herbsaint, a licorice-flavored liqueur. If
making your own pasta seems too labor-
intensive, purchase sheets of fresh pasta.

Filling
12 ounces freshly shucked oysters, oyster
   liquor reserved
1 cup dry white wine
1/4 cup plus 1-1/2 teaspoons minced
   shallots
1 eggplant
1-1/2 teaspoon minced garlic
2 tablespoons minced celery
2 tablespoons dry bread crumbs
2 tablespoons diced green onions
1-1/2 teaspoons chopped fresh oregano
1 teaspoon hot sauce
Salt and pepper to taste

Pasta

Makes 20 ravioli

3 large eggs
1 tablespoon olive oil
1 teaspoon salt
2 cups unbleached all-purpose flour
1 egg mixed with 1 tablespoon water for
   egg wash
Cornmeal for sprinkling

Sauce:
1/3 cup heavy (whipping) cream
Reserved oyster cooking liquid
1/2 teaspoon minced shallots
Pinch of minced garlic
1 tablespoon minced green onions
2 tablespoons Herbsaint or Pernod
1 tablespoon pasta water from boiling
   pasta
2 teaspoons unsalted butter

To make filling: Place the oysters and
their liquor in a medium saucepan, add
the wine and 1/4 cup of the shallots,
bring to a simmer, and cook for 3
minutes or until the oysters are firm.
Strain the oysters and reserve the cooking
liquid for the sauce.

Oyster and Eggplant Ravioli, Haley Gabel, Ristorante Bacco

Prick eggplant with fork. Place on cookie
sheet in 350°F oven and bake for 1 hour,
or until cooked through completely.
Scoop out flesh. Drain in sieve. Chop.

Mince the oysters. Sauté the garlic, celery,
and the remaining 1-1/2 teaspoons
shallots until translucent. Combine with
the oysters and all the remaining
ingredients until well mixed. Roll the
filling into 1-inch balls. Set aside.

To make the pasta: Combine the eggs,
olive oil, and salt in a food processor.
Pulse to mix well. Add 2 cups of flour
and process until mixture holds together.
Remove from processor and cover with
plastic wrap, if not using right away.

Cut pasta in half. Put 1/2 of pasta
through pasta machine on widest setting.
Repeat with second half. Continue to
turn pasta through machine, moving
rollers closer together each time until you
reach the desired thickness. Cut pasta into
two even sheets. Lightly coat one pasta
sheet with the egg wash, then place balls

of filling 2-1/2 inches apart on the sheet
of pasta. Cover the filling with the
remaining sheet of the pasta and cut into
equal squares. Use your fingers to press
the edges together (removing any air
pockets) and place the squares on a
cornmeal-dusted baking sheet. Sprinkle
the ravioli with a little cornmeal.

Place the ravioli in a large quantity of
boiling salted water and cook for 2-1/2 to
4 minutes, or until al dente, then drain,
reserving two tablespoons of the pasta water.

To make the sauce: In a small saucepan
combine the cream and reserved oyster
cooking liquid and cook over medium
heat to reduce by half, about 3 to 4 minutes.

In another small saucepan, sauté the shallots,
garlic, and green onions and deglaze with
Herbsaint or Pernod. Add the cream mixture
to the vegetable mixture and cook over medium
heat to reduce until thick, about 4 minutes.
Add the cooked ravioli and blend in the
butter, thin sauce with 2 tablespoons
reserved pasta water. Serve at once. ■

CHRISTIANE ENGERAN FISHER
Chez Daniel, Metairie

Christiane Engeran Fisher radiates a kind of breathless enthusiasm for food, cooking, restaurants, and everything about her chosen profession.

Her first job—washing dishes and preparing salads at Jacmel Inn, Hammond, Louisana—would have been the last job for many. Washing dishes is backbreaking, and prepping salads both boring and labor-intensive. But, says Engeran Fisher, "Mostly I learned how to work quickly and efficiently, and I observed what the chefs did, knowing that one day I wanted to *be* them."

Her second job, as pastry and pantry assistant at Bayona restaurant in New Orleans, convinced her that she had to go to culinary school. "I was very impressed with all of the specialty items and knew I had to go to school to learn about them."

Engeran Fisher finished her first year at the New England Culinary Institute in Essex, Vermont, learning what she calls "the backbone" of both traditional and contemporary cooking. She returned for a year to work at Bayona. "I wanted to challenge my knowledge, to see how much I really learned. Before I left I was sautéing and feeling very confident for my last year of school."

She graduated from the New England Culinary Institute in late 1992 and did a culinary apprenticeship at Cayenne restaurant in Southhampton, New York, where she began to create some of the daily menu specials that bear the stamp of her style.

At Chez Daniel, Engeran Fisher is now sous-chef, responsible for creating weekly menu changes and special-occasion menus, and for maintaining quality. She also oversees two kitchen apprentices, whose position—on the bottom rung of the culinary ladder—she herself occupied just a few years ago.

Her featured recipes are Abita Saffron Crêpes with Crab Meat and Mushroom Filling, and Caviar Sauce (appetizer), and Sautéed Duck Breast with Gingered Fig Sauce, Braised Fennel, and Celeriac-Potato Timbale.

Abita Saffron Crêpes with Crab Meat and Mushroom Filling, and Caviar Sauce

From Christiane Engeran Fisher of Chez Daniel, Metairie, LA

Serves 2

Traditionally, French crêpe batter is light, delicate and almost bland, creating a thin pancake, the perfect wrap for dozens of fillings. (Classics include seafood, cheese, spinach, and mushrooms.) Conversely, traditional beer batter is a hearty, gutsy mixture most often used to dip foods before frying. In this unusual recipe, two worlds meet in one surprise package. The thin French crêpe borrows flavor and color from saffron, orange, and Abita beer, from a microbrewery in the town of Abita Springs north of New Orleans. Each crêpe is stuffed with a spicy mushroom-crab meat mixture and tied with thin ribbons of green onion.

Crêpes

Makes 12 to 14 crêpes

2 cups all-purpose flour
1 tablespoon salt
2 eggs beaten
1-3/4 (14 ounces) Abita beer or other
   flavorful dark beer
4 strands saffron
Zest of 1/2 orange
4-1/2 tablespoons melted butter

Filling (for 2 crepes)

2 tablespoons (1 ounce) olive oil
2 shallots, thinly sliced
1/2 Vidalia or other mild white onion,
    thinly sliced
2 minced garlic cloves
1 julienned Roma tomato
1/4 cup (1 ounce) fresh cèpes mushrooms
    julienned
1/4 cup (1 ounce) fresh shiitake mushrooms,
    julienned
1/4 cup (1 ounce) fresh oyster mushrooms,
    julienned
1/4 cup (1 ounce) fresh domestic mushrooms,
    julienned
2 tablespoons (1 ounce) Armagnac or
    another good brandy
3 to 4 thyme sprigs, chopped
4 basil leaves, cut into chiffonade
1/4 cups (2 ounces) mushroom or chicken stock
1/2 cup (8 ounces) fresh crab meat
1 tablespoon (1 ounce) ground dried
    green peppercorns
1 tablespoon (1 ounce) ground dried pink
    peppercorns
Pinch of salt
Small pinch of freshly cracked black pepper
2 ounces Brie cheese

Caviar Sauce

1 tablespoon butter
1 minced shallot
1/4 cup warm Armagnac
1/2 cup shrimp stock or bottled clam juice
1/2 cup crème fraîche (see Techniques)
1/2 teaspoon Romanoff red caviar
1/4 teaspoon Romanoff black caviar (optional)
Leaves from 1 baby leek or 1 bunch green
    onions

To make the crêpes: Sift the flour and the salt into a medium mixing bowl. Add the eggs and beer, mixing until smooth. Strain the mixture into another medium bowl. Stir in the saffron, zest, and melted butter. Let set one hour.

Use a small cast-iron crêpe pan, or a teflon-lined pan, 8 to 10 inches in diameter. Heat your skillet on a medium to high flame. Do not grease the skillet. The melted butter in the batter will suffice to prevent the crêpes from sticking. (the first few may stick.). Hold the pan slightly tilted and pour about 3 tablespoons of batter on the high side. Quickly tilt the pan so that the batter has a chance to coat the whole bottom before hardening. Shake the pan to force the batter all over. The thinner the coating, the better the crêpes. Cook the crêpes on medium heat for approximately 50 seconds. Then bang the skillet a few times on the pot holder or a folded towel to release the crêpe. Flip the crêpe over or turn it with a spatula and cook approximately 30 seconds on the other side. You will notice that the side that was browned first is nicer than the other. When stacking them, place the nicer side underneath so that it shows on the outside after the crêpe is folded.

To make the filling: In a large sauté pan or skillet, heat the olive oil. Add the shallots, onion, and garlic; sauté until onions begin to color, about 4 to 5 minutes. Add the tomato and mushrooms, then sauté for 4 to 5 minutes. Pour in the Armagnac, avert your face, light the liquid with a long match, and shake the pan until the flames subside. Remove from heat carefully. Add the thyme and the basil. Add the mushroom or chicken stock, then the crab meat, and sauté for 2 to 3 minutes. Add the green and pink peppercorns, then season lightly with salt and pepper. Finish by topping with Brie cheese.

To make the caviar sauce: Melt the butter, sweat shallots in a small sauté pan or skillet and sauté for 4 to 5 minutes, or until soft. Pour in the Armagnac, avert your face, light the liquid with a long match and shake the pan until the flames subside. Cook over medium heat to reduce slightly; add the shrimp or bottled clam juice stock and cook to reduce by about half. Add the crème fraîche. Strain the sauce through a fine-meshed sieve. Stir in the red caviar, then add the (optional) black caviar. (It will darken the light orange-colored sauce). Keep warm.

Putting the crêpe together: Blanch the leek or green onion leaves in boiling water for 3 to 4 minutes, drain and pat dry, and cut in half lengthwise. On a work surface, place 2 pieces of leaf about 1-1/2 inches apart. Place a crêpe over the leaf pieces. Fill the crêpe with about one 1 cup of filling. Fold the crêpe gently over the filling, tie both leaves, and gently lift the filled crêpe onto a plate. With a spatula pool the caviar sauce around the plate and pour a little onto the crêpe. Garnish the plate with the caviar. Repeat for each serving. ∎

Abita Saffron Crêpes with Crab Meat and Mushroom Filling, and Caviar Sauce, Christiane Engeran Fisher, Chez Daniel

Michael Fennelly
Mike's on the Avenue, New Orleans

"Cross-cultural dabbling—it's what I like to do," says Michael Fennelly, chef-proprietor of Mike's on the Avenue and author of *East Meets Southwest* (San Francisco: Chronicle Books, 1991). The cookbook was written while he was executive chef at SantaCafe in Santa Fe, listed by Mimi Sheraton in 1990 in her Top 50 Restaurants of the Year.

Curiously, this chef who has been praised by *Gourmet, The New York Times, Connoisseur, Food and Wine, Travel and Leisure,* and a dozen other publications, did not start his career in the kitchen. Until 1985, he was an art director and designer. One day he realized that "I had always cooked to make myself happy, and that I should be doing this professionally. It's a good vehicle for all different aspects of my creativity." In addition to his education in visual arts, design, and architecture, Fennelly is a painter, sculptor, and graphic artist. At Mike's on the Avenue he not only created the menu but designed the restaurant, the artwork in it, the neckties, T-shirts, logo, and signage.

Fennelly first commanded the attention of the food media and the dining public during his five-year tenure as executive chef at SantaCafe (where he also designed the restaurant's logo and graphics). His move to New Orleans was in response to a culinary gravitational pull: "It's a whole new area. The ingredients available here make cooking a pleasure."

At Mike's on the Avenue he serves forth an eclectic cuisine. His approach to cooking is spontaneous. "That has to do with my training in art, which enables me to not really have any preconceived rules." He challenges the home cook to be creative as well. "That's where inspiration comes from, taking ideas and expanding and changing them. Recipes are really for guidelines."

He's a firm believer that restaurant dining and home cooking can coexist, because "going out to eat has taken on a whole new persona as a form of entertainment. The experience of home is to eat and be nurtured and warmed by your environment—and to be at rest, whatever rest denotes to you."

His recipes in this book are Crawfish Spring Rolls with Three-chili Dipping Sauce (appetizer), Painted Pasta Ribbons with Louisiana Soft-shell Crab and Roasted Poblano-Ginger Beurre Blanc (entrée), and Asian Napoleon (dessert).

Crawfish Spring Rolls with Three-chili Dipping Sauce

From Mike Fennelly of Mike's on the Avenue, New Orleans, LA

Serves 8 to 10

This is chef Mike Fennelly's answer to the ever-popular egg roll. His recipe uses crawfish instead of pork or shrimp, and the hot Asian-inspired dipping sauce is a great flavor match. Do try the chef's suggestion and wrap cooked spring rolls in a crisp lettuce leaf with pasta and mint. They're unforgettable!

Spring Rolls
1 red bell pepper, seeded, deribbed, and cut into 1/4-inch-wide strips
1 pound crawfish tail meat
1 small carrot, peeled, and finely julienned
1/2 cup julienned Napa cabbage
1/4 cup julienned spinach leaves
3 cloves garlic, finely chopped
1 celery stalk, finely julienned
1 tablespoon chopped fresh cilantro
1/4 cup chopped red onion
Salt and freshly ground black pepper to taste
1 package (1 pound) rice paper wrappers (see Note)
4 egg whites, lightly beaten

Three-Chili Dipping Sauce
6 cloves garlic
1/4 cup sugar
3 Anaheim chilies
2 fresh jalapeño chilies, seeded, and deribbed
1/4 teaspoon red pepper flakes
Juice of 2 limes
1/2 cup Vietnamese fish sauce
1 cup water
1 teaspoon distilled white vinegar

Peanut oil for deep frying
Julienned carrot strips for garnish
1 head red leaf or butter lettuce, optional
8 ounces linguine, cooked, drained and cooled (optional)
1 bunch fresh mint, stemmed (optional)

To make the spring rolls: In a large bowl, gently toss together the bell pepper, crawfish, carrot, cabbage, spinach, garlic, celery, cilantro and onion. Season with salt and pepper. Place a rice paper round on work surface. Brush the surface of the wrapper with egg white. Let stand a few seconds to soften. Place a heaping spoonful of filling about one fourth of the way in from the top edge of the wrapper. Spread the filling into a rectangular shape about 3/4 inch wide and 5 inches long. Fold over the top of the wrapper to cover the filling, then roll up one turn, fold in the sides, and finish rolling. Repeat until all the filling is used. Set aside.

To make the dipping sauce: Combine the garlic, sugar, chilies, red pepper flakes, and lime juice in a blender or food processor. Process until minced. Add the fish sauce, water, and the vinegar and mix well. Set aside.

To cook the spring rolls: Pour the oil into a large, heavy saucepan or deep fryer to a depth of at least 4 inches. Heat the oil to 375°F. Drop the spring rolls into the oil a few at a time and fry until golden brown, about 4 minutes; do not crowd the pan. Remove with a slotted spoon to paper towels to drain briefly. Cut each roll into 3 pieces.

To serve, divide the sauce among individual bowls. Place spring rolls on sauce. Garnish with carrot strips. The spring rolls may be eaten plain, or they may be wrapped inside a lettuce leaf with a small amount of pasta and a few mint leaves. In either case, dip them into the sauce and enjoy!

Note: Rice paper rounds, usually measuring from 6 to 8 inches, are sold in 1-pound packages in shops carrying Southeast Asian foods. You will need only part of a package to make these rolls. Wrap the remaining rounds tightly and refrigerate. ∎

Pecan Wood-smoked Shrimp Quesadillas & Charbroiled White Tuna with Crab Meat and Three-pepper Relish, Horst Pfeifer, Bella Luna

Pecan Wood-smoked Shrimp Quesadillas

From Horst Pfeifer of Bella Luna, New Orleans, LA

Serves 6

This is what happens when a creative chef introduces southwestern flavors and Italian ingredients to shrimp.

12 large peeled shrimp
6 tablespoons goat cheese
1/2 teaspoon pepper
1/2 teaspoon salt
1/4 teaspoon cayenne pepper
6 flour tortillas
3 tablespoons roasted, diced Poblano chili (see Techniques)
3 tablespoons minced sun-dried tomatoes
2 tablespoons fresh cilantro and Italian parsley, mixed together
6 tablespoons shredded mozzarella

How to smoke shrimp: Place 1 tablespoon dry pecan wood chips in a stove top smoker. Place rack in the smoker. Add the shrimp to the smoker. Cover the smoker and smoke the shrimp over medium heat for 10 minutes. The shrimp may be smoked outdoors on a barbecue grill with pecan wood chips placed on top of hot charcoal.

Blend the pepper, salt and cayenne into the goat cheese and spread 1 tablespoon of the goat cheese on each tortilla. Sprinkle 1-1/2 tablespoon diced chili, 2 shrimp, 1 tablespoon minced dried tomatoes and 1 teaspoon minced herbs over half of each tortilla. Top with 1 tablespoon mozzarella and fold in half. Repeat to fill all tortillas.

Grill the tortillas on a griddle until the inside is hot and outside is lightly browned and crisp, about 1 to 2 minutes on each side.

To Serve: Cut each quesadilla into 3 triangles to serve, 3 triangles per person. ∎

Shrimp and Andouille Cheesecake with Creole Mustard-Tomato Coulis

From Emeril Lagasse of Emeril's and NOLA

Makes 1-9-inch cheesecake
Serves 12

No wonder that Emeril Lagasse is called The Cheesecake King in New Orleans. Here is just one of his many recipes for savory appetizer cheesecakes.

Crust
1 cup (4 ounces) grated Parmesan cheese
1 cup fresh bread crumbs
1/4 teaspoon Emeril's Creole Seasoning (recipe follows)
1/2 cup (1 stick) melted butter

Coulis
1 teaspoon olive oil
1 teaspoon minced garlic
2 teaspoons minced shallots
8 Roma (pear) tomatoes, peeled, seeded and diced
1/2 teaspoon Emeril's Creole Seasoning (recipe follows)
2 tablespoons Creole mustard

Filling
1 pound chopped andouille sausage
1 tablespoon olive oil
1 cup chopped onion
1/2 cup diced red pepper
1/2 cup diced green pepper
1 pound chopped shrimp

28 ounces cream cheese at room temperature
1 cup (4 ounces) grated Gouda cheese
1/2 cup heavy (whipping) cream
4 eggs, beaten

To make the crust: Combine the Parmesan cheese, bread crumbs and Creole seasoning in a medium bowl. Add the butter and mix just until the dry ingredients are moist; don't overmix. Press into the bottom of a 9-inch spring-form pan. Set aside.

To make the coulis: In a medium saucepan, heat the oil and sauté the garlic and shallots until tender, about 2 to 3 minutes. Add the tomatoes and cook for 3 to 5 minutes. Add Creole seasoning and Creole mustard. Purée in blender or food processor and strain through a fine-meshed sieve. Let cool.

Shrimp and Andouille Cheesecake with Creole Mustard-Tomato Coulis, Emeril Lagasse, Emeril's and NOLA

To make the filling: Preheat the oven to 350°F. In a large sauté pan or skillet, sauté the andouille. Drain off the excess oil and set aside. In another large sauté pan or skillet, heat the olive oil. Sauté the onions, peppers, and shrimp until the onions are translucent, about 3 minutes, and set aside.

In a large bowl, beat the cream cheese and Gouda until smooth. Add the heavy cream, andouille and shrimp-onion mixture; blend in the eggs. Pour into the crust and place the pan in a baking pan. Add 1 inch of warm water and bake for 1 hour and 5 minutes or until set. Cheesecake should feel firm when touched with fingers.

Emeril's Creole Seasoning

Makes about 2/3 cup

2-1/2 tablespoons paprika
2 tablespoons dried garlic
2 tablespoons black pepper
1 tablespoon cayenne pepper
1 tablespoon dried thyme
1 tablespoon dried oregano
1 tablespoon dried onion

Blend all of the ingredients in a blender or food processor. Transfer to a small jar, seal tightly, and store in a cool, dry place. ▪

EMERIL LAGASSE
Emeril's and NOLA, New Orleans

Emeril Lagasse is the embodiment of the spirit of Louisiana's new garde chefs, and the food at his restaurants, Emeril's and NOLA, is at the very apex of the new culinary style. He calls his food "new New Orleans" cuisine. Critics call it—and him—top notch. He was named one of the top twenty-five chefs in the country by *Food and Wine* magazine; to Who's Who of Cooking in America, by *Cook's* magazine; the Best Southeast Regional Chef, by the James Beard Foundation; he was the Distinguished Visiting Chef at his alma mater Johnson & Wales University in Providence, Rhode Island. Emeril's was named Restaurant of the Year in 1990 by *Esquire* magazine, and in 1994 won the Ivy Award from *Restaurants & Institutions* magazine. His cookbook, *Emeril's New New Orleans Cooking*, (New York: William Morrow, 1993), has received critical acclaim.

Lagasse's background is down to earth, which is where he has his feet firmly planted today. He grew up in the small town of Fall River, Massachusetts. His mother was Portuguese and his father French-Canadian. Food and the family dinner table were central to his life. In childhood, Lagasse worked at a local Portuguese bakery, and as a teen he turned down a music scholarship in order to work his way through the culinary program at Johnson & Wales Unversity, from which he holds a doctorate degree.

After polishing his cooking skills in France (in Paris and Lyon), he returned to the States and cooked in fine restaurants in New York, Boston, and Philadelphia. He was offered the position as head chef at Ella and Dick Brennan's historic Commander's Palace in New Orleans where for 7-1/2 years he lightened and brightened the menu.

He opened Emeril's in 1990, and in 1993 he opened NOLA, a less pricey, more informal restaurant. Both serve up tempting fare with Southwestern, Asian, and New England accents, translated into the Creole genre. Lagasse's featured recipes are Shrimp and Andouille Cheesecake with Creole Mustard-Tomato Coulis (appetizer), Louisiana Crab and Vegetable Hash with Vanilla Bean Sabayon (entrée), Chicken Roulades with Andouille Cornbread Stuffing, Baby Vegetables, and Roasted Garlic Sauce (entrée), and Three-berry Tart with Vanilla Cream (dessert).

KEIL MOSHIER
Bistro la Tour, New Orleans

At 25, Keil Moshier became executive sous-chef at Bistro la Tour, the latest step in a culinary journey of discovery initiated by his father, a police officer who had been a cook in the army. "It all comes from my father. Growing up all I ever did with him was cook—on camping trips, at home. I loved cooking with him. When he passed away, something just clicked." Moshier, who had been a business major at a local college in his home state of Michigan, changed colleges—transferring to the New England Culinary Institute—and careers. Since then, "I've never looked back and I've never even considered doing anything else. I just want to learn as much as I can about this industry."

His quest for knowledge has taken him to the kitchens of the Windsor Court Hotel in New Orleans; the Amway Grand Plaza Hotel in Grand Rapids, Michigan, and Peter Island Resort in the British Virgin Islands.

He describes his style as "kind of nouvelle. I like things very simple—nothing really heavy." At the same time he says that people who come to dine at Bistro la Tour are coming for French food, so there are "no complaints about a little butter and cream."

Within the framework of his classical training, Moshier loves to experiment and develop recipes. For example, fresh lamb scraps left over from making a pâté can be sautéed with rough-cut peppers, onions and leeks, and a little blackberry brandy, and served with minted rice pilaf and a minted blackberry-shallot sauce.

French cooking as done by a new garde chef in the city of New Orleans undergoes a subtle transformation. "It's interesting to do French cooking here. We alter it to suit our personal tastes. We're able to do that because American chefs are cooking in the United States now for Americans. We're not trying just to copy the French or the Italians."

Moshier's featured recipe for French Bistro Tart (appetizer) appears in this chapter.

French Bistro Tart

From Keil Moshier of Bistro la Tour, New Orleans, LA

Serves 8

An appetizer pizza by another name is a French bistro tart. These savory little pizzas, topped with tomatoes, herbs and cheese, are sure winners.

Pâté Brisée
3 cups all-purpose flour
Pinch of salt
Pinch of sugar
1 cup (2 sticks) plus 2 tablespoons cold unsalted butter
1/2 cup vegetable shortening
5 tablespoons cold water

To make pâté brisée: In a medium bowl combine flour, salt, and sugar. With a pastry cutter or your fingers, cut in the butter and shortening until the mixture resembles oatmeal. Add cold water and mix until all the ingredients are moistened. Form into a ball. Cover and chill for 30 minutes. Preheat the oven to 375°F. On a lightly floured surface, roll out the dough to a 1/8-inch thickness. Cut into 3-inch rounds. Prick the dough all over with a fork. Place on a baking sheet and bake until dough is tan.

1 cup chopped plum tomatoes
1/2 cup minced fresh basil
1/4 cup minced fresh thyme
1 cup crumbled goat, feta, or shredded mozzarella cheese
Sliced plum tomatoes and black olives for garnish
8 teaspoons olive oil
Salad (recipe follows)

Top the dough with the chopped tomatoes, basil, thyme, and cheese, and garnish with sliced tomatoes and black olives. Drizzle with a little olive oil. Bake for 4 to 5 minutes, or until cheese is melted. Serve with salad. ▪

Salad

Serves 8

1 cup olive oil
1/2 cup balsamic vinegar
1/2 teaspoon crushed garlic
1 tablespoon soy sauce
Pinch of salt and pepper
4 cups salad greens
In a medium bowl, whisk together the oil, vinegar, garlic, soy sauce, and salt and pepper until the mixture is emulsified. Toss the salad greens in enough vinaigrette to coat, about 1/2 cup. Store left-over vinigrette in a tightly-sealed container in the refrigerator. ▪

Goat Cheese in Filo Provençal

From André Poirot of Begue's, New Orleans, LA

Serves 1

Herbes de Provence, which gives the vegetables in this colorful appetizer their special character, is a mixture of dried herbs from southern France. Commercial mixtures vary in content and may include many, if not all, of the following: savory, thyme, rosemary, marjoram, sage, lavender, and sometimes fennel seeds. In a pinch, mix your own from 4 parts thyme, and 1 part each of savory, rosemary, marjoram, and basil.

1-1/2 ounces fresh goat cheese
1 teaspoon cracked black pepper
1 tablespoon herbes de Provence
4 sheets filo dough
4 tablespoons virgin olive oil
1 tomato, sliced 1/4 inch thick
1 zucchini, sliced 1/4 inch thick
1 yellow squash, sliced 1/4 inch thick
1/2 cup shredded lettuce

Cut the cheese into 3 medallions and sprinkle them with a little cracked black pepper and herbes de Provence. Brush each sheet of filo dough with olive oil, and cut into 3 equal pieces. Enclose each cheese medallion in a section of the filo.

Preheat oven to 400°F. Place the vegetable slices on a baking sheet, brush them with 2 tablespoons of olive oil, and season with salt, pepper, and herbes de Provence. Bake for 5 to 6 minutes, or until tender. Meanwhile, in a medium sauté pan or skillet, heat the remaining 2 tablespoons of olive oil over medium heat

and cook the filo packets until browned on both sides, about 3 to 4 minutes. Place the vegetables around the edge of a heated plate. Place the lettuce in the center of the plate. Place the filo packets atop the bed of lettuce. ▪

Crawfish Cakes with Lemon Butter Sauce

From Dick Brennan, Jr., of Palace Café, New Orleans, LA

Serves 4 (2 cakes per person)

Here is a zesty alternative to the ever-popular crab cakes. Chef Dick Brennan makes his cakes with crawfish, which is readily available in Louisiana. Crawfish is becoming more popular outside Louisiana, and more fish markets now stock it.

Crawfish Cakes
1/2 cup (1 stick) butter
2 cups diced onions
1 cup diced celery
1 cup diced red bell pepper
1 cup diced green bell pepper
1 tablespoon Worcestershire sauce
1 tablespoon Louisiana hot sauce
1 pound fresh crawfish tail meat
1/2 cup (2 ounces) Romano cheese, grated
One cup dried bread crumbs
Salt and pepper to taste

4 tablespoons olive oil
Lemon Butter Sauce
Juice of 2 lemons
1/4 cup dry white wine
1 cup (2 sticks) butter, cut into tablespoons
4 tablespoons all-purpose flour for dusting

To make the crawfish cakes: In a large sauté pan or skillet, melt the butter and sauté the vegetables until tender, about 5 minutes. Add the Worcestershire, hot sauce, and crawfish tail meat, and sauté for 2 to 3 minutes or until crawfish are heated through. Remove from heat. Add the Romano cheese and bread crumbs, and mix thoroughly. Season with salt and pepper. Transfer the mixture to a 12" x 18"-inch baking sheet and spread out evenly. Refrigerate for at least 45 minutes.

Form into 8 round cakes about 1/2 cup each. Dust with flour. In a large sauté pan or skillet, heat the olive oil and sauté 4 cakes at a time for 3 to 4 minutes on each side, or until golden brown.

To make the sauce: Place the lemon juice and white wine in a medium saucepan. Cook over medium heat to reduce the liquid by half. Lower heat, and whisk in 1 tablespoon of butter at a time. ▪

To serve: Ladle sauce onto four 6-inch plates. Place 2 crawfish cakes on each plate.

French Bistro Tart, Keil Moshier, Bistro la Tour

Soft-shell Crawfish with Creole Mustard Sauce

*From Bob Roth of The Steak Knife,
New Orleans, LA*

Serves 4

Soft-shell crawfish are now available in specialty fish stores. Like soft-shell crabs, they are a seasonal delicacy. In order to grow, the crustacean must shed its hard outer shell. The crustaceans are caught before the soft new shell underneath has a chance to harden. The whole point of this dish is the paper-thin edible shells that, when battered and deep fried, produce double crispness surrounding the sweet, succulent crawfish meat inside. The spicy batter and Creole mustard sauce, however, aren't half bad, so if you can't find soft-shell crawfish, try this dish with shelled fresh crawfish tails.

16 live soft-shell crawfish

Batter
6 eggs, beaten
3/4 cup all-purpose flour
1/2 cup milk
1/2 cup Louisiana hot sauce
1 teaspoon salt
1 teaspoon pepper

2 cups corn flour seasoned with 1 tablespoon Creole seasoning
1 quart peanut oil for frying
1 quart vegetable oil for frying

Creole Mustard Sauce
1/2 cup mayonnaise
1/2 cup Creole mustard or hot, spicy mustard
1/2 teaspoon prepared horseradish
1 teaspoon Worcestershire sauce
Juice of 1 lemon

To clean the crawfish, cut off the tip of the head behind the eyes. Remove the two rock-like calcium deposits behind the tip of the head. Rinse the crawfish carefully so you don't wash out the fat in the head. Pat dry with paper towels.

To make the batter: Whisk all of the ingredients together until smooth.

Dip the crawfish in the batter, then into the corn flour. Heat the oils in a large sauté pan or skillet and cook the crawfish until golden brown on both sides, about 3 to 4 minutes.

To make the sauce: Whisk all of the ingredients together until thoroughly blended. Put 1/4 cup of the sauce on each serving plate. Place 4 fried crawfish in the sauce.■

Grilled Shrimp with Coriander Sauce, and Black Bean Cakes

*From Susan Spicer of Bayona,
New Orleans, LA*

Serves 4

Susan Spicer, chef-owner of Bayona restaurant in New Orleans, shares a recipe that tastes great, is quick and easy to prepare, and a breeze to garnish and present. Add a salad and corn bread for a complete lunch for two.

16 medium to large shrimp, heads removed, peeled, and deveined
1/4 cup olive oil
1 teaspoon minced garlic
1/2 teaspoon ground cumin
1/2 teaspoon ground coriander
1/2 teaspoon salt
1/2 teaspoon black pepper

Coriander Sauce
1 tablespoon minced shallots
1/2 teaspoon grated orange zest
1/2 teaspoon ground coriander
2 tablespoons orange juice
1/4 cup dry white wine
2 tablespoons sherry wine vinegar
3/4 cup (1-1/2 sticks) butter at room temperature, cut into 12 pieces
1 tablespoon minced fresh cilantro
Salt and pepper to taste

Black bean cakes (recipe follows)

Toss the shrimp with the oil, garlic, and seasonings. Skewer 4 for each portion and marinate for 20 minutes.

Grilled Shrimp with Coriander Sauce, and Black Bean Cakes, Susan Spicer, Bayona

To make the sauce: In a small saucepan, simmer the shallots, orange zest, ground coriander, orange juice, wine, and vinegar, until reduced by half. While still hot, place the mixture in blender and blend for 5 seconds. Add butter one piece at a time. Stir in the cilantro, and season with salt and pepper. Keep warm over hot water.

Broil or grill the shrimp for 2 to 3 minutes on each side, until pink and opaque. Nap with sauce and serve with black bean cake topped with sour cream.

Black Bean Cakes

Makes 8 cakes

1 pound black beans, washed and soaked overnight in cold water to cover
3 to 4 tablespoons peanut oil
2 onions, chopped
2 bell peppers, seeded, deribbed, and chopped
2 jalapeño chilies, seeded and minced (optional)
2 tablespoons minced garlic
2 teaspoons ground cumin
1 bay leaf
1 teaspoon chili powder
2 tablespoons honey
1/4 cup cider vinegar
Salt, pepper, and Tabasco sauce to taste
Flour for dusting
8 teaspoons sour cream for garnish
Cilantro sprigs for garnish

Drain the washed and soaked beans and place them in a 1 gallon pot with cold water to cover. Bring to a boil, lower heat, and simmer for 1 hour; skimming every now and then; stir frequently. In a medium sauté pan or skillet, over medium heat, heat the oil and the onions, peppers, optional jalapeños, and garlic until soft, about 5 minutes; add to the beans along with cumin, the bay leaf, chili powder, honey, vinegar, salt, pepper, and Tabasco. Add more water, if necessary, to keep the beans from sticking to the bottom of the pot. Continue cooking and stirring over low heat until beans and vegetables begin to break down.

Preheat oven to 350°F. Purée the beans in a food processor, then spread the purée in a 12- x 18-inch baking pan and place them in the oven for 10 minutes. Let cool, and form beans into small cakes, about 1/2 cup each.

Shrimp Carrie, Tom Weaver, Christian's Restaurant

Dust with flour, shaking off the excess. In a large sauté pan or skillet, heat the peanut oil and cook the cakes in batches until crisp, about 2 to 3 minutes on each side. Place in a warm oven until all the cakes are cooked. Garnish with a spoonful of sour cream and sprig of cilantro. ∎

Shrimp Carrie

From Tom Weaver of Christian's Restaurant, New Orleans, LA

Serves 4

What is a gifted Louisiana chef's idea of fish and chips? Deep-fried sweet potato chips with sautéed shrimp, topped with a red sweet pepper vinaigrette.

Red Sweet Pepper Vinaigrette
1-1/2 cups red bell peppers, seeded, deribbed, and diced
1/2 cup sugar
1/2 cup water
1/2 cup distilled white vinegar
1 teaspoon Dijon mustard
1 cup olive oil
1 teaspoon salt
1/4 teaspoon white pepper
1 pound medium shrimp, peeled and deveined

3/4 cup clarified margarine (see Techniques)
1-1/2 teaspoon salt
1/4 teaspoon cayenne pepper
1/2 teaspoon black pepper
8 cups peanut oil
2 large sweet potatoes, peeled and julienned

To prepare the vinaigrette: Place the red peppers, sugar, water, and vinegar in a medium saucepan and bring to a boil. Reduce heat and simmer for 5 minutes. Remove from heat, place in a stainless steel bowl and let cool. Add the Dijon mustard and olive oil slowly while whisking until blended. Add the salt and white pepper and set aside.

Brush the shrimp with the clarified margarine and season with salt, cayenne, and black pepper. Grill over medium coals for 2 minutes on each side until pink and opaque; set aside and keep warm. In a large heavy pot or deep-fryer, heat the peanut oil to 350°F and cook the sweet potatoes for 1 minute or until crisp. Remove with a slotted spoon and drain on paper towels. Place sweet potatoes in the center of each plate. Surround each mound with about 9 shrimp and spoon red sweet pepper vinaigrette over the shrimp. ∎

Commander's Tasso Shrimp with Five-pepper Jelly

From Jamie Shannon of Commander's Palace, New Orleans, LA

Serves 6

Chef Jamie Shannon of the legendary Commander's Palace restaurant in New Orleans combines butterflied jumbo shrimp with spicy tasso ham, deep-fries the combination and plates it with a spicy butter sauce and pepper jelly. The pepper jelly is a nice accent for grilled fish, roast chicken, or lamb, so double the recipe and store it in a sterilized jar in the refrigerator. When doubling the recipe, keep the amount of cayenne the same unless you share the Louisiana love of hot stuff – in which case, double it along with other ingredients.

8 ounces tasso ham, cut into 32 matchsticks
30 jumbo shrimp, deveined and butterflied (see Techniques)
2 eggs
2 cups milk
2 cups all-purpose flour
8 cups vegetable oil

Crystal Butter Sauce
1/2 cup Crystal hot sauce or pepper sauce
1/2 cup dry white wine
1/2 tablespoon minced shallots
1/4 tablespoon minced garlic
2 cups (4 sticks) unsalted butter
Pepper Jelly (recipe follows)

Frisée, red oak leaf lettuce leaves, or watercress sprigs for garnish.

Place a piece of tasso inside slit in the shrimp and secure with toothpick. In a large bowl, beat the eggs and milk together until blended. Dip each shrimp into this mixture and then dredge in the flour.
Heat the oil to 350°F in a deep-fat fryer or large heavy pot. Deep-fry shrimp in batches about 3 to 4 minutes or until golden brown. Remove with slotted spoon.

To make butter sauce: Combine the hot sauce, wine, shallots, and garlic in a small saucepan and cook over medium heat until the mixture is reduced by half. Let cool to warm, then slowly add the butter,

New Orleans Barbecued Shrimp, Gerard Maras, Mr. B's

4 tablespoons at a time, stirring constantly. The key to this sauce, like all butter sauces, is to keep the heat warm at all times, not too hot or too cold. Periodically place pan over low heat to keep the sauce just warm enough to melt the butter.

To Serve: Arrange 1/4 cup of the pepper jelly on the base of each of six salad plates to be used. Place the butter sauce in a small bowl and dip shrimp into sauce and coat evenly. Place 5 shrimp on each plate in a circular design and garnish with suitable greens, such as frisée or watercress.

Pepper Jelly
1-1/2 cups white distilled vinegar
2 tablespoons balsamic vinegar
3/4 cup corn syrup
1 yellow bell pepper, finely diced
1 red bell pepper, finely diced
1 green bell pepper, finely diced

1 jalapeño chili, finely diced
1/8 teaspoon cayenne pepper

Combine the white and balsamic vinegars and corn syrup in a large sauce pan and bring to a boil. Reduce heat to a slow boil and cook until liquid is reduced by half, about 10 to 15 minutes. Add the peppers, chili, and cayenne, and simmer 10 minutes. Remove from heat and let cool. ∎

New Orleans Barbecued Shrimp

From Gerard Maras of Mr. B's,
New Orleans, LA

Serves 2

It just doesn't get any better than Chef Maras' spicy shrimp with French bread for dipping up—and cutting down the heat in—the sauce. If ever a dish was meant to be served with cold beer, this is it. Have an empty bowl ready to hold the shrimp shells, and provide plenty of paper napkins, because this is a peel-your-own dish.

14 large unpeeled shrimp with heads
6 tablespoons cold, unsalted butter
1-1/2 teaspoon ground black pepper
1-1/2 teaspoon cracked black pepper
1 teaspoon Creole seasoning (recipe
    follows)
3 tablespoons Worcestershire sauce
1 teaspoon chopped garlic
Juice of 1 lemon
Hot French bread

Preheat the oven to 450°F. Place the shrimp, 3 tablespoons of the butter, the seasonings, and garlic in a sauté pan or ovenproof skillet large enough to hold the shrimp in one layer. Place the shrimp in the oven for 2 minutes. Turn the shrimp and return to the oven for 2 to 3 minutes. Remove the shrimp from the oven and place over medium heat. Add the lemon juice and stir in the remaining 3 tablespoons butter, 1 tablespoon at a time. Serve the shrimp in a bowl and pour the sauce over the shrimp. Serve with hot French bread for dipping.

Creole Seasoning

Makes 2/3 cup

2 tablespoons salt
2 tablespoons garlic powder
1 tablespoon ground black pepper
1 tablespoon cayenne pepper
1 tablespoon dried thyme
1 tablespoon dried oregano
2-1/2 tablespoons paprika
1 tablespoon onion powder

Blend all of the ingredients in a bowl. Store in a sealed container.∎

GERARD MARAS
Mr. B's, New Orleans

"Getting out on the farm and seeing the product is about as exciting to me as being in the kitchen," says Gerard Maras, executive chef at Mr . B's restaurant. His fascination with food started in childhood: "My grandparents were from Poland and I still remember the weekends at their house and the food they cooked: interesting, savory, good cooking. My mother and sister were incredible cooks and food was central to all our major holidays. We reveled in it!"

Maras was born in Blackwell, Oklahoma, and he financed his college education by working in New York restaurants. By the time he graduated from State University of New York in Oswego, New York, Maras was hooked on foodservice. At twenty-four he became the head chef of the Gaslight Restaurant in Fayetteville, New York. From New York he moved to Florida and worked with European chefs, honing his skills to become head chef at Fitzgerald's in West Palm Beach, and Harpoon Louie's in Jupiter.

When Maras moved to New Orleans, he moved into the kitchens at Commander's Palace as a sous-chef, where his unique talents prompted the Brennan family to promote him to executive chef at Mr. B's. Under his aegis the restaurant has won an Ivy Award from *Restaurants & Institutions* magazine and a Fine Dining Hall of Fame Award from *Nation's Restaurant News.*

Maras reassures the nonprofessional cook about trying his recipes. "Although in the restaurant we can do a lot of things because we have the equipment, the staff, and we don't have to shop all around town for product, we still base our food on older cooking techniques that were basic and simpler. We've gotten away from many of those five-step dishes."

But he does encourage the home chef to do what he does: search for the best. "Absolutely buy the best! It's worth paying a little extra. And use things in season at their peak. That way you don't have to cover it with sauce—you can feature it."

Maras's featured recipes in this book are New Orleans Barbecued Shrimp (appetizer), Roasted Leg of Duckling with Spring Leeks, and New Potatoes (entrée), and Sour Cream Pound Cake with Lemon Crème Sauce (dessert).

Oysters Gabie

From Greg Sonnier of Gabrielle, New Orleans, LA

Serves 4

Seasoned bread crumbs are always a great topping for baked seafood. Chef Greg Sonnier gives a lagniappe to his topping for baked oysters by adding artichokes and pancetta, a spicy, unsmoked Italian bacon.

1 lemon, halved
4 tablespoons olive oil
2 large artichokes
4 ounces pancetta, finely diced
1 tablespoon butter
1/4 cup chopped green onions (white part only) or shallots
1 tablespoon minced garlic
2 tablespoons fresh minced parsley
Salt and pepper
Juice of 1 lemon
1/4 cup plus 2 tablespoons dry bread crumbs
1/4 cup plus 2 tablespoons grated Parmesan cheese
16 to 20 large plump oysters, liquor reserved

Place the halved lemon and two tablespoons of the olive oil in a large pot of boiling water. Add the artichokes and cook until tender, about 20 minutes.

Drain and cool. Pull off the leaves and scrape off the pulp at their bases. Dig out the choke with a spoon and dice the remaining heart. Set aside with the scraped pulp.

Preheat the oven to 450°F. In a medium sauté pan or skillet, heat 1 tablespoon olive oil and cook the pancetta until brown; add the remaining tablespoon of oil and the butter. Sauté the green onions or shallots, garlic, and parsley until tender, 3 to 4 minutes. Add the diced artichokes and lemon juice. If the dressing looks too dry, add a little oyster liquor to moisten. Sauté for about 2 minutes. Adjust the seasoning. Remove from heat, add 1/4 cup of the bread crumbs and 1/4 cup of the cheese and toss lightly.

Place 4 or 5 oysters into each of 4 individual casseroles. Top with the artichoke dressing. Sprinkle with the remaining cheese and bread crumbs. Bake until browned, 10 to 15 minutes. Serve with hollandaise sauce over the dressing.

Hollandaise Sauce

Makes 1-1/4 cups

2 egg yolks
2 tablespoons dry white wine
1 tablespoon fresh lemon juice
Pinch of salt

Pinch of cayenne
1 cup warm clarified butter (see Techniques)
Warm water as necessary

In a double boiler over simmering water, whisk the egg yolks, wine, lemon juice, salt, and cayenne, until thick, about 5 to 6 minutes, being careful not to overcook the eggs. Add the warm butter in a thin stream, continually whisking until all the butter has been incorporated. If the sauce is too thick, add warm water 1 tablespoon at a time. Adjust the seasoning and serve. ■

Oysters, Prosciutto, and Roasted Peppers with Creole Mustard Sauce Meunière

From Jay Kimball of Romair's, Terrytown, LA

Serves 4

This is a creative and tasty update of the old-fashioned, but always popular, angels on horseback hors d'oeuvre (oysters wrapped in bacon, skewered and broiled). Corn flour, which is finely milled white or yellow corn, serves admirably as a crisp batter for fried foods.

8 ounces prosciutto, cut into 1/2-inch slices
2 red, green, or yellow roasted peppers, cut into 16 strips (see Techniques)
16 large oysters
1 tablespoon seafood seasoning (recipe follows)
1 cup corn flour
1 teaspoon salt
1 cup oil

Creole Mustard Sauce
1/3 cup beef broth
1 teaspoon fresh lemon juice
1/2 teaspoon Creole mustard
Dash of Worcestershire sauce
Dash of heavy (whipping) cream
3 tablespoons unsalted butter

Cut the prosciutto into 16 cubes. Place the end of a pepper strip on a metal skewer, add a cube of prosciutto, and an oyster, and wrap by skewering the other end of the pepper. Repeat until the skewer is filled. Or, use tooth picks. In a bowl, combine the seafood seasoning, corn flour and salt. Roll the skewered food in the corn flour mixture. In a large sauté pan or skillet, heat the oil to 350°F

Oysters Sautéed in Cumin, Hubert Sandot, L'Economie

and cook the skewered food for 2 to 3 minutes on each side, or until light golden brown. Remove with a slotted spatula and drain on paper towels.

To make the sauce: In a small saucepan, bring all of the ingredients except the butter to a boil over medium heat. Whisk in the butter a tablespoon at a time, until smooth.

To serve: Remove prosciutto, pepper, and oysters from skewers and divide among 4 plates. Drizzle with the Creole mustard sauce.

Seafood Seasoning

Makes about 1/2 cup

6 teaspoons paprika
4 teaspoons ground garlic
4 teaspoons black pepper
2-1/2 teaspoons ground onion
1-1/2 teaspoon fine thyme
1-1/4 teaspoon fine oregano
1-1/4 teaspoon basil
1 teaspoon cayenne
Salt, to taste

In a small bowl, combine all ingredients. Store tightly sealed in a cool, dry place.

Oysters Sautéed in Cumin

From Hubert Sandot of L'Economie, and Martinique, New Orleans, LA

Serves 4

This is one of those recipes in which the sum is much greater than the parts. Although it is simple to prepare, the combination of wine, cumin and a touch of soy sauce results in a captivating, complex flavor. Serve this à la minute dish from its sauté pan or skillet, and accompany with French bread to catch the pan sauce.

2 tablespoons butter
8 mushrooms
2 garlic cloves, minced
16 oysters
1/2 cup dry white wine
1 teaspoon ground cumin
1/2 teaspoon soy sauce

In a sauté pan or skillet over medium-high heat, melt the butter and sauté the mushrooms and garlic for 2 to 3 minutes. Add the oysters and sauté for 3 minutes. Add the white wine, cumin and soy sauce, and simmer for 1 minute. Arrange on four small plates and serve. ∎

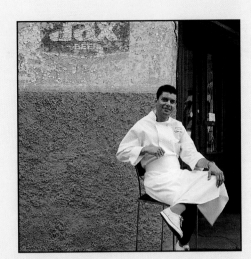

HUBERT SANDOT
L'Economie and Martinique, New Orleans

Hubert Sandot dreamed of opening a restaurant from the time he was fourteen years old. After getting his bachelor's degree in economics and social studies, he went to work at the Hôtel George V in Paris, learning the ropes for five years by starting as a night manager. By 1985 he was food and beverage director of the five-star Hôtel Barzac in Paris.

"Then I took a break," he says; he went to Japan where he married his wife and also worked as a fashion model. By 1989 they had decided to come to the States. "We bought a car and crossed the country twice— west to east and east to west—to find the place we liked best." Santa Barbara was love at first sight, but the cost of opening a restaurant was prohibitive. They loved New York, too, but finally decided it was too much like Paris and Tokyo. Atlanta was tempting, but New Orleans got their vote, and in 1989 they opened L'Economie, an intimate fifty-five-seat restaurant.

Some food writers describe Sandot's style of cooking as "Neo Creole." "I'm French," he says, "and I can't turn my back on my culture. However, I use no cream and almost no butter in my cooking. I never went to cooking school and, although I could do classic dishes, I don't. I'm not interested in those." Instead, Sandot's food (which has gained such a following that he just opened a second restaurant, Martinique) is light French food. He uses no meat stock, only fish stock, and does not use flour to thicken sauces, depending instead on long reductions of wine. One of the secrets of his sauces is honey. "Where appropriate it gives sauces a very heavy and rich look. I use only a little butter, and for the rest high quality olive oil, sesame oil, and cold-pressed walnut oil from France."

His customers are seventy-five percent local. "In New Orleans when they like a restaurant, they really support it. If they don't like you, you know it very fast. And even if they like you and something goes wrong, you will hear about it right away!" Sandot says that people in New Orleans love food and know a lot about it, and for him that makes cooking in New Orleans "A very nice challenge."

His featured recipes in this book are Oysters Sautéed in Cumin (appetizer), Rack of Lamb with Apricot Sauce (entrée), and Figs in Vanilla and Pepper Sauce, Flambéed with Pernod (dessert).

Sea Scallops with Roasted Red Pepper Sauce, Robert Krol, Crozier's

Sautéed Oysters with Sweet Potatoes

From Bernhard Gotz of Fillets, New Orleans, LA

Serves 4

Chef Bernhard Gotz, the author of this recipe, shows his classical European culinary training by piping the sweet potatoes from a pastry bag to border the plate. This elegant touch is well worth the extra few minutes it takes. To simplify the recipe without sacrificing flavor, make scoops of sweet potato purée with a melon baller or teaspoon.

Sweet Potatoes
2 sweet potatoes, peeled and cut into eighths
4 tablespoons butter at room temperature
Pinch of ground nutmeg
Pinch of ground cinnamon
Salt and pepper to taste

Oysters
3 tablespoons olive oil
2 minced shallots
1 teaspoon minced garlic
16 large oysters, shucked
1 cup Madeira wine or dry sherry
1 teaspoon minced fresh dill
1 teaspoon minced fresh thyme
1 teaspoon minced fresh tarragon
1 tablespoon minced fresh parsley
3/4 cup (1-1/2 sticks) butter at room temperature
Curry powder to taste
Salt and pepper to taste
Green onions for garnish

To make the sweet potatoes: In a large saucepan, boil the sweet potatoes for 6 to 8 minutes or until tender. Drain and dry them in a warm oven five minutes, to remove all water from the potatoes. Put the potatoes through a ricer or purée with a food processor. Add the butter and seasonings. Keep warm.

To prepare the oysters: In a large sauté pan or skillet, heat the olive oil and sauté the shallots and garlic until translucent, about 3 minutes. Add the oysters and Madeira and cook over medium heat to reduce the mixture by half, about 4 to 5 minutes. Remove the oysters and add the herbs to the sauce; simmer for 5 minutes. Remove from heat and whisk in the butter and seasonings. Return the oysters to the pan and keep warm until serving time.

Place the warm potato mixture in a pastry bag fitted with a star tip and pipe a border on each plate. Place 4 oysters in the center of each plate and garnish with chopped green onions. ∎

Sea Scallops with Roasted Red Pepper Sauce

From Robert Krol of Crozier's, Metairie, LA

Serves 4

Roasted red bell peppers and cream make the perfect sauce for quickly sautéed sweet scallops.

2 red bell peppers
1 tablespoon butter
1/2 teaspoon minced garlic
2 cups heavy (whipping) cream
1/2 teaspoon salt
Pinch of pepper
Olive oil
8 sea scallops

Roast the peppers in 400°F oven until very dark. Place in a closed paper bag for 15 minutes. Peel the peppers, and remove the seeds and ribs. Purée in a blender or food processor until very smooth. Add the pepper purée, butter, and garlic to a hot medium saucepan and cook for 3 minutes. Add the cream and cook to reduce the sauce for 3 minutes. Add the salt and pepper and keep warm.

In a large sauté pan or skillet, heat the olive oil until almost smoking, add the scallops and cook on one side for 2 minutes; turn and cook for 2 minutes. Transfer 2 scallops to each serving plate and cover with pepper sauce. ▪

ROBERT JAMES KROL
Crozier's, Metairie

"If you can work at Crozier's, you can cook anywhere in the United States," says head chef Robert James Krol. Referring to Crozier's chef-proprietor, Gerard Crozier, Krol adds, "He's both the toughest and the best. But once you get past the first three or four years, and get the consistency down to his satisfaction, then he allows you some leeway."

Gerard Crozier says that's a fair statement. By his own admission he's tough. He and his wife and partner Eveline came to the States in 1970 from France, where he received training at Michelin-rated two- and three-star restaurants. In 1972, they moved from Milwaukee to New Orleans where "food is a priority," and where ninety percent of his customers are locals. "If ninety percent of your customers are tourists, it's not the same. When your clientele is local, then you cannot afford to make mistakes."

"Robert came up the same way I did," Crozier says. "He started out washing dishes the same way I did thirty-four years ago. He's a very professional man. We're happy with him and he's happy with us."

Krol says that he had a job as a dishwasher in the summertime when he was in high school. "I knew the chef at the restaurant where I worked and I wanted to be like him: a chef. He told me, 'Just keep it up and if you're good enough, you'll make it.'"

Before coming to Crozier's, Krol worked as *saucier* at La Louisiane and was head chef at Montalbano's, both in New Orleans. At Crozier's the menu is fancy French bistro food, and he never gets tired of cooking it. "If you can cook French food, you can cook anything. And you can see how much of a foundation it is for the food of New Orleans."

Krol's recipes in this book are Sea Scallops with Roasted Red Pepper Sauce (appetizer), and Chocolate Mousse Cheesecake (dessert).

Clancy's Quail

From Kevin Graham of the Windsor Court Hotel, New Orleans, LA

Serves 1

Okay, so you want to impress someone? This is the dish to do it with! (See the television program, where Windsor Court's chef Kevin Graham makes it look easy.)

Two 4-ounce quails
1 tablespoon salt
1 tablespoon sugar
2 ounces foie gras
2 ounces whipped cream
1 teaspoon Madeira or dry sherry
Salt and pepper to taste
Kumquat Relish (recipe follows)

Rub quails with salt and sugar mixture and let marinate for 20 minutes. Slow smoke over low coals for one hour.

Remove the skin from one of the quails, then gently remove all of the meat. Finely chop or grind the meat and set aside. Press the foie gras through a fine-meshed sieve and combine with the cream and Madeira. Fold in the chopped quail meat. Season with salt and pepper and refrigerate.

To Serve: Slice the meat off the remaining quail breast and cut each side into 7 slices. Set aside. Remove the bones from the carcass and re-form the breast with the foie gras mousse. Cover with the reserved breast slices, overlapping them at an angle; the breast should take on the appearance of being braided. Arrange the quail on plates with kumquat relish. ∎

Kumquat Relish
1/4 cup sugar
8 kumquats, thinly sliced
1 tablespoon Champagne vinegar
1 tablespoon dry vermouth

Place the sugar in a sauté pan or skillet over medium to high heat. Stir to caramelize evenly. When the sugar turns a golden brown, add kumquats, Champagne vinegar and vermouth. Cook until the sugar is melted and most of liquid is evaporated, about 5 minutes. Remove and let cool. ∎

Rabbit Tenders with Tasso and Shrimp Fettuccine

From Randy Barlow of Kelsey's, New Orleans, LA

Serves 2

Fresh rabbit is always best, but frozen rabbit is better than no rabbit at all. A full-service meat market or butcher shop can order rabbit if they don't stock it. Boneless, skinless chicken breasts, pounded to flatten, may be substituted for rabbit tenderloin. The flavor won't be the same, but no one will complain.

Tasso is a Cajun specialty. It is made from cured pork, cayenne, several herbs and spices, then smoked. The result is a firm, smoky, and tangy meat that is principally used for seasoning.

2 rabbit tenderloins, butterflied
Salt and pepper to taste
1 cup flour for dusting
3 eggs, beaten with 1 cup milk
1 cup dried bread crumbs
1/4 cup oil
2 cups heavy (whipping) cream
2 ounces chopped tasso ham
8 ounces peeled raw shrimp
2 tablespoons butter
1 bunch green onions, chopped
8 ounces fettuccine, cooked until al dente
2 tablespoons grated Romano cheese
2 tablespoons grated Parmesan cheese

With the flat side of a meat mallet or the base of a wine bottle, pound the rabbit until about 1/2 inch thick. Season with salt and pepper. Dust with flour, dip in the egg-milk mixture, then into the bread crumbs.

In a large sauté pan or skillet, heat the oil over medium-high heat and cook the rabbit until golden brown on each side, about 2 to 3 minutes per side. Remove the rabbit from the pan. Pour off the oil; add the cream, tasso, shrimp, butter, and green onions. Cook until the shrimp turns pink and opaque, about 4 to 5 minutes. Add the cooked pasta and toss. Add grated cheeses and toss. Serve the rabbit over the shrimp fettuccine. ∎

Rabbit Tenders with Tasso and Shrimp Fettuccine, Randy Barlow, Kelsey's

PATTI CONSTANTIN
Constantin's, New Orleans

Food writers have described Patti Constantin's imaginative cooking as "nouvelle Creole." "If I had to say what my style was, I'd call it Continental Creole," she says. "But my mother cooked like this before people even gave it a name."

She remembers her Scottish-Irish mother as an inspired cook who garnished plates lavishly for family meals. "She was into having textures and variety on one plate, and I guess it kind of rubbed off on me."

Before opening Constantin's with her husband and restaurant manager Paul, Constantin worked in New Orleans restaurants ranging from La Bonne Bouche to Gautreau's.

Constantin's was recommended by *Cook's* magazine, *The New York Times* and the *Chicago Tribune*, and her style of cooking has been lauded by national and local food media. Constantin is somewhat bemused by the media attention she has received: "My whole intention was to please people with food. I had no idea that news people would call and interview me. I hardly advertised and never hired a publicist."

The foundation of her cooking is flavor and texture. "I can't stand to just eat one thing. I want a combination of textures and flavors: dimensional food. And when it comes to a choice between flavor and appearance, flavor comes first. Food shouldn't be too beautiful to eat."

She loves fresh ingredients. "I'm an advocate of using as fresh a product as I can." And she recommends it to the nonprofessional cook: "Buy the best-quality product you can. That doesn't mean you have to buy a filet as opposed to a round steak—which you can make taste good. But when you do buy a filet, buy the best you can get."

Constantin and her husband have three children, who seem to be following in their culinary footsteps. One day she heard her preschool child give someone a recipe over the phone for panéed chicken. "He really had it down," she says.

Her dream is to someday open up a small specialty restaurant—smaller and even more labor-intensive than Constantin's (closed in favor of a catering business), where she can prepare "food extravaganzas" for guests.

Constantin's featured recipes are Rabbit Strudel (appetizer), Grilled Baby Wild Boar T-Bones (entrée), and Snappy's Polar Chip (dessert).

Rabbit Strudel

From Patti Constantin of Constantin's, New Orleans, LA

Serves 6

Say strudel and most people think of a sweet, fruit-filled flaky dessert, but this savory rabbit pastry gives strudel new meaning. It is accompanied with a rich sauce based on the Creole vegetable trinity of onions, celery and green pepper.■

Roast Rabbit and optional stock
1 whole rabbit
1 yellow onion, coarsely chopped or sliced
3 cloves garlic, coarsely chopped
1/2 teaspoon black pepper
1/2 teaspoon cayenne pepper
1/2 teaspoon salt
1/2 cup dry vermouth
4 fresh thyme sprigs
12 cups water (optional)

Filling
2 bunches spinach stemmed
2 cloves garlic, minced
3 minced shallots
1/2 teaspoon chopped fresh thyme
5 cups (1-1/4 pound) grated mustard seed Havarti
Salt, red and black pepper to taste

1 package filo dough
3/4 cup dried bread crumbs
2 cups (4 sticks) butter melted

Sauce
2 tablespoons olive oil
2 onions chopped
6 cloves garlic, minced
2 stalks celery, chopped
1 green bell pepper, seeded, deribbed and chopped
1 cup dry white wine
2 cups rabbit stock or chicken broth
1 teaspoon fresh minced thyme
1 teaspoon fresh minced marjoram
1 teaspoon minced fresh flat-leaf parsley
Juice of lemon
1 red bell pepper, roasted and puréed
Salt, black and red pepper to taste

To roast the rabbit: Place the rabbit in a roasting pan with all of the remaining ingredients except the water. Cover with aluminum foil. Bake at 375°F for about 30 minutes or until tender. Let cool. Pick all the meat off of the rabbit and cut the meat into pieces.

To make rabbit stock: (optional): Place the bones and any scraps from the rabbit in a small stock pot, cover with water, and boil to reduce by half. Strain and set aside.

To make the filling: Blanch the spinach in boiling water and cover for 3 to 4 minutes. Let cool. Drain and squeeze all the moisture out of the spinach. Chop and set aside. Sauté the garlic and shallots until translucent. Add the thyme, spinach and cheese. Add the seasonings.

Place a sheet of filo on a work surface. Brush with butter and sprinkle lightly with bread crumbs. Repeat to make 3 to 5 layers. Cut into 3 lengthwise strips . Place the filling in a line down the center of each strip. Place the chopped rabbit down center of the filling. Fold the sides over, then roll up jelly roll fashion. Cover and chill for 30 minutes. Preheat the oven to 375°F. Bake until lightly browned, about 15 minutes.

To make the sauce: In a large skillet or sauté, pan or heat the oil and sweat the onions, garlic, celery, and green bell pepper. Add the wine and cook over medium heat to reduce by half, about 5 to 8 minutes. Add the stock or broth, herbs, and lemon juice. Simmer until almost all liquid is evaporated. Stir in the roasted red pepper purée. Add the seasonings.

To serve: Pool some sauce on each plate. Cut each strudel diagonally into 4 slices and serve 2 slices on a pool of sauce. ∎

Rabbit Tenderloin with Sautéed Spinach and Creole Mustard Sauce

From Frank Brigtsen of Brigtsen's Restaurant, New Orleans, LA

Serves 4

To reduce time and preparation but still enjoy this flavorful dish, omit the rabbit sausage accompaniment. Or shape the sausage mixture into small patties and poach them in simmering water in a large sauté pan or skillet. When the sausage is cooked through, drain off the water, and brown the patties on both sides.

Creole Mustard Sauce
3/4 cup heavy (whipping) cream
1/4 cup Creole mustard or another hot, spicy mustard
1/4 cup sour cream

1 cup all-purpose flour
5 teaspoons Chef Paul Prudhomme's Pork and Veal Cajun Magic® or another Cajun seasoning
4 rabbit tenderloins
3/4 cup vegetable oil
2 tablespoons unsalted butter
2 teaspoons raw sesame seeds
1 bunch spinach, stemmed
1 teaspoon Chef Paul Prudhomme's Vegetable Cajun Magic® or another Cajun seasoning
1/4 cup rabbit stock or chicken broth

To make the mustard sauce: In a 4-cup saucepan, bring the cream to a low boil over medium heat. Whisk in the mustard and sour cream and simmer for 5 minutes. Keep warm.
Mix the flour with 1 teaspoon of the seasoning. Season each tenderloin evenly with the remaining 4 teaspoons of seasoning. In a 10-inch skillet, heat the oil to 360°F. Coat each tenderloin with the seasoned flour and fry until golden brown, about 2 minutes on the first side and 1 minute on the second side. Remove from the pan with a slotted spatula and drain on paper towels. Discard the oil and place the skillet over medium-high heat. Add the butter and sesame seeds and let the seeds brown for about 10 seconds. Add the spinach and vegetable seasoning and cook until the spinach wilts, about 2 minutes. Add the stock or broth and cook 1 more minute.

Place 1/4 cup of the warm mustard sauce on each of four plates and divide the spinach evenly among the plates. Make 4 or 5 small slices in each tenderloin and place each over a bed of spinach. Serve with sliced rabbit sausage (recipe follows). ∎

Rabbit Sausage

From Frank Brigtsen of Brigtsen's Restaurant, New Orleans, LA

Serves 4

2 pounds fresh rabbit meat, ground
1 pound fresh pork butt or shoulder, ground

2-1/2 teaspoons salt
1/2 teaspoon ground black pepper
1/2 teaspoon ground cayenne pepper
1/4 teaspoon ground white pepper
1/2 teaspoon ground cumin
2 teaspoon finely-chopped fresh sweet thyme
1 tablespoon finely-chopped fresh oregano
1 tablespoon finely-chopped fresh sweet basil
3 tablespoons finely-chopped fresh flat-leaf parsley
1 tablespoon minced garlic
1 cup thinly-sliced green onions
1/2 cup finely-chopped yellow onion
1 egg
3/4 cup rich rabbit or chicken stock (see Techniques)
1/2 cup finely ground French bread crumbs
2 tablespoons grated Parmesan cheese
7 natural pork casings

Combine all ingredients, except the pork casings. In a large mixing bowl, blend thoroughly, using your hands. Transfer mixture to a plastic container, cover, and refrigerate for 24 hours. Pipe the sausage mixture into the pork casings.

Preheat oven to 300°F. Place the sausage links in a shallow pan with 1 inch of water. Bake uncovered for 1 hour. Place sausage links under the broiler and cook until browned on top, about 5 minutes. Slice into desired portions and serve.

Rabbit Strudel, Patti Constantion, Constantions's

Main Courses:
Fish and Shellfish, Poultry and Game Birds, Meat and Game

A lthough appetizers, as we pointed out in "Flexible First Courses: Appetizers," may sometimes be substituted for an entrée, they will never replace main courses altogether. The entrée is still the star of the show, the main event. The entrées in this chapter are all showstoppers. Some are elegant and labor-intensive, some require moderate time and culinary skill, and some are downright easy.

The majority of the entrée recipes that follow are well within the range of the average cook. For example Chili-rubbed Pork Tenderloin with Savory Wild Mushroom Bread Pudding, (André Begnaud, Emeril's), takes almost as long to say as it does to cook. Rack of Lamb with Apricot Sauce (Hubert Sandot, L'Economie) and Swordfish with Roasted Red Pepper Vinaigrette (Randy Windham, Le Bistro) could hardly be easier. And Scaloppine of Chicken with Stir-fried Vegetables (André Poirot, Begue's) is an elegant one-dish meal. You will find other one-dish entrées that, once assembled, tend themselves. They are great for weekends and big, informal parties: Roasted Chicken Stuffed with Crawfish Country Rice, and Creamy Pan Gravy (Greg Sonnier, Gabrielle), Osso Bucco (Bob Roth, The Steak Knife), and two updated traditional favorites, Maw Maw's Chicken Stew and Cajun Smothered Duck (Gigi Patout, Patout's).■

Veal Tenderloin Crusted with Fresh Herbs and Coarse-ground Black Pepper, Michael Uddo, G&E Courtyard Grill

JAMIE SHANNON
Commander's Palace, New Orleans

When Jamie Shannon, executive chef at Commander's Palace, says "Seventy percent of our products come from within a one-hundred-mile radius," he is echoing a lesson he learned as a child growing up on the New Jersey seashore.

He spent summers on his grandparents' farm, located about six miles from his boyhood home of Sea Isle. There he saw herbs and vegetables grown, chickens and hogs raised, and homemade sausage smoked in the chimney. He also tasted great homemade fare such as perogi, stuffed cabbage, black walnut pie, and fresh peach brandy. At home in Sea Isle, his godfather owned a lobster boat and Jamie learned early to clean fish, to set crab traps—and to recognize perfectly fresh seafood. In the Shannon household he grew up with fresh seafood as a staple, along with fresh pastas and cheeses from local street vendors and homemade dishes such as pasta fagiole and boiled codfish with olives and potatoes.

His first restaurant job was in a local cafeteria where everything was made from scratch, and he worked his way up from busboy to cook. Next, he worked as a sous-chef in a restaurant in Wildwood, New Jersey, that specialized in seafood.

Shannon attended the Culinary Institute of America in Hyde Park, New York, on a full scholarship and, while there, under the tutelage of chef Tim Ryan, decided to specialize in American cuisine. After graduation, Shannon worked in the *saucier* section of Trump Towers Hotel and Casino in Atlantic City, preparing traditional French cuisine. At the suggestion of Tim Ryan, in 1984 Shannon went to New Orleans for a first-hand experience with regional American cuisine.

Shannon joined Commander's Palace as *saucier* and gradually moved to the position he now holds as executive chef. Under Shannon's direction, Commander's culinary staff makes its own Worcestershire sauce, sausages, and cheeses. He is committed to fresh, seasonal products, and says, "For American cuisine to grow, we're going to have to support local producers. And be flexible as chefs and customers—and not demand what's not available. The best cuisine is to cook and eat what's in our own backyard."

Shannon's featured recipes in this book are Commander's Tasso Shrimp with Five-pepper Jelly (appetizer), Creole Bouillabaisse (entrée), and Creole Cream Cheese Cheesecake with Caramel Sauce (dessert).

Creole Bouillabaisse

From Jamie Shannon of Commander's Palace, New Orleans, LA

Serves 8

Although every country has its seafood soup, none is more famous than the bouillabaisse of France. Today we tend to place it on a culinary pedestal, forgetting that it began as a simple fisherman's stew. Traditionally it was composed of a fish broth flavored by onions, garlic, tomatoes, herbs, and saffron to which was added the fish from the day's catch that could not be sold. The seafood was then quickly cooked (*bouillir*, to boil; *baisser*, to turn down). Standard accompaniments were and still are French bread and *rouille*, a fiery garlic-chili sauce.

Chef Jamie Shannon's Creole bouillabaisse incorporates chili in the broth, and his assortment of seafood includes shellfish, trout, and his own signature seafood sausage. This dish is a meal in itself, needing only garlic bread, a salad, and a bottle of French rosé, Beaujolais, or Riesling. If you're pressed for time, omit the seafood sausage. But at some point do try it, because it adds a new dimension.

Broth Base
1/2 cup olive oil
1/4 cup chopped garlic
4 gumbo crabs (small blue crabs)
1/2 pound shrimp shells, fresh, not frozen, and heads
1 jalapeño chili, minced and seeded
4 stalks celery, no leaves, coarsely chopped
2 carrots, peeled and coarsely chopped
3 leeks, split, cleaned, and coarsely chopped
3 red bell peppers, seeded, deribbed, and coarsely chopped
4 large white onions, coarsely chopped
6 ripe tomatoes
2 quarts fish stock or 1 quart water and 1 quart white wine
2 fresh thyme sprigs
8 basil leaves, stemmed and coarsely chopped
Pinch saffron

Bouillabaisse
1/2 cup olive oil
3 tablespoons minced garlic
24 mussels, scrubbed and debearded

8 slices of seafood sausage (recipe follows)
1 8-ounce boneless trout or sheepshead
    fillet, cut into 8 pieces
3/4 cup dry white wine
8 cups of Broth Base (recipe follows)
24 medium oysters, shucked
2 leeks, split, cleaned, and julienned
2 tomatoes, peeled and chopped
1 carrot, peeled and chopped
1 red pepper, seeded, deribbed, and
    julienned
8 new red potatoes, quartered and
    blanched for 4 to 5 minutes
24 jumbo shrimp, peeled, tails left on
1 pound crab fingers (the small pincher
    from the first joint of the crab claw)
Salt and pepper to taste

1/4 cup chopped fresh parsley for garnish

To make the broth base: In a large pot,
heat the olive oil over medium heat and
sauté the garlic until brown. Add the crabs
and the shrimp shells, and sauté over high
heat for 10 minutes. Add all the vegetables
and continue to sauté until tender, about
20 minutes. Add the stock or water and
wine, herbs, and saffron, and simmer for
1 hour. Purée in batches and strain.
This may be made up to 2 days ahead,
covered and stored in the refrigerator.

To make Bouillabaisse: In a large
casserole, heat 1/4 cup of the olive oil
over medium heat and sauté garlic until
browned, about 1 minute. Add the
mussels, shrimp, seafood sausage, and
fish, and cook for about 5 minutes. Pour
in the white wine and cook, scraping
the bottom of the pan to remove any
browned juices. Add 8 cups of base and
bring to a boil. In a medium sauté pan or
skillet, heat 1/4 cup of the olive oil over
medium heat and sauté the vegetables
until tender. Add the oysters and crab
fingers to the broth and seafood mixture.
Add the sautéed vegetables to the
mixture. Season with salt and pepper.■

To serve: Pour the hot bouillabaisse into
bowls, top with parsley.

Creole Bouillabaisse, Jamie Shannon, Commander's Palace

Seafood Sausage

Makes 1 large or 8 small sausages

1 pound shrimp, crawfish, crab meat, or
    fish pieces, or a combination
1/4 cup chopped onion
2 tablespoons chopped celery
1 tablespoon chopped bell pepper
1/2 tablespoon minced garlic
1/4 cup shopped andouille sausages
3 tablespoons salt
1 teaspoon ground black pepper
1/4 teaspoon cayenne pepper
1/2 teaspoon dried red pepper flakes
1/2 teaspoon paprika
2 eggs
2 tablespoons water

Chop the fish and/or shellfish into small
cubes and place in a medium mixing
bowl. Stir in all of the rest of the
ingredients. Cut a large piece of plastic
and place the seafood mixture on it.

Shape the mixture into a long cylinder
and roll the plastic around it tightly; seal
the ends. Bring a large pot of water to
180°F. Place the sausage into the water
and cook at simmer for 20 to 30 minutes.
Remove from the water and let cool for 10
minutes. To serve, remove the plastic and
slice. The sausage may be served as a first
course with Creole mustard or used in
Creole Bouillabaisse.

Painted Pasta Ribbons with Louisiana Soft-shell Crab and Roasted Poblano-Ginger Beurre Blanc

From Mike Fennelly of Mike's on the Avenue, New Orleans, LA

Serves 6

Chef Mike Fennelly, proprietor of Mike's on the Avenue in New Orleans, showcases soft-shell crab in an artful dish that tastes as good as it looks. A suggested shortcut for busy cooks: Purchase fresh or dried tricolor pasta to replace the three homemade pastas. The squid ink may be purchased from the fish market.

Black, Yellow, and Red Chili Pasta Dough
3 cups semolina flour
1-1/2 cups all-purpose flour
3 teaspoons salt
2 tablespoons squid or cuttlefish ink, mixed with 3 tablespoons water

6 eggs
4-1/2 tablespoons olive oil
15 threads saffron, mixed with 3 tablespoons water
1-1/4 cup finely ground Chimayó chili or other medium-hot finely ground chili

Roasted Poblano-Ginger Beurre Blanc
1 tablespoon minced fresh ginger
3 tablespoons minced shallots
3 cups dry white wine
1/4 cup heavy (whipping) cream
2 cups (4 sticks) cold unsalted butter, cut into 1-inch pieces
Juice of 1 lemon
1 poblano chili, roasted, peeled, seeded, deribbed, and cut into julienne
Salt and white pepper to taste

1 cup all-purpose flour
1/2 teaspoon salt
1 teaspoon red chili powder
6 large soft-shell crabs, cleaned
12 sea scallops

1 tablespoon clarified butter (see Techniques)
Peanut oil for deep frying
Sliced green onions and fresh chives for garnish

To make the black pasta dough:
Combine 1 cup of the semolina flour, 1/2 cup of the all-purpose flour, and 1 teaspoon of the salt in a food processor. With the machine running, gradually add the diluted squid or cuttlefish ink and 2 of the eggs through the feed tube. Then slowly add about 1-1/2 tablespoons olive oil, or just enough for the mixture to form a mass that holds together. Turn the dough out onto a lightly floured board and knead until smooth, at least 5 minutes. The dough should be firm and not sticky. Form into a smooth ball, cover with plastic wrap, and refrigerate for 2 hours.

To make the yellow pasta dough: Follow the same method substituting the saffron-water mixture for the diluted squid or cuttlefish ink.

To make the red chili pasta dough: Follow the same directions, substituting the red chili for the saffron-water mixture.

On a lightly floured surface, divide each color pasta into 2 equal pieces and flatten with the palm of your hand to 1/4-inch-thick pieces about 3 by 7 inches. Top each piece of red dough with a piece of black dough, then top each stack with a piece of yellow dough. Roll each stack of dough like a jelly roll and firmly press the seams together. Place in a plastic bag and refrigerate for 1 hour. Cut each pasta roll into 1/4-inch-thick slices and flatten each with the palm of your hand. Following the manufacturer's instructions, run each pasta disc through a pasta machine until it is 1/16-inch thick. Each sheet of pasta should be 8 to 10 inches long.

To make the beurre blanc: Place the ginger, shallots, and white wine in a medium saucepan and cook over medium heat to reduce by one-third, about 10 minutes. Whisk in the cream and cook for 3 minutes. Remove from heat and whisk in the butter one piece at a time; add the lemon juice, julienned chili, salt and pepper. Keep warm over hot water.

To make the crabs and scallops: Mix the flour, salt, and red chili powder in a medium bowl. Dredge the crabs in this mixture.

Painted Pasta Ribbons with Louisiana Soft-shell Crab and Roasted Poblano-Ginger Beurre Blanc, Mike Fennelly, Mike's on the Avenue

Bring a large pot of water to a boil. Drop sheets of pasta into boiling water and boil for 5 minutes, or until al dente. Meanwhile, in a large heavy skillet or deep-fryer, heat 3 inches of peanut oil to 375°F. Drop the soft-shell crabs into the hot oil and cook them for 3 minutes; remove with tongs and drain on paper towels. In a large sauté pan or skillet over high heat, heat the butter, and cook the scallops for 2 minutes on each side, or until slightly browned. Drain the pasta and place 1 long ribbon on each serving plate. Ladle about 3 tablespoons of beurre blanc onto each ribbon. Place 2 cooked scallops and one crab on each ribbon. Garnish with green onions and chives. ▪

Risotto Mille e Una Notte

From Fernando Saracchi of Ristorante Bacco, New Orleans, LA

Serves 6

The recipe title translates as "thousand-and-one-nights risotto." Perhaps chef Fernando Saracchi is hinting that this risotto, made with prosciutto, mushrooms, green peas, and spinach, is so good that we can eat it more than a thousand times without getting tired of it. In a traditional Italian meal, risotto is served as a first course, but this recipe makes a generous, filling entrée.

1 bunch spinach, blanced and puréed
12 cups chicken stock or broth
1-1/4 cups (2-1/2 sticks) unsalted butter
1/2 cup chopped onions
2-1/4 cups (1 pound) Arborio rice
1 cup dry white wine
2/3 cup carrots, peeled and diced
2/3 cup chopped prosciutto, plus 12 slices
1/2 cup diced fresh porcini mushrooms
1/3 cup green peas
1 cup (4 ounces) grated Parmesan cheese
Salt and pepper to taste
Whole slices of prosciutto for garnish.

To make the spinach purée: Remove the leaves from the spinach. Pat the leaves dry. Blanch the leaves in boiling water for 2 to 3 minutes. With a slotted spoon, transfer the spinach to a bowl of cold water. Drain the spinach. Purée the spinach in a blender or food processor.

In a large saucepan, bring the chicken stock or broth to a simmer. In a large, heavy saucepan, melt 3/4 cup of the butter over medium heat and sauté the onion for 3 to 4 minutes or until pale golden. Add the rice and stir for 1 minute. Add the wine and cook until it has about evaporated, about 5 to 6 minutes. Add the diced carrots, diced prosciutto, and mushrooms. Add 1/2 cup hot chicken stock or broth and cook, stirring constantly with a wooden spoon until the broth has evaporated. Repeat, adding 1/2 cup of hot stock of broth at a time. When the rice has been cooking for about 15 minutes, add the peas and the spinach purée. Continue to cook, stirring and adding the stock or broth until the rice is tender, but still slightly chewy. When the rice is done, stir in the remaining 1/2 cup of butter and all the grated Parmesan cheese. Add salt and pepper. Garnish each wide rimmed soup bowl with whole slices of prosciutto and serve the risotto warm. ▪

Catfish Louisiana

From Patrick Mould of Hub City Diner, Lafayette, LA

Chef Patrick Mould's recipe is the very spirit of Louisiana cookery. To perfectly fried catfish fillets he adds the lagniappe of a shrimp sauce, good enough to stand on its own spooned over white rice–not a bad idea.

Serves 4

Sauce
4 tablespoons oil
2 tablespoons flour
1/4 small onion, chopped
1/2 celery stalk, chopped
1/4 bell pepper, seeded, deribbed, and chopped
1 garlic clove, minced
1 cup shrimp stock or bottled clam juice
1/4 cup dry white wine
1/4 teaspoon seasoned salt
1/4 teaspoon paprika
1/4 teaspoon Tabasco or hot pepper sauce
Salt to taste
4 ounces cooked small shrimp
1 tablespoon chopped green onion
1 tablespoon chopped fresh parsley

Catfish
Oil for deep frying
2 eggs
1/2 cup milk
1/2 cup buttermilk

Catfish Louisiana, Patrick Mould, Hub City Diner

1 tablespoon seasoned salt
Four 8-ounce catfish fillets
3 cups all-purpose flour

To make a white roux: Heat 2 tablespoons oil in a small sauté pan and add the 2 tablespoons flour. Cook over low heat, stirring, for about 3 to 4 minutes. Set aside. In a medium saucepan, heat the remaining 2 tablespoons cooking oil over medium heat and sauté the onion, celery, and bell pepper for 1 minute. Add garlic and sauté for 1 minute. Be careful not to burn the garlic. Add the shrimp stock, white wine, seasoned salt, paprika, Tabasco, and salt. Whisk in the white roux and cook until the sauce thickens, about 3 minutes. Add the cooked shrimp, green onion, and parsley. Simmer for 1 minute. Keep warm.

To make catfish: In a large heavy pot or deep-fryer, heat 6 inches of oil to 350°F. Beat the eggs, milk, and buttermilk until combined. Add 1-1/2 teaspoon seasoned salt. Stir the remaining 1-1/2 teaspoon seasoned salt into flour. Dredge the fillets in the flour, then dip into the egg batter, then back in the flour. Drop the fillets in the hot oil and fry until golden brown, about 3 to 4 minutes.

To Serve: Top the fried catfish with the sauce and serve with steamed rice. ▪

Catfish Pecan with Meunière Sauce, Dick Brennan, Jr., Palace Café,

Catfish Pecan with Meunière Sauce

From Dick Brennan, Jr., of Palace Café, New Orleans, LA

Serves 6

Before commercial catfish farming began in 1965, catfish was mostly a Southern specialty. Now farm-raised catfish of excellent quality is available year round, and its firm, sweet white flesh–low in calories, fat and cholesterol –is becoming a national favorite. Chef Dick Brennan of Palace Café in New Orleans shares his version of one of Louisiana's favorite ways to serve fish: sautéed in a pecan crust and served with a spicy meunière sauce.

Catfish Pecan
Six 5- to 7-ounce catfish fillets
3 cups roasted pecans (see Techniques)
1 cup dried bread crumbs
1 cup all-purpose flour
1 teaspoon salt
1/2 teaspoon pepper
3 eggs
1/2 cup milk
Seafood seasoning (see page 41)
Olive oil

Meunière Sauce
2 cups fish stock or bottled clam juice
Juice of 1/2 lemon
1teaspoon Worcestershire sauce
Dash of Louisiana hot sauce
1 tablespoon heavy (whipping) cream
1/2 cup (1 stick) unsalted butter
Roasted whole pecans

To make the catfish: Preheat the oven to 450°F. Trim all fat from the catfish fillet. In a blender or food processor, grind the pecans and bread crumbs until fine. Pour into a pie pan. Place the flour in another pie pan and stir in the salt and pepper. In a medium bowl, beat together the eggs and milk. Season the catfish with the seafood seasoning, dredge in the flour, dip in the egg mixture and coat with the pecan mixture. Film the bottom of large ovenproof sauté pan or skillet with olive oil over medium heat. Add fish and brown on both sides. Bake in the oven for about 5 minutes.

To make the sauce: In a medium saucepan, cook the fish stock, lemon juice, Worcestershire sauce, and hot sauce. Add the heavy cream and cook to

reduce for 1 or 2 minutes. Remove from the heat and whisk in the butter. Serve over the cooked fish and sprinkle with roasted whole pecans. ■

Grouper Iberville

From Tom Weaver of Christian's Restaurant, New Orleans, LA

Serves 6

Grouper is a sea bass with a mild, white, and lean flesh. In this recipe, grouper is baked in a zesty Creole sauce, and the preparation is simple and foolproof.

Creole Sauce
2 tablespoons olive oil
4 small onions, cut into large dice
2 small bell peppers, cut into large dice
3 stalks celery, cut into medium dice
2-1/2 teaspoons minced garlic
2 large fresh tomatoes, peeled, seeded, and diced (see Techniques)
1 teaspoon minced fresh thyme
1 teaspoon minced fresh oregano
1 teaspoon minced fresh basil
1/2 cup dry white wine
3/4 cup fish stock or bottled clam juice
1-1/4 cup tomato purée
3 teaspoons salt
1/8 teaspoon dried red pepper flakes
Pinch cayenne pepper

Hollandaise
6 egg yolks
1 teaspoon red wine vinegar
2 teaspoons water
3/4 cup warm clarified butter (see Techniques)
Salt and cayenne pepper to taste

3 pounds fresh grouper fillets, cut into 8-ounce portions
1 pound medium shrimp, peeled and deveined
1 bunch green onion, thinly sliced
Vegetable garnish (recipe follows)

To make the Creole sauce: Heat the olive oil in a medium saucepan. Add the onions, bell peppers, and celery, and cook over medium heat until tender, about 5 minutes. Add the garlic, tomatoes, thyme, oregano, basil, white wine, and fish stock or clam juice, and simmer for about 10 minutes. Add the tomato purée, salt, red pepper flakes, and cayenne pepper, and simmer for about 30 minutes or until thick. Set aside.

To make the hollandaise sauce: Put the egg yolks, vinegar, and water in a double boiler over hot water and whisk until thick and creamy. Do not curdle the egg yolks. Add the butter a little at a time in a small stream while beating. If too thick, thin with warm water. Season with salt and cayenne. Keep warm over hot water.

Preheat oven to 400°F. Place about 3 cups of Creole sauce in the bottom of a large ovenproof sauté pan or skillet or heatproof casserole. Place the fish fillets over the sauce, divide the shrimp, and put equal amounts on top of each fish fillet. Top the shrimp with the remaining sauce. Heat over high heat until the sauce simmers. Cover and bake in 400°F oven for about 12 minutes or until fillets begin to flake. Divide fillets and shrimp among six plates. Top each with 5 tablespoons of hollandaise sauce, sprinkle with sliced green onions, and garnish with vegetables.

Vegetable Garnish

Serves 6

2 large carrots
1 large turnip
1 large rutabaga
4 tablespoons butter
1 teaspoon sugar
1/4 teaspoon salt
1/4 teaspoon white pepper
1 cup parsley sprigs, minced

Peel the carrots, turnip, and rutabaga. Cut the carrots into crosswise pieces, then cut each piece in half lengthwise. Cut each piece into an egg-shaped round. Cut the turnip and rutabaga in half, then cut each half into fourths. Shape the same way as the carrots. In a medium saucepan, boil the vegetables in salted water to cover for 6 to 8 minutes until crisp-tender; drain well. Heat the butter in a medium sauté pan or skillet over medium heat, add the vegetables, and sauté for about 1 minute. Add the sugar, salt, white pepper, and parsley and sauté for about 2 to 3 minutes. ∎

DICK BRENNAN, JR.
Palace Café, New Orleans

Dick Brennan, Palace Café's exective chef and partner, grew up in the restaurant business a block away from Commander's Palace. "When I was a teenager I started working with Paul Prudhomme. He treated me like family. 'You don't take shortcuts!' he used to admonish me." This business has a natural attraction for all the Brennans.

When it came time for college, Brennan was momentarily drawn to "do what all my friends were doing," so he attended Louisiana State University in Baton Rouge to study business administration, and Loyola University in New Orleans, where he graduated with a degree in finance.

His business background has been put to use in his restaurant career. Interwoven with his college studies were stints in some stellar restaurants: In addition to working at Commander's from 1975 to 1983, he helped open Mr. B's in 1979 and was a chef's apprentice in the summer of 1980 at Delmonico's restaurant in Mexico City, Mexico. In 1983, he apprenticed under Larry Forgione, chef-owner of An American Place in New York. "He was the guru of American food, and his attention to the detail of his food products—who produced them, where and how they were grown, where they came from—was impressive."

After working under Forgione, Brennan went to France for almost two years and worked as a chef's apprentice in restaurants such as Au Quai d'Orsay, Gerard Besson, Chiberta, La Marée, Taillevent, and Tour d'Argent. His ego survived the sometimes-harsh French culinary tutelage with ease. "I grew up in a big family. And if I got egotistical, I got put back in line pretty fast." By 1986, the die was cast: he became general manager of Brennan's of Houston, where he stayed until 1990. In 1990, he opened Palace Café.

"We opened Palace Café because we wanted to re-create the grand old cafés with their charcuterie and house-made products, but we wanted to do it using local products." Today, at Palace Café, Brennan cures his own sauerkraut for his choucroute plate, which includes andouille sausage and house-made pickled (not smoked) pork. He also uses his sauerkraut in the café's Reuben sandwich, which contains rémoulade sauce, thinly sliced housemade pickled pork, and housemade mozzarella. Brennan's featured recipes for appetizer Crawfish Cakes with Lemon Butter Sauce, Catfish Pecan with Meunière Sauce, (entrée), and White Chocolate Bread Pudding (dessert), demonstrate his cooking philosophy at Palace Café: "We'll take an idea—and we'll make it us."

Pan-roasted Snapper with Crab Meat, Roasted Garlic, and Sun-dried Tomato Butter

From Frank Brigtsen of Brigtsen's Restaurant, New Orleans, LA

Serves 6

Louisiana has such an embarassment of riches from rivers, lakes, and sea that creative chefs instinctively call on this bounty for new recipes. Here, chef Frank Brigtsen tops a sautéed fillet of snapper with crab meat in a highly flavorful butter.

Roasted Garlic and Sun-dried Tomato Butter
1 cup (2 sticks) unsalted butter, at room temperature
1/4 cup finely chopped oil-packed sun-dried tomatoes
1/4 teaspoon salt
1 teaspoon minced fresh basil
1/8 teaspoon cayenne pepper

2 tablespoons roasted garlic (see Techniques)

Six 7-ounce snapper fillets with skin
3 teaspoons seafood seasoning (recipe on page 41)
1 cup all-purpose flour
1/2 cup clarified butter (see Techniques)

1 cup fish stock or bottled clam juice
1-1/2 cups (16 ounces) fresh crab meat, picked over for shells

To make the butter: In a blender or food processor, blend all of the ingredients until smooth. Refrigerate until ready to serve. (This may be done one day ahead.)

Preheat the oven to 450°F. Season each snapper fillet lightly with 1/2 teaspoon seafood seasoning and dust the skin side of each fillet with flour. Heat 2 large ovenproof sauté pans or skillets over medium-high heat and add 1/4 cup clarified butter to each. Place the fish in the hot butter, skin-side down, and cook for 1 minute. Bake for 7 to 8 minutes, or until fish begins to flake.

Place a fillet on each of six heated plates. Discard the butter and return the sauté pans or skillets to high heat. Add 1/2 cup of stock or clam juice to each pan and bring to a boil. Add half of the garlic and tomato butter to each pan and cook until the butter is almost melted, about 1 to 2 minutes. Add 3/4 cup of crab meat to each pan and cook just until the crab meat is heated through, about 1 minute.

To serve: Divide the crab meat and sauce evenly over the top of each snapper fillet. Serve immediately. ∎

Pan-roasted Snapper with Crab Meat, Roasted Garlic, and Sun-dried Tomato Butter, Frank Brigtsen, Brigtsen's Restaurant

Caramelized Salmon with Mirliton Slaw, David McCelvey, NOLA

Caramelized Salmon with Mirliton Slaw

From David McCelvey, NOLA, New Orleans, LA

Serves 4

Move over coleslaw, chef David McCelvey has come up with an alternative to you! Mirliton (also known as chayote squash) was cultivated in Central America by the ancient Aztecs and Mayans, and this mild green gourd is quickly becoming available year round. It can be prepared as you would any summer squash, but its firm texture allows it to stay crisp in salads.

Mirliton Slaw
2 mirlitons (chayote squash)
1 peeled carrot
1 sliced red onion
1 cucumber
1 tablespoon rice wine vinegar
1 tablespoon shredded fresh basil
Juice of 1 lime

Twelve 2-ounce salmon fillets
Soy sauce for brushing
Salt and pepper to taste
Sugar for dredging
2 tablespoon oil
1 to 2 tablespoons piri piri (recipe follows)

To make the slaw: Boil the mirlitons until tender, about 20 minutes. Cut the carrot and mirilton into julienne. Blanch the onion slices in boiling water for 2 to 3 minutes, drain. Rinse in cold water and drain again. Peel, seed and julienne the cucumber. Combine all the rest of the ingredients and set aside.

Brush the salmon with soy sauce and season with salt and pepper. Dredge in sugar. In a large sauté pan or skillet, heat the oil over medium-high heat and sauté the salmon until caramelized, about 4 minutes on each side.

Serve salmon with mirliton slaw and sprinkle with piri piri.

Piri Piri
4 jalapéño chilies
2 poblano chilies
1 habañero chili
1-1/2 tablespoon dried red pepper flakes
Pepper to taste
1-1/2 cup olive oil
1 tablespoon minced garlic

Seed and coarsely chop the chilies. Combine all of the ingredients except garlic in a small saucepan and simmer for 10 minutes. In a blender or food processor purée the mixture with the garlic and set aside. Let the sauce cool to room temperature and store in a bottle covered with plastic wrap for seven days before using. The piri piri may be kept for 2 months.

KEVIN GRAHAM
Windsor Court Hotel, New Orleans

"A whole career can be based on one little moment," muses Kevin Graham, award-winning executive chef of the Windsor Court Hotel and author of two best-selling cookbooks: *Simply Elegant* (New York: Grove Weidenfeld, 1991), and *Body Conscious Cuisine: Kevin Graham's Fish & Seafood Cookbook* (New York: Stewart, Tabori & Chang, 1993). His third cookbook, *Pulse of Life*, a cookbook about grains and legumes, is in the works.

For this native of Cheshire, England, the seminal moment was meeting and working under the German chef Klaus Rhulickhe. "He was a brilliant chef whose attitude was impeccable and whose technique was enviable. He caught me at the right moment and instilled in me discipline and commitment. I consider myself very fortunate to have been caught at that moment," says Graham.

Graham graduated from Hollings College in Manchester, England, and worked at famous European hotels including the Savoy in London, Hotel Negresco in Nice, and the Picadilly in Manchester, England. Before migrating to New Orleans, Graham successfully operated his own restaurant in Cheshire. In New Orleans, Graham was executive chef for the private City Club, then the Omni Royal Orleans hotel, and later executive chef at the Omni's Sagamore Resort in Saratoga Springs, New York.

Some food writers have described Graham's culinary style as "New Orleans grande cuisine." Graham, however, says that because the Windsor Court is an international hotel with global clientele, "We don't limit the menu to dishes indigenous only to Louisiana." His entrée, Dover Sole Medusa, is based on French classical technique (poaching) and a contemporary French sauce (beurre blanc), but is infused with his own sense of humor. (The fish fillets curl during poaching and the chef tops it off with a frizzle of fried fennel, whimsical allusions to Medusa's locks.)

"I'm incredibly proud to be classified as an American chef," says Graham. "I much prefer the attitude in the New World toward food. It's much freer. And what keeps me on the edge is just being able to see what's going on in kitchens here. Good food is not a threat. I can learn something from what other guys are doing.

"The beauty of our business," says Graham, "is that it is a creative pursuit—one that give us and others instant gratification."

Graham's other featured recipes are Clancy's Quail (appetizer), and Chocolate Mousse with Harlequin Cookie Mask (dessert).

Dover Sole Medusa

From Kevin Graham of Windsor Court Hotel, New Orleans, LA

Serves 4

When the sole – skinned, beheaded, and filleted up to the tail – are cooked, they curl up, somewhat like Medusa's locks. However, they taste much better than Medusa looked, and although you may be momentarily stunned by the brilliant simplicity of this dish, you won't be turned to stone, we guarantee.

4 Dover sole, (or flounder) about
  1 pound each, cleaned and scaled
4 cups fish stock or bottled clam juice
4 fresh fennel sprigs
1/2 cup olive oil
1/4 cup capers, drained
Salt and freshly ground black pepper
  to taste
1-1/2 cup beurre blanc (recipe follows)

Skin the sole and remove the heads. Using the point of a sharp knife, cut through the flesh along the side fins. Working at an angle, with the knife almost flat, cut the flesh away from the ribs. Turn the fish over and repeat the process to end up with 2 whole fillets still attached to the fish at the tail. Beginning two inches from the tail, cut both fillets into 8 lengthwise strips.

In a large saucepan, bring the fish stock or clam juice to a rolling boil. Holding 1 sole by the tail, carefully lower the fish into the simmering stock. The strips should curl gently. Cook for 1 to 2 minutes, then remove the fish from the pan and drain on paper towels. Repeat with the remaining fish. Keep warm.
In a small, heavy saucepan, heat the olive oil to 350°F and cook the fennel sprigs just until crisp, about 2 to 3 minutes. Remove from the pan and drain on paper towels.
Season the fish with salt and pepper and arrange one fillet on each of four plates with the tail at 12 o'clock. Sprinkle the capers over the sole and garnish with the deep-fried fennel sprigs. Pour beurre blanc around the fish. ∎

Dover Sole Medusa, Kevin Graham, Windsor Court Hotel

Beurre Blanc

6 minced shallots
1-1/2 cup dry white wine
1/2 cup heavy (whipping) cream
1-1/2 cup (3 sticks) cold unsalted butter,
  cut into 1-inch pieces
Salt and white pepper to taste

In a medium saucepan, cook the shallots and white wine over high heat until the wine has almost evaporated. Add the cream and cook over low heat until reduced to a very small amount.

Over low heat, whisk in 4 pieces of butter one at a time, adding more as the butter blends into the sauce. Strain and keep warm over hot water if not used immediately.

Swordfish with Roasted Red Pepper Vinaigrette

From Randy Windham of Bistro at Maison de Ville, New Orleans, LA

Serves 4

The firm, almost meatlike texture and mild flavor of swordfish has made it one of America's most popular fish. This recipe pairs a contemporary vinaigrette with swordfish steaks. The combination is hearty enough to lure even diehard meat-lovers.

Roasted Red Pepper Vinaigrette
1 red bell pepper, roasted, peeled, seeded, deribbed and chopped (see Techniques)
1 garlic clove, roasted and minced (see Techniques)
2 tablespoons balsamic vinegar
1/8 teaspoon salt
1/4 cup olive oil
1/4 cup extra-virgin olive oil
Pepper to taste

2 tablespoons olive oil
Four 7-ounce swordfish steaks, 1 inch thick

To make the vinaigrette: In a blender or food processor, purée the pepper, garlic, vinegar, and salt until smooth. Pour in the oils slowly while the motor is running. Add the pepper.

Heat the olive oil in a large non-stick skillet. Sauté the swordfish for 4 to 5 minutes on each side, until cooked through. Transfer to warm serving plates and top with a little of the roasted red pepper vinaigrette. ■

RANDY WINDHAM
Bistro at Maison de Ville, New Orleans

When managing director Alvin P. Danner of the Hotel Maison de Ville announced the appointment of Randy Windham as executive chef in December 1991, he cited Windham as a prime example of the talented, bright, creative young culinary pros who have maintained the Bistro's classic style. "We trust them with responsibility and let them develop," Danner said, pointing to Windham predecessors John Neal and Susan Spicer. "We did not plan to become the graduate school for culinary 'stars'," Danner continues, "but as reputations go, that is not a bad track record."

The Bistro's latest star attended the New England Culinary Institute on scholarship. During school he served externships at 21 Federal restaurant on Nantucket Island, and at his future place of employment, the Bistro at Maison de Ville. After graduation he worked in the SoHo, New York, bistro, Onda, belonging to Karen Hubert and Len Allison, and later at their Long Island restaurant, Len Allison on Shelter Island. Before returning to the Bistro at Maison de Ville as sous chef, Windham spent five years at the Ritz-Carlton Buckhead in Atlanta.

Typical of his generation of chefs and heavily influenced by his family's farm life, Windham's culinary philosophy is to buy the best and freshest ingredients, especially, whenever possible, those that are organically grown.

He calls his style of cuisine Mediterranean. "However, it has a touch of American, a touch of Italian and a good measure of French, with a bent toward French country cooking."

His featured entrée recipe for Swordfish with Roasted Red Pepper Vinaigrette is one of the most colorful in the book and one of the most accessible to the home cook. His other featured recipes are Grilled Shrimp with Polenta (appetizer), and Créme Brûlée (dessert).

Swordfish with Roasted Red Pepper Vinaigrette, Randy Windham, Bistro at Maison de Ville

Garlic-crusted Trout with Sweet Pepper and Shrimp Sauce

From Jay Kimball of Romairs,
New Orleans, LA

Serves 4

Prepared concentrated shrimp stock is available frozen from fish markets and, when reconstituted according to package directions, can be a timesaver in preparing the shrimp sauce in this recipe. The crisp garlic bread crumb crust preserves the moistness of tender trout fillets without deep frying.

Sweet Pepper and Shrimp Sauce
1 tablespoon extra-virgin olive oil
1 tomato, peeled and finely diced
1 roasted red pepper, peeled, seeded, deribbed and finely diced
1/3 cup finely diced onion
1 teaspoon salt
Pinch cayenne pepper
1 teaspoon fresh lemon juice
1 teaspoon fresh lime juice
1/4 cup shrimp stock or bottled clam juice
12 to 15 large shrimp
1/3 cup shredded fresh basil

Garlic-crusted Trout with Sweet Pepper and Shrimp Sauce, Jay Kinball, Romairs

Garlic Bread Crumbs

1 teaspoon salt
1 teaspoon black pepper
2 tablespoons grated Romano cheese
1 teaspoon minced garlic
1 teaspoon minced fresh thyme
1 teaspoon minced fresh parsley
1/3 loaf stale French bread, cubed (2 cups)

4 skinless trout fillets
3 tablespoons extra-virgin olive oil

To make the sauce: In a large sauté pan or skillet over a medium heat, heat the olive oil and sauté the tomato, pepper, onion, salt, and cayenne for 1 minute. Add the lemon and lime juices and shrimp stock. Cook over medium heat until reduced by half, about 4 minutes. Cut shrimp in half lengthwise. Add the shrimp and basil to the sauce. Cook until the shrimp turn pink, about 2 to 3 minutes.

To make the coating: Preheat the oven to 500°F. Place all the ingredients for coating in a blender or food processor and blend until fine.

To prepare fillets: Press the trout fillets firmly into the coating to coat evenly. In a large ovenproof sauté pan or skillet, heat the oil to smoking and cook the fillets on each side until browned, about 2 minutes for each side. Bake for 4 to 5 minutes or until crust is crisp.

To Serve: Place 1 fillet on each of four serving plates and surround with the sweet pepper and shrimp sauce. ■

JAY KIMBALL
Romairs, Terrytown

While attending Louisiana State University in New Orleans, Jay Kimball worked first at Jacques restaurant in the Sheraton, then at Dajonell's, a restaurant known for its contemporary French cuisine. When Kimball graduated from LSU he attended the Culinary Institute of America in Hyde Park, New York, where he concentrated on classes that would sharpen his skills in classical and contemporary French and also Italian cuisines.

After the Culinary Institute, Kimball returned to New Orleans and set about putting all that culinary theory to practice. First he worked with an old school friend at the friend's Italian family restaurant. Next he went to the French Quarter to work at Maximo's, one of the city's contemporary bistros. After Maximo's, Kimball moved to Gabrielle to assist chef-proprietor Greg Sonnier as sous-chef. Kimball is now executive chef at Romairs restaurant on New Orleans's West Bank, where he and partner Jason Romair meld the tastes and traditions of south Louisiana with the flavors and flair of Italy. Romairs' menu offers a captivating Creole-Italian cuisine that can be seen in Kimball's featured recipes. His appetizer, Oysters, Prosciutto, and Roasted Peppers with Creole Mustard Sauce Meunière, is a skewered assortment of peppers, prosciutto cubes, and oysters, reminiscent of the Tuscan spiedini, accented by a traditional Creole sauce. Kimball's entrée, Garlic-crusted Trout with Sweet Pepper and Shrimp Sauce, features a boneless trout fillet coated with a zesty crumb crust redolent of garlic, herbs, pepper, and Romano cheese. It is then sautéed in extra-virgin olive oil, and sauced with a tomato, roasted pepper, and shrimp sauce flavored with cayenne and fresh basil.

FRANK BRIGTSEN
Brigtsen's Restaurant, New Orleans

Frank Brigtsen is a New Orleans native of Norwegian descent who decided on a culinary career in 1973 while attending Louisiana State University. Two years earlier he had apprenticed under Paul Prudhomme at Commander's Palace, and by 1980, Brigsten became the first night chef at Prudhomme's new restaurant, K-Paul's Louisiana Kitchen. During his tenure at K-Paul's, he became executive chef.

In 1986, Frank and his wife Marna opened Brigtsen's Restaurant in uptown New Orleans. Since then it has received dozens of awards, among them: Gene Bourg's top Five Bean award in *The Times-Picayune*, *Travel & Holiday* magazine's Good Value Dining Award, Gault-Millau's Lauriers du Terroir award, and Top Cajun Restaurant in the Zagat Survey. Brigsten himself was named one of America's Top Ten New Chefs in 1988, and Chef of the Year in 1990 by the New Orleans chapter of Chefs in America.

During this time he also took his talents traveling as guest chef aboard Cunard's *Sea Goddess* as she sailed the Caribbean and Mediterranean seas.

When asked what was different about the new garde of Louisiana chefs to whom he belongs, he says, "From my perspective as a native of New Orleans, who worked for Paul Prudhomme, I feel he brought the great regional cooking of Louisiana to national attention and he paved the way as well for others to follow him. My roots are still in Louisiana cooking, but chefs my age across the country have been exposed to so many styles of cooking that, in a sense, the boundaries have been dropped. It may be," he concludes, "difficult for some people to categorize or put a label on our style of cooking. When I'm asked I just say I do modern Louisiana cooking."

By his admission modern Louisiana cooking turns out sometimes to be what he calls pan-American. "We change our menu daily and we just follow our instincts and sensibilities. And we have fun with it and we don't limit ourselves." Brigtsen's two entrée recipes, Pan-roasted Snapper with Crab Meat, Roasted Garlic, and Sun-dried Tomato Butter, and Blackened Yellowfin Tuna with Roasted Vegetable Salsa, and Smoked Corn Sauce, show his facility for grafting ethnic offshoots onto Louisiana roots. His featured dessert recipe, Banana Bread Pudding with Banana Rum Sauce and Whipped Cream, demonstrates his talent for updating traditional favorites.

Blackened Yellowfin Tuna with Roasted Vegetable Salsa, and Smoked Corn Sauce

From Frank Brigtsen of Brigtsen's Restaurant, New Orleans, LA

Serves 6

What would a book about Louisiana cooking be without a recipe for blackening, a preparation method made famous by chef Paul Prudhomme? Well, here it is, and it's a good one, too. The vegetable salsa and smoked corn sauce add both texture and flavor and could accompany grilled fish or chicken, as well.

Roasted Vegetable Salsa

Makes 2 cups

2 large tomatoes
1 large red or yellow bell pepper
1 medium red onion
1 small jalapeño chili
1-1/2 teaspoon fresh lime juice
3/4 teaspoon minced fresh cilantro
1/2 teaspoon salt
1/2 teaspoon minced garlic
1/4 teaspoon Louisiana Gold hot sauce
  or other hot pepper sauce
1/8 teaspoon ground cumin

Smoked Corn Sauce

6 ears of corn
4 tablespoons unsalted butter
1 cup finely chopped yellow onions
1 teaspoon salt
1/4 teaspoon ground white pepper
1/8 teaspoon cayenne pepper
1/8 teaspoon minced fresh garlic
1/8 teaspoon ground cumin
1/8 teaspoon minced fresh sage
1 small bay leaf
1 cup heavy (whipping) cream

Blackened Yellowfin Tuna

Four 8-ounce yellowfin tuna steaks,
  1 inch thick
4 teaspoons melted, clarified butter
  (see Techniques)
4 teaspoons Paul Prudhomme Seafood
  Magic® or Creole seasoning

To make the vegetable salsa: Place the vegetables on a hot grill or directly in the flame of a gas stove. Cook and turn until the vegetables are charred all over. When done, place the vegetables in a bowl and

Blackened Yellowfin Tuna with Roasted Vegetable Salsa, and Smoked Corn Sauce, Frank Brigtsen, Brigtsen's Restaurant

cover. Set aside for 15 to 20 minutes. Under running water, peel the vegetables and remove all seeds. Cut into 1/4-inch dice. Combine the diced vegetables and all the remaining salsa ingedients to blend throughly.

To make the corn sauce: Husk the corn and smoke the whole ears of corn over medium coals sprinkled with 1/2 cup presoaked hickory chips in a covered barbeque grill, turning the corn several times for 30 to 40 minutes or until light brown. Do not over-smoke. Let cool, then cut the kernels from the cobs and set kernels aside.

Heat a heavy saucepan over medium heat. Melt the butter and cook the onions until translucent, about 3 minutes, stirring constantly. Add the corn and cook until tender, about 10 to 15 minutes, stirring constantly. Reduce heat to low and add the salt, white pepper, cayenne, garlic, cumin, sage, and bay leaf. Cook for about 3 more minutes, stirring constantly and scraping the bottom of the pan with a spoon. Add the cream and bring to a boil. Reduce heat and let simmer for 5 minutes.

To cook the tuna: Dip the tuna steaks in melted butter and season with Seafood

Magic® or Creole seasoning. Heat a cast iron skillet to the smoking point. Add the steaks and cook 3 to 4 minutes on each side for medium rare (should be pink inside).

To serve: Pool each of six serving plates with 1/4 cup corn sauce, top with a tuna steak and top the fish with 1/4 cup vegetable salsa. ■

Bella Luna, New Orleans

German-born Horst Pfeifer is one of the youngest chefs ever to receive a European master chef's certificate. He is qualified to and indeed has worked in Michelin one- and three-star restaurants. But he prefers to work at Bella Luna, the 160-seat restaurant and pasta shop he owns in New Orleans.

"When I was working in Munich, Germany, at the three-star restaurant Tantris, we had twenty-five cooks and twenty-five waiters to take care of sixty reservations. Very few restaurants can do this. I learned cooking, and I wanted to serve a great quality food at a fair price. I didn't want to cook for a few very select people. It's much more gratifying to please a lot of people with very good food."

Pfeifer arrived in New Orleans via Germany (where he received his chef's degree), the Swiss Alps and Italy (where he worked in resorts), Munich (where he worked at Tantris and received his master chef's degree), and Texas (where he was executive chef at Austin's Courtyard and at Barton Creek in Austin).

"I love pasta," he says, adding that the custom fillings he makes for the house-made pasta at Bella Luna are virtually endless. He even encourages customers to bring in their own fillings for ravioli.

Even though Pfeifer cooks professionally, he still cooks at home, and he is a firm believer that everyone else should do likewise. "It is not only possible, but very important for people to cook at home. The family meal is very important and you should make time to have it. When you go out to eat, that's when you should get dressed up and order a multi-course meal. When you cook at home, do something real simple. Bring home a nice piece of fish, cook it simply, make a nice salad and have a simple dessert." Pfeifer's recipe for Charbroiled White Tuna with Crab Meat and Three-pepper Relish is just the place to start following his advice. But then, his appetizer recipe for Pecan Wood-smoked Shrimp Quesadillas is also a good place to start.

Charbroiled White Tuna with Crab Meat and Three-pepper Relish

From Horst Pfeifer of Bella Luna, New Orleans, LA

Serves 6

"White tuna" is a Louisiana euphemism for escolar, a large fish with oily flesh and a delectable flavor that is caught in the Gulf of Mexico. For Bella Luna, chef Horst Pfeifer buys escolar that range up to twenty-six pounds and prepares the steaks himself.

Cajun Spices

makes about 2 cups

1 cup paprika
1/4 cup cayenne pepper
1/4 cup garlic powder
1/4 cup onion powder
2 tablespoons sweet dried basil
2 tablespoons dried oregano
2 tablespoons dried thyme

1/2 cup olive oil
2-1/2 pounds escolar or salmon steaks
36 shiitake mushrooms stemmed
1 teaspoon minced garlic

Crab Meat and Three-pepper Relish
1 each red and yellow bell pepper and
    poblano, roasted, peeled, seeded,
    deribbed and diced
1/4 cup sesame oil
1/4 cup soy sauce
1/4 cup balsamic vinegar
2 tablespoons diced fresh ginger
1 pound fresh cooked crab meat
Cracked black pepper to taste

2 tablespoons butter
36 baby carrots, peeled and blanched for
    3 to 4 minutes
2 tablespoons minced fresh cilantro
2 tablespoons minced fresh chives, plus
    1 tablespoon for garnish
2 tablespoons minced fresh basil for garnish

To make Cajun spices: Combine all the ingredients in a blender or food processor until blended. Store in an airtight jar.

Cut the fish into 1/2 inch thick steaks and place in a shallow non-aluminum container. Mix together 1/4 cup of the olive oil and the Cajun spices. Pour over the fish. In a medium bowl toss the

66 THE LOUISIANA NEW GARDE

shiitakes with 1/4 cup olive oil and the garlic. In another bowl, mix together the sesame oil, soy sauce, vinegar, and ginger and let sit for 10 to 15 minutes. Stir in the peppers and crab meat. Season with cracked black pepper.

Meanwhile grill the mushrooms and fish over medium coals for 2 to 3 minutes, or until lightly seared. In a medium saucepan, melt the butter and sauté the carrots for 3 to 4 minutes until lightly browned. Toss with the cilantro and 2 tablespoons of the chives.

To serve: Place the carrots, mushrooms, and grilled fish on dinner plates. Top with the relish and garnish with fresh chives and basil. ▪

Chicken Roulades with Andouille and Cornbread Stuffing, Baby Vegetables, and Roasted Garlic Sauce, Emeril's, New Orleans, LA

MICHELLE NUGENT
Bayona, New Orleans

Michelle Nugent, executive sous-chef at Bayona, has always had the kind of job where she was "consumed by the work that I was doing." She was fifteen years old when she realized that there was more to eating than hamburgers and potato chips. "I spent a summer with a woman from Vietnam who set before me my first lunch composed of salad, Chablis, and a Brie so ripe that it was running off the table. I said to myself, 'This is real!'" Since then, Nugent has been involved only with real food, some of the most real at Bayona, owned by Chef Susan Spicer. "Susan has trained me from the ground up; I've been working with her off and on for about seven years," says Nugent.

Nugent started her foodservice career as a kitchen assistant at the New Orleans whole-food bakery with the unlikely name of Billabong. She moved from Billabong Bakery to the Bistro at Maison de Ville, where she was lead cook working all stations, under the supervision of chef Spicer.

In 1988, she moved to Santa Rosa, California, to be pastry chef and *garde-manger* at Restaurant Matisse. It was here she became "really excited about produce. The chef was familiar with local farmers—he was a farmer himself—and we had an overabundance of perfect produce, fish, vegetables, grains. He served on big white plates and he just let me go, encouraging me to make things as beautiful as possible." Nugent is also an artist, painting in acrylic and watercolor, so the chef's suggestion was well received.

In 1990, Nugent returned from California to help Spicer open the 110-seat, trend-setting Bayona. Her training was in classical French cooking, but she has also concentrated on Southern French and Northern Italian, and she has an affinity for curries and chilis. That Asian affinity can be seen in her featured entrée, Tuna with Japanese Noodles and Soy Dipping Sauce.

Tuna with Japanese Noodles and Soy Dipping Sauce

From Michelle Nugent of Bayona, New Orleans, LA

Serves 8

This recipe artfully combines ingredients and flavors borrowed from Asian cooking: Japanese, Indonesian, and a touch of Thai. Soba and somen are Japanese noodles, here tossed with peanut sauce as a bed for seared tuna fillets, which are in turn topped with an aromatic dipping sauce. All of the Asian ingredients are available from Asian markets.

Dipping Sauce
1/2 cup soy sauce
1 tablespoon sesame oil
2/3 cup peanut oil
3 tablespoons fresh lime juice
3 tablespoons rice wine vinegar
2 teaspoons chili paste
1 tablespoon molasses
1 tablespoon water
1 tablespoon minced fresh lemongrass (optional)
2 teaspoons minced fresh ginger
1/2 bunch green onions, chopped
1/2 teaspoon minced garlic (optional)

Peanut Sauce
1 cup roasted peanuts
Juice of 2 limes
1 scant teaspoon sambal oelek (Indonesian chili paste)
1 teaspoon minced garlic
6 tablespoons rice wine vinegar
1 cup peanut oil
2 tablespoons ketjap manis (Indonesian soy sauce)
2 tablespoons soy sauce
2 tablespoons minced fresh cilantro

Carrot slices, snow peas, and red bell pepper slices
8 ounces soba (buckwheat) noodles
8 ounces somen noodles
Fresh cilantro sprigs for garnish

Eight 6-ounce tuna fillets, about 3/4 inch thick

To make the dipping sauce: Whisk all of the ingredients together. Cover and refrigerate for 30 minutes.

To make the peanut sauce: In a blender or food processor, pulse the first five ingredients until puréed, then pour in the oil slowly with the motor running. Stir in the ketjap manis and soy sauce, then the cilantro. Set aside.

Steam the vegetables over boiling water for 3 minutes, or until crisp-tender. Set aside. In two separate large pots cook the somen and soba noodles in a large amount of boiling salted water for about 3 minutes, or until tender. Drain and toss with 1 cup peanut sauce.

Grill the fillets over hot coals for 2 minutes on each side (the tuna will be medium rare). Make a bed of noodles in the center of each plate and place a fillet on top. Garnish with the steamed vegetables and cilantro sprigs and top with a little of the dipping sauce.▪

Louisiana Crab and Vegetable Hash with Vanilla Bean Sabayon

From Emeril Lagasse of Emeril's and NOLA, New Orleans, LA

Serves 4

Chef Emeril Lagasse stretches a familiar dish—hash—and a dessert sauce—sabayon—to new limits. This hash is made of crab meat with sweet potatoes, celery, green pepper, onion, and sweet corn. And sabayon is transformed into a savory sauce with a surprising spice: vanilla.

Louisiana Crab and Vegetable Hash

1 pound fresh cooked claw crab meat
1 ear shucked corn
1 tablespoon olive oil
1/3 cup chopped red bell pepper
1/3 cup chopped green bell pepper
1/4 cup chopped onion
1/4 cup chopped celery
1/2 cup sweet potato, shredded and peeled
1/3 cup finely-shredded leeks, white part only
1 tablespoon minced garlic
Salt and pepper to taste
1 teaspoon Creole seasoning

Vanilla Bean Sabayon
2 egg yolks
2 tablespoons minced shallots
1 vanilla bean, split lengthwise
1/3 cup Champagne
1/4 cup extra-virgin olive oil
Creole seasoning for garnish

To make the hash: Pick through the crab meat to remove any pieces of shell and cartilage. Cut the kernels from the corn. In a large nonstick sauté pan or skillet, heat the olive oil over medium heat and sauté the bell peppers, onion, celery, sweet potato, leeks, and corn for 4 to 5 minutes, or until slightly soft. Stir in the garlic, salt, pepper, and Creole seasoning. Add the crab meat and cook for 2 minutes, or until heated through. Keep warm.

To make the sauce: Place the egg yolks and shallots in a double boiler. Scrape the pulp from the vanilla bean and add the pulp to the yolks. Whisk together, and add the Champagne. Whisk over simmering water for 3 to 4 minutes, or until thick. Let cool for 3 minutes. Whisk in the olive oil and add salt and pepper. Mound the hash in the center of each serving plate and spoon the sabayon over the hash. Sprinkle the rim of each plate with Creole seasoning.▪

Louisiana Crab and Vegetable Hash with Vanilla Bean Saboyon, Emeril Lagasse, Emeril's and NOLA

Chicken Maximilian

From Mark Hollger of Santa Fe Restaurant, New Orleans, LA

Serves 1

Chicken Maximilian is an innovative version of the Mexican classic, chiles relleños. Chilies are stuffed with cheese, then wrapped in a chicken breast, deep fried and baked. Chef Mark Hollger of Santa Fe Restaurant in New Orleans says this dish began as a special creation for a banquet. Through word of mouth, it became so often requested, even when it's not on the menu, Hollger and his kitchen crew are prepared to produce it for the inevitable special requests. Try it and you'll see why.

One 8-ounce boneless skinless chicken breast
Salt, pepper, paprika, minced garlic, and minced fresh cilantro to taste
1 Anaheim chili, roasted and peeled (see Techniques)
1/4 cup shredded cheddar cheese
1/4 cup shredded Monterey Jack cheese
Flour for dusting
2 eggs beaten with 1 tablespoon milk
1 cup dried bread crumbs
Vegetable oil

Sauce

2 tablespoons butter
1/4 teaspoon minced garlic
1/2 cup diced assorted bell peppers
1/2 cup brown gravy (see Techniques)
1 tablespoon red wine

Preheat the oven to 375°F. Flatten the chicken breast with a meat pounder to 1/2-inch thick. Sprinkle the chicken with the salt, pepper, paprika, garlic, and cilantro. Split open the chili and remove the seeds. Combine the cheeses into a football shape and place it inside in the chili. Roll the stuffed chili in the chicken breast. Dust the chicken roll with flour. Dip into the egg mixture and then the bread crumbs. Pour the oil to a depth of 3 inches into a large heavy pot or deep fryer. Heat to 350°F and cook the chicken roll for 3 to 4 minutes or until browned. Bake in the oven for 20 minutes.

To make sauce: In a medium sauté pan or skillet over medium heat, melt the butter, and cook the garlic and peppers for 3 to 4 minutes, or until softened. Add the brown gravy and red wine. Cook for 2 to 3 minutes.

To Serve: Pour the sauce onto a platter. Cut the chicken rolls into slices and arrange the slices on the sauce. May be served with Mexican-style rice. ▪

Chicken Maximilian, Mark Hollger, Santa Fe Restaurant

Chicken Roulades with Andouille Cornbread Stuffing, Baby Vegetables, and Roasted Garlic Sauce

From Emeril Lagasse of Emeril's, and NOLA, New Orleans, LA

Serve 4

Anyone who likes roast chicken with stuffing and gravy will love chef Emeril Lagasse's stuffed chicken roulades with roasted garlic sauce. Don't let the length of the recipe daunt you; preparation is simple and direct.

Roasted Garlic Sauce

Makes about 1-1/2 cups

3 heads whole garlic
1/4 cup olive oil
1 teaspoon minced garlic
2 teaspoons minced shallots
2 cups brown chicken stock or chicken broth
1 bay leaf
6 whole black peppercorns
1 fresh thyme sprig
1 tablespoon Plugra or other unsalted butter
Salt and fresh-ground pepper to taste

Cornbread Stuffing

2 tablespoons olive oil
1 small onion, diced
1 tablespoon minced garlic
2 tablespoons minced shallot
2 celery stalks, diced
1 green bell pepper, seeded, deribbed and diced
1 red bell pepper, seeded, deribbed and diced
2 tablespoons Emeril's Creole Seasoning or other Creole Seasoning.
8 ounces skinless andouille sausage, chopped
1/2 cup chicken broth
Crystal® hot sauce or another hot pepper sauce to taste
Worcestershire sauce to taste
2 cups crumbled cornbread

4 skinned and boneless whole chicken breasts
4 teaspoon Emeril's Creole Seasoning or other Creole-style seasoning.

Baby Vegetables

2 pounds baby zucchini
2 pounds baby patty pan squash
4 ounces haricots verts or baby green beans
2 tablespoons olive oil
1 teaspoon minced garlic
1 teaspoon minced shallots
Salt and white pepper to taste

To make the Garlic Sauce: Preheat the oven to 275°F. Trim the outer papery skin from the whole garlic heads but leave the heads intact. Bake for 30 minutes, until brown. Let cool. Squeeze the roasted garlic cloves from their skins, and set aside. In a medium sauté pan or skillet over medium heat, heat the oil and sauté the minced garlic and shallots until almost dry. Add the chicken stock, bay leaf, peppercorns, and thyme, and bring to a boil. Add half of the roasted garlic to the pan and reduce heat to a simmer. Cook to reduce the sauce by half, about 5 to 6 minutes. Swirl in the butter, remove from heat and strain through a fine-meshed sieve. Adjust seasoning and add the remaining roasted garlic.

To make the cornbread stuffing: In a large sauté pan or skillet over medium heat, heat the olive oil and sauté the vegetables in olive oil until tender, about 4 to 5 minutes. Season with Creole seasoning. While the vegetables are cooking, cook the andouille over medium heat in a separate sauté pan or skillet for 3 to 4 minutes. Combine the vegetables, hot sauce, Worcestershire, and sausage in a large bowl. Add the cornbread and mix well. Add broth as necessary to moisten stuffing.

To make the baby vegetables: Blanch the vegetables in salted boiling water to cover for 4 to 5 minutes. Drain and let cool. In a large sauté pan or skillet heat the olive, oil and sauté the garlic and shallots until softened, about 3 minutes. Add the baby vegetables to the pan and heat through. Add salt and pepper and keep warm.

To make the chicken roulades: Heat oven to 350°F. With the flat side of a meat mallet or the bottom of a heavy bottle, pound the breasts to flatten them. Season each breast. Place one fourth of the stuffing in the center of each breast and roll it around the stuffing, overlapping the edge. Place in a lightly greased baking pan and bake for 25 to 35 minutes. Remove and let stand 2 to 3 minutes before serving.

To Serve: Serve the chicken roulades with the roasted garlic sauce and baby vegetables on the side. ∎

MARK ULRICH HOLLGER
Santa Fe Restaurant, New Orleans

The chef-proprietor of Santa Fe Restaurant describes his choice of career tongue-in-cheek with a verse:

We may live without poetry, music, and art;
We may live without conscience and live without heart;
We may live without friends; we may live without books;
But civilized man cannot live without cooks.
He may live without books—what is knowledge but grieving?
He may live without hope—what is hope but deceiving?
He may live without love—what is passion but pining?
But where is the man who can live without dining?

Hollger was born in a small town in a wine-producing area of southern Germany just before World War II. "Food was a commodity then that was very much appreciated," says Hollger, and it was here that he learned his love of and respect for food.

At fifteen, Hollger started his culinary apprenticeship ("My mother said, 'You're interested in eating, maybe you'd be interested in cooking?'"), learning every position from pastry kitchen to fish station to soups and sauces in the major hotels of Frankfurt, Lucerne, and Stockholm. He was also chef in resorts in the Virgin Islands and Bermuda.

From Bermuda he considered it "a short jump to Texas," where he found something completely different: Mexican food. "Texas is where I tasted and learned how to make my first good Margarita. When people ask me how can a German or Austrian cook Mexican food, I remind them that for a time—from 1864 until his death in 1867—Kaiser Maximilian ruled Mexico." He describes Mexican food as mildly addictive "Once you've tasted good Mexican food, then once in a while, you crave it, you just have to have it."

Hollger picked New Orleans with a flip of a coin: "Heads it was Las Vegas, tails, New Orleans." He moved to the Big Easy in 1977. Before opening Santa Fe he worked as a waiter for two years at Brennan's, "to learn the front of the house," and operated an ice cream parlor selling ice cream and sandwiches. One day, about seven years after he moved to the city, a friend told him that a local hotel had a bunch of chairs for sale. He bought them. "I started Santa Fe on a very low budget and very low key. I wanted it to be a local place, for people in the neighborhood."

GREG SONNIER
Gabrielle, New Orleans

Greg Sonnier, chef-proprietor of Gabrielle, started cooking—really cooking—at the age of eight. Both parents worked, and he bridged the gap by preparing family dinners.

He earned a bachelor's degree at Loyola University in New Orleans, but cooking proved to be his calling. The New Orleans restaurant community is a very small community, after all, almost like a family, and young chefs tend to work at many of the same places. For example, Sonnier's first three-year training period began where so many young New Orleans chefs got their start—at K-Paul's Louisiana Kitchen under the guidance of Paul Prudhomme.

In 1986, Sonnier moved to Brigsten's and worked under Frank Brigsten for the next six years. "I learned the basics and developed my own taste while working at K-Paul's. Then I learned to develop my creative side under chef Frank Brigtsen," says Sonnier.

Sonnier and his wife and pastry chef-partner, Mary, named their restaurant after their small daughter Gabrielle. The menu at Gabrielle is an appetizing mix of traditional Creole, Cajun, and Louisiana country dishes with some deft ethnic accents. Among more traditional dishes are Roasted Chicken Stuffed with Crawfish Country Rice, and Creamy Pan Gravy (an entrée recipe featured in this book), Panéed Rabbit with Shrimp Bordelaise Pasta, and Sautéed Rabbit Tenderloin and Andouille Sausage. Testifying to Sonnier's creativity are dishes such as Crawfish Enchilada con Queso Sauce, Grilled Lemon Fish with Smoked Corn Salsa and Avocado Sauce, and Sesame-breaded Shrimp with Chinese Mustard Sauce.

Sonnier's other featured recipe in this book is Oysters Gabie (an appetizer).

Scaloppine of Chicken with Stir-fried Vegetables

From André Poirot of Begue's,
New Orleans, LA

Serves 2

Good and good for you, this recipe uses skinless chicken and olive oil in place of butter, making it low in cholesterol but not low in color, flavor, or appeal. It's hearty but not heavy, and it's also quick to make.

3 small new red potatoes, halved
2 skinless, boneless chicken breast halves
4 tablespoons flour for dredging
1/2 teaspoon salt
1/2 teaspoon pepper
2 tablespoons olive oil
1 cup mixed julienned carrots, zucchini, and yellow squash
1 tablespoon dry white wine
2 tablespoons pesto (recipe follows)
1 tablespoon plain low-fat yogurt
1 teaspoon minced fresh chives

Cook the potatoes in boiling salted water to cover until tender, about 7 to 8 minutes; drain, and set aside. Meanwhile, with the flat side of a meat mallet or the bottom of a heavy bottle, pound the breast until flattened. Mix together the flour, salt, and pepper. Lightly dredge the chicken in the seasoned flour. In a medium sauté pan or skillet, heat 1 tablespoon of the olive oil and sauté the chicken for 2 to 3 minutes on each side, or until opaque throughout. Set aside and keep warm. In another medium sauté pan or skillet, heat the remaining 1 tablespoon olive oil and sauté the vegetables until crisp-tender, about 3 to 4 minutes. Mix the wine and pesto, yogurt, and chives, in a small saucepan and heat through. Serve each breast with half of the potatoes and vegetables. Drizzle the pesto over the chicken.

Pesto Sauce

Makes about 2 cups

1 cup packed fresh basil leaves
1/2 cup pine nuts, toasted (see Techniques)
1/2 cup (2 ounces) grated Parmesan or Romano cheese
1/2 cup olive oil

Place the basil, pine nuts, and cheese in a blender or food processor. Slowly pour in the oil with the motor running to make a smooth sauce. ∎

Maw Maw's Chicken Stew

From Gigi Patout of Patout's, New Orleans, LA

Serves 5 or 6

Even comfort food is filled with flavor in Louisiana, as in chef Gigi Patout's chicken stew with rice. The chicken is browned in chicken fat, three kinds of pepper give the dish zing, and a depth of flavor is provided by a mahogany brown roux. This is traditional Louisiana cooking at its best. Serve with hot cooked rice.

One 5-pound hen
2 tablespoons salt
1 tablespoon cayenne pepper
2 teaspoons black pepper
2 teaspoons white pepper
5 cups dark roux (recipe follows)
3 large yellow onions, chopped
2 large bell peppers, chopped
2 celery stalks, chopped
8 cups chicken stock or broth
6 ounces fresh mushrooms, sliced
2 bunches green onions, chopped
Parsley, stemmed and minced

For the stew: Pull off the neck and back fat from the hen and reserve; cut the hen into 10 to 12 small serving pieces. Mix the salt and peppers in a small bowl. Season the chicken pieces well with about a third of this mixture.

In a large, heavy skillet, preferably cast iron, cook the chicken fat over medium heat until the fat is melted. Add the chicken pieces and brown well on all sides over medium-high heat. Remove the chicken from the pan. Add the roux and half of the onions, bell peppers, and celery to the skillet, cook 4 to 5 minutes, remove from the heat, and let cool.

Place the chicken stock or broth in a heavy 6-to 8-quart stockpot. Add the remaining onions, bell peppers, and celery, and bring to a boil over high heat. Reduce heat to medium and begin whisking or stirring in the roux 1 cup at a time, making sure each cup dissolves completely before you add more, until you have a medium-thick sauce. Stir in the rest of the salt and pepper mixture and simmer over low heat, stirring often, for 45 minutes to 1 hour. Add the chicken pieces and continue to simmer until the hen is tender, about 1-1/2 to 2 hours, depending on the toughness of the bird. Remove from heat and let stand for 5 to 10 minutes to allow the fat to rise to the top. Skim off and discard as much fat as possible and

return the stew to a simmer over medium-high heat. Add the mushrooms, green onions, and parsley, and simmer 3 to 5 minutes more. Serve the chicken on plates with rice and gravy.

Roux

2 cups high-grade vegetable oil
3 to 3 1/2 cups all-purpose flour

Place the oil in a large heavy skillet over medium heat. Heat it to about 350°F. Using a wooden spoon or a whisk, quickly stir in 3 cups of flour all at once, being careful not to splatter yourself. Once the flour is thoroughly mixed in, check the consistency: It should form a smooth paste that is neither runny nor clumpy or grainy. Since the absorbency of flour varies greatly, as does the body of oils, it is impossible to give an exact proportion of flour to oil. If the roux is too thin, stir in a bit more flour; if it is too thick, stir in a little oil. With the roux still over a medium heat, stir continuously, being sure to scrape the sides and bottom of the pot. The flour will slowly begin to brown. Simply continue to cook and stir until it reaches the desired stage of doneness. A dark roux will take 50 to 70 minutes. It should be dark brown, but not black. Judge your roux's doneness by the color, not time, which will vary according to your equipment and ingredients. When it has reached the desired color, remove it from the heat and let it cool. ∎

Roasted Chicken Stuffed with Crawfish Country Rice, and Creamy Pan Gravy

From Greg Sonnier of Gabrielle, New Orleans, LA

Serves 4

Simple, economic, and delicious, this is a perfect dish for Sunday dinner. Once you put it in the oven it will tend itself. If you have a crowd, just double or triple the recipe.

Crawfish County Rice
2 tablespoons butter
1/2 cup finely chopped onion
1/2 cup finely chopped bell pepper
1/4 cup finely chopped celery
1 bay leaf
1 tablespoon seafood seasoning (recipe on page 41)
1 cup short-grain rice
2-1/4 cups chicken stock or broth
1 cup crawfish tails or small shrimp
1/2 cup sliced green onions (green part only)

Salt to taste (optional)
4 boned chicken leg and thigh quarters
Salt and pepper to taste

3/4 cup dry white wine
1 cup heavy (whipping) cream

To make Crawfish Country Rice: In a large, heavy saucepan, melt the butter and sauté the vegetables until tender. Add the bay leaf and seafood seasoning, then add the rice and sauté for about 1 minute, or until opaque. Add the stock or broth slowly, stirring constantly, and bring the stock or broth to a boil. Reduce heat to low, cover, and simmer for about 20 minutes, or until the rice is tender. Add the crawfish or shrimp and green onions and salt, if you like. Stir and spread out on a baking sheet to cool.

Preheat the oven to 400°F. When the rice is completely cooled, stuff the chicken quarters with the rice, overlapping the skin at the end to hold the rice inside. Season the outside of the chicken and place it in a buttered ovenproof skillet or roasting pan. Bake the chicken 45 minutes to 1 hour, or until browned. Place on a warm serving dish.

Pour off the fat from the pan, pour in the wine, and cook and stir over medium heat to scrape up all the browned juices from the bottom of the pan. Add the cream and cook to reduce until the sauce has thickened. Adjust seasoning and serve over chicken. ∎

Roasted Chicken Stuffed with Crawfish Country Rice, and Creamy Pan Gravy, Greg Sonnier, Gabrielle

Grilled Cornish Hen with Voodoo Barbecue Sauce, Daniel Landry, J. Lillian

grill and cook for 15 minutes. Turn the hens, basting with barbecue sauce, and cook 10 minutes. Remove from grill and baste on both sides.

Voodoo Barbecue Sauce

Makes 3 quarts

8 cups (64-ounces) ketchup
1 cup molasses
1/2 cup vinegar
1/2 cup Tabasco sauce or other hot pepper sauce
1 cup Creole mustard or Dijon-type mustard
3/4 cup packed brown sugar
5 tablespoons liquid smoke (optional)
3 tablespoons Worcestershire sauce
1 tablespoon minced garlic
1/2 tablespoon garlic powder
12-ounce bottle of Voodoo or other dark beer

Combine all ingredients. Sauce may be kept in refrigerator up to two weeks, and may be used for other barbecue meats. ∎

Sautéed Duck Breast with Gingered Fig Sauce, Braised Fennel, and Celeriac-Potato Timbales

From Christiane Engeran Fisher of Chez Daniel, Metairie, LA

Serves 4

Chef Christiane Engeran Fisher brings together a variety of flavors and texture in this innovative recipe. Sweet ripe figs combine with ginger and balsamic vinegar to create a piquant sauce for sautéed duck breast, which is served with timbales of celeriac and potato, and fennel braised with onion.

Celeriac-Potato Timbales
1 large celeriac (celery root)
3 potatoes
3 eggs, beaten
1/3 cup heavy (whipping) cream
Salt and pepper to taste

Braised Baby Fennel
Olive oil
1 onion, chopped
3 fennel bulbs, stemmed and sliced
1/4 cup chicken or beef stock or broth

Grilled Cornish Hens with Voodoo Barbecue Sauce

From Daniel Landry of J. Lillian, New Orleans, LA

Serves 8

When a Louisiana chef dubs a barbecue sauce "Voodoo," watch out! Multiply this recipe to be sure you have enough grilled Cornish hens on hand, because when this dish is featured at a cookout, folks are bound to come back for seconds. Serve with potato salad and coleslaw.

Four 1-pound Cornish hens

Marinade
1/4 cup cooking oil
1/2 cup dry white wine
1 minced garlic clove
1 minced onion
1/2 teaspoon salt
1/2 teaspoon coarsely ground black pepper
1/4 teaspoon dried thyme
3 to 4 canned chipotle chilies

1 cup hickory chips
Voodoo Barbecue Sauce (recipe follows)

Cut the tail from the hens. Cut through breast cavity, cut around to backbone, and separate leg bone. Repeat procedure with other half of hen, and remove backbone.

To make the marinade: Mix together all of the ingredients and chill for several hours in covered jar. Shake well, then pour over the hens. Cover and chill for about 3 hours, turning the hens at least once during this time period. Remove from the refrigerator 30 minutes before grilling.

Place the hens on a grill over hot coals sprinkled with dry hickory chips.

Turn the hens with tongs and baste evenly with barbecue sauce. Cover the

Gingered Fig Sauce
1/2 cup sugar
1/4 cup water
2 tablespoons red wine vinegar
2 tablespoons balsamic vinegar
12 ripe figs, cut in half
1/2 teaspoon minced fresh ginger
4 cups chicken broth

4 duck breasts
Fresh figs for garnish

To make the timbales: Preheat the oven to 400° F. Peel and chop the celeriac and the potatoes. Place in a medium saucepan with salted water to cover, and cook over medium heat until tender. Drain and mash until smooth. Add the eggs and cream, and mix until blended. Season with salt and pepper. Fill each of four well-buttered 2-ounce timbale molds to the top with this mixture. Set the timbales in a baking pan, add 1 inch of warm water, and bake for 20 minutes, or until set. Set aside.

To make the fennel: Reduce oven temperature to 350°F. In a heatproof casserole or ovenproof skillet, heat the olive oil over medium heat and sauté the onion until translucent, about 3 minutes. Stir in the fennel and pour in the stock or broth. Bake for 15 minutes. Keep warm in the turned-off oven with the timbales.

To make the sauce: In a medium, heavy saucepan, combine the sugar and water. Cook over high heat until the mixture begins turning an amber color. Pour in the vinegars and stir well so that no sugar remains on the bottom. Add the figs and ginger. Stir in the stock or broth and cook over medium heat until thickened. Purée in a blender and strain through a fine-meshed sieve. Set aside and keep warm.

In a large sauté pan or skillet over high heat, cook the duck breasts, fat side down, for 2 to 3 minutes. Lower heat and cook 3 or 4 minutes, or until medium rare.

Thinly slice the duck on the diagonal and arrange on each of four plates. Unmold the timbales and put one on each plate. Arrange the onion and fennel next to the timbale. Pour the sauce over the duck and garnish with ripe figs.∎

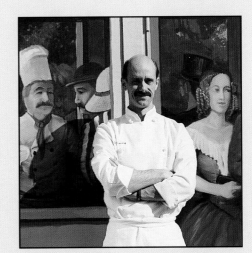

DANIEL K. LANDRY
J. Lillian, New Orleans

"Who is J. Lillian?" is the advertising slogan used to arouse curiosity in anyone in New Orleans not already familiar with this new restaurant star of the Garden District. It opened in 1993, and the answer to its rise to fame lies in the question: "Who is Daniel Landry?"

For starters, he's the executive chef who, still in his thirties, has fifteen years of restaurant experience under his toque.

Landry graduated from the University of Southwestern Louisiana in Lafayette with an accounting degree, giving him a business edge for his first venture in 1980 as chef-owner of Parrot's Food & Spirits in Houma, Louisiana, where he was jack-of-all-trades for policies, recipes, menus, training procedures, and operations manuals. Landry moved to Vincent's restaurant, again as chef-owner, in 1985, creating a progessive Louisiana cuisine there. Contemporary Creole cuisine was an established specialty at DeNovo restaurant, where he was executive chef, and subsequently at Isadora Restaurant (both in New Orleans), where his reputation grew for innovative new American-Creole cuisine with cross-cultural influences.

Perhaps to prove he could excel big, Landry became executive chef for a franchised chain, Owen Brennan's, developing recipes, food production systems, training kitchen personnel, and designing complete kitchen facilities to produce food for up to fourteen hundred covers per day.

After serving as executive chef at New Orleans's Royal Cafe in 1990, and executive chef at The Bombay Club in the same city in 1992, Daniel Landry became executive chef at J. Lillian, a fine one-hundred-seat restaurant with a mysterious namesake.

At J. Lillian, Landry is forging his own Louisiana cuisine, based on, but not restricted to, Cajun, Creole, and Continental New Orleans cookery. His menus feature fresh pizzas of the day, with eclectic toppings such as duck sausage and tasso, and pastas of the day composed of equally unexpected but appetizing combinations. Two menu favorites are his Rabbit Wellington, and Duck and Turnip Potpie.

Landry's recipe for Grilled Cornish Hen with Voodoo Barbecue Sauce may not reveal who J. Lillian is—but it says a lot about Daniel Landry.

Lisa Hanson
Bistro la Tour, New Orleans

Lisa Hanson studied for two years at the Food Service Institute of New Orleans, receiving her associate degree in culinary arts. Shortly thereafter she went to work for Kevin Graham when he was executive chef at the Omni Royal Orleans hotel. She worked with Graham at the Omni for four and one-half years, then moved to the Windsor Court Hotel where she again worked under Graham as a line cook for the next three years.

When she walked into her job at Bistro la Tour, she walked into a chapter of New Orleans history. The restaurant is located in the heart of the French Quarter at 720 Rue St. Louis, a property originally owned by one Samuel Hermann, who sold it to Pierre Soulé in 1833. Soulé built the current building as his private residence. (He was president of the new St. Louis Hotel, which was then under construction just down the street.) The building that houses Bistro la Tour was in for a checkered future: Right after World War I, the infamous Panama Hattie opened a "sporting house" there that did business until World War II. After the war the Kelso Club, a private club for local celebrities, opened and held sway until the early sixties. After a brief life as Sinatraville, and another as an Asian restaurant, Bistro la Tour was born.

The menu is a mix of French bistro and Creole fare, ranging from traditional salade niçoise and quiche du jour to Crawfish Etouffée and Jambalaya la Tour.

Hanson's touch can be seen in her featured recipe, Duck Stew, a Parisian bistro favorite re-created for the menu. The "stew" is not the duck but the tantalizing mixture of tomatoes, onions, and chopped black and green olives that are stewed in Port wine.

Duck Stew

*From Lisa Hanson of Bistro la Tour,
New Orleans, LA*

Serves 1

The duck leg and the breast are from a whole duck that has been roasted until half done. The duck leg could be braised, while the duck breast is sautéed to medium rare and fanned out over a cooked tomato-olive relish that is finished with a port reduction. This recipe proves that elegant can be easy.

1 tablespoon butter
2/3 cup diced onions
1-1/2 cups chopped black and green olives
1 cup diced tomatoes
1/4 cup port
2 tablespoons duck fat or vegetable oil
1/2 duck breast, half roasted
1 duck leg, half roasted

In a large saucepan, melt the butter over medium heat and sauté the onions until translucent, about 3 minutes. Add the olives and tomatoes. Cook for 2 to 3 minutes. Add the port and cook for another 2 minutes. Keep warm.

In a large sauté pan or skillet, heat the duck fat or oil over medium heat and sauté the duck breast (skin side down) and leg until the duck skin is crisp.

To serve: Pour the tomato and olive sauce on a serving plate. Slice the duck breast on a bias and fan slices over the sauce. Set the duck leg on the side of the fanned breast.■

Roast Leg of Duckling with Spring Leeks, and New Potatoes

*From Gerard Maras of Mr. B's,
New Orleans, LA*

Serves 4

The spring leeks called for in this recipe, also known as wild leeks or wild ramps, are a rare treat if you can find them. They grow wild from Canada to the southern United States and look like a scallion but taste much stronger, like garlic and onion mixed into one. They can be found in specialty produce markets from March to June. Baby leeks are an excellent substitute.

Two 4-pound ducklings
Salt and pepper to taste

Forcemeat
6 ounces boneless pork from leg or shoulder
4 ounces boneless veal
1 teaspoon minced fresh thyme
1 teaspoon minced fresh sage
1 teaspoon minced fresh oregano
1 ounce minced wild mushrooms such as
    morels, chanterelles, cèpes, or shiitakes
1 garlic clove, minced
1 teaspoon salt
1/2 teaspoon black pepper
1 egg yolk
3 tablespoons heavy (whipping) cream
Four 5-inch by 5-inch pieces caul fat*
Salt and pepper to taste

Duck Stock
Reserved bones from 2 ducks
1 cup dry white wine
1 leek, chopped
1 small onion, chopped
1 celery stalk, chopped
2 bay leaves
1 thyme sprig
4 peppercorns

Sauce
1 teaspoon olive oil
1 tablespoon minced onion
2 tablespoons dry white wine
2 cups duck stock or chicken stock
1/2 teaspoon each minced fresh thyme,
    oregano, and sage
1 tablespoon cold unsalted butter

New Potatoes
3 tablespoons olive oil
12 new potatoes, halved
Salt and pepper to taste
3 tablespoons fresh rosemary leaves

Spring Leeks
Baby leeks or spring leeks (1/2 cup per person)
1/3 cup water
2 tablespoons unsalted butter
Salt and pepper to taste

Remove the breasts and legs from ducks and reserve the breasts. Remove the bones from the legs by cutting down to the bone with a sharp knife on each side, then cutting under the bone to free it from the meat. Pop the joint and remove the first bone. Cut around the top of the second bone with a sharp knife. Turning the meat inside out, cut along the bone to the last knuckle. With heel of a French knife, cut bone off at bottom. Season the meat with salt and pepper inside and out. (Reserve all bones for stock.)

To make the forcemeat: Preheat the oven to 300°F. Grind the pork and veal through a 3/8-inch grinder blade into a non-aluminum bowl set in a larger bowl of ice. Add the herbs, minced mushrooms, garlic, salt, and pepper. Mix well with a wooden spoon. Stir in the egg yolk and gradually add the cream until mixed to a paste. Place the forcemeat into a large pastry bag and force the mixture into the duck leg, filling the cavity left by the two bones. Lay the duck leg on the caul fat and wrap to encase the entire leg tightly. Season with salt and pepper. Bake for about 30 minutes. Let rest for 10 minutes before slicing.

To make the duck stock: Preheat the oven to 375°F. Chop the bones, then place them in a roasting pan, and bake until evenly browned, about 20 minutes. Transfer the bones to a 6-quart stock pot. Add the white wine to the roasting pan and cook and stir over medium heat to scrape up all the browned juices at the bottom. Pour the liquid into the stock pot. Add the leek, onion, celery, bay leaves, thyme, and peppercorns. Simmer for 5 minutes. Add enough water to just cover the bones, bring to a boil, then reduce heat to a simmer. Cook for 1 hour, then strain the stock. Cook over medium heat to reduce by one fourth, about 10 minutes. Strain the stock through and fine-meshed sieve, spoon off the fat and set the stock aside.

To make the sauce: In a medium saucepan or sauté pan, heat the olive oil, over medium heat and sauté the onion, until translucent, about 3 minutes. Add the white wine and cook to reduce by half, about 2 to 3 minutes. Add the stock, bring to a boil, and cook to reduce by one third, about 4 minutes. Add the herbs and cook for 1 minute, swirl in the cold butter. Keep warm.

Duck Stew, Lisa Hanson, Bistro la Tour

To make the potatoes: Heat the olive oil in a large sauté pan or skillet until smoking. Add potatoes and toss to start browning, about 4 to 5 minutes. Season with salt, pepper, and rosemary. Place the potatoes in 350°F oven for 15 minutes; remove, keep warm.

To make the leeks: Cut the leeks into 1-inch diagonal pieces. Place in a saucepan with remaining ingredients. Cook over high heat until tender, about 3 minutes. Strain the leeks and keep warm.

To serve: Slice the duck legs. Place on each of four plates. Serve the leeks and potatoes alongside.

*Caul fat is a lacy net of pork abdominal membrane. It may be purchased from a local butcher.∎

Roast Duck with Hunter's Sauce

From Randy Barlow of Kelsey's, Gretna, LA

Serves 2

This is a classic recipe in the best sense of the word. A traditional hunter-style brown sauce, flavored with bacon and wild mushrooms, accompanies roast duck. Serve with green vegetable, wild rice, and a bottle of fine red wine.

One 3 to 5 pound duck

6 celery stalks, chopped
2 medium onions, chopped
6 medium carrots, peeled and chopped
1 teaspoon dried oregano
1 teaspoon dried basil
Salt and pepper to taste

Hunter's Sauce

8 ounces bacon (about 6 to 8 slices), chopped
1 large onion, chopped
8 ounces shiitake, oyster or other wild mushrooms or white cultivated mushrooms, chopped
1 cup dry white wine

6 cups of duck stock made from reserved vegetables and bones (see Techniques) or chicken stock
1 cup diced tomatoes
Salt and pepper to taste

Preheat the oven to 350°F. Remove the neck and giblets from the duck. Loosely stuff the cavity of the duck with chopped vegetables, herbs and seasonings, and place the remaining vegetables on the bottom of a roasting pan. Set the duck on the vegetables. Bake for 2 to 2-1/2 hours, or until a thermometer inserted in the duck registers 190°F. Let cool. Split in half and remove the vegetables and bones, reserving them to make stock, if you like.

To make the sauce: In a large sauté pan or skillet, cook the bacon until crisp. Remove bacon with a slotted spoon, leaving the bacon fat, and discard the bacon. Add the onion and cook over medium heat until translucent, about 3 minutes. Add the mushrooms and cook until browned, about 2 to 3 minutes. Add the white wine, stock, and tomatoes. Lower heat to medium-low and cook for 30 minutes. Season with salt and pepper.

Serve one half duck on each plate with Hunters sauce and wild rice. ∎

Cajun Smothered Duck, Gigi Patout, Patout's

Cajun Smothered Duck

*From Gigi Patout of Patout's,
New Orleans, LA*

Smothered is another term for fricassée, a dish of poultry that has been sautéed, then stewed with vegetables. This hearty recipe for duck with bell pepper, green onion, and parsley has a lagniappe: it makes its own gravy.

Serves 4 to 6

1 tablespoon salt
2 teaspoons ground red pepper
2 teaspoons ground black pepper
1 teaspoon ground white pepper
3 large ducks
1-1/2 cups all-purpose flour
1/2 cup vegetable oil
3 medium onion, chopped
2 bell peppers, seeded, deribbed, and
   chopped
1 celery stalk, chopped
1 cup chicken stock or broth
1 cup chopped green onions
1/2 cup minced fresh parsley

In a small bowl, mix together the salt and ground peppers. Season the ducks inside and out with about half of this mixture. Place the flour in a large flat pan and dredge the ducks to coat them lightly on all sides. Heat the oil in a Dutch oven or other large, heavy pot over medium-high heat and brown the ducks well on all sides. Remove the ducks to a platter and discard all but 1 tablespoon of the oil. Add the onions, bell peppers, and celery, reduce heat to low, and sauté for 2 to 3 minutes. Return the ducks to the pot, stir well, and add the stock or broth. Cover the pot and let cook over the lowest possible heat until the ducks are very tender, about 1-1/2 hours. This may also be cooked in the oven at 350°F for about 1-1/2 hours. Stir once during cooking to be sure nothing is sticking to the pot. Remove from heat and let stand a few minutes to allow the fat to rise to the top. Skim and discard the fat and stir in the green onions and parsley. Serve on individual plates, with rice alongside and gravy over all. ▪

GIGI PATOUT
Patout's, New Orleans

Chef Gigi Patout has a way of making bold moves very smoothly, so you hardly notice anything big is happening until it has. Before becoming a chef at her family's original Patout's restaurant in New Iberia, Louisiana, she held an executive position in a firm that fabricated off-shore oil rigs. She had moved from receptionist to management level by the time she was twenty-five years old.

In 1979, when she stepped into Patout's, the family restaurant, she started, characteristically, as hostess—and wound up as chef.

By 1985, she won the Best of Show for her Redfish Eugenie at the Culinary Classics, an annual competition between fifty-two of the region's best chefs, organized by the Chefs de Cuisine Association of Louisiana. Several California food experts served as judges, including Ruth Reichl, then with the *Los Angeles Times*, and Patricia Unterman with the *San Francisco Examiner*. Reichl was so impressed with Patout's Redfish Eugenie that she visited the family's Louisiana namesake restaurant.

Her subsequent article about Louisiana regional cooking stirred interest in Los Angeles. Patout and her brothers Mitch and André were invited to be guest chefs at Pax in La Jolla and Chez Mélange in Redondo Beach, California. The next big step, in 1988, was to open a branch of Patout's in Los Angeles (subsequently closed).

Gigi is now executive chef at Patout's Cajun Corner in New Orleans, a complex of three restaurants—Cajun Cabin, Patout's restaurant and Patout's Gallery—plus Jelly Rolls, a large banquet facility. And she is still cooking and serving some of the dishes that have made her famous, including the two entrées featured in this cookbook, Cajun Smothered Duck and Maw Maw's Chicken Stew, and her hearty appetizers, Cabbage Rolls and Maque Choux.

RICHARD W. HUGHES, JR.
Pelican Club, New Orleans

When Gene Bourg, writing in *The Times Picayune,* described Richard Hughes's style of cooking at the Pelican Club as "Excellent...a mix of Louisiana earthiness and New American polish," he unintentionally described the chef-proprietor's career. Hughes, a Louisiana native, went from New Orleans to New York, where he orchestrated Eddie Murphy's New Year's Eve party (for 700 of the star's closest friends) and a reception for Henry Kissinger—and back to New Orleans.

Hughes received his education and culinary training in Louisiana. He has a bachelor of fine arts degree from Louisiana State University in Baton Rouge and attended classes in Hotel and Restaurant Administration at the University of New Orleans. His first apprenticeship was at La Provence in Lacombe, Louisiana; then he moved to New Orleans where he progressed to *saucier* at Winston's at the Hilton, night chef at The Sazerac in The Fairmont, and executive chef at Dante by the River, where he stayed for three years.

Next stop, the Big Apple, where he opened three high-volume restaurants with combined annual sales of $7 million. He planned food concepts, recipes, kitchen organization, and kitchen staff hiring and training for Memphis, Coastal, and 107 West from 1983 to 1989.

The Big Apple grew a little sour for a number of reasons: Hughes and his wife had a new baby to raise and "I wanted to have a restaurant where I could have complete control."

In 1990, Hughes came back to his roots and opened the Pelican Club to quick acclaim: In 1991, it was given four stars by New Orleans food critic Tom Fitzmorris and was voted one of the 30 Top Grand Restaurants by *New Orleans Magazine.* His wine list received *The Wine Spectator's* Award of Excellence.

Pelican Club's menu is based on skillful renditions of traditional Lousiana favorites. But from these standards he segues to such signatures as Crawfish Chili with White Beans, and Whole Striped Bass Oriental Style. "My partner and chef de cuisine Chin Ling is from Singapore," says Hughes by way of explanation. Hughes' entrée recipe, Filets Mignons with Shiitake Mushrooms and Cabernet Sauce, and Garlic Mashed Potatoes with Roasted Onion, shows part of his range. His other recipe in this book is Quail Salad with Pâté (appetizer).

Filets Mignons with Shiitake Mushrooms and Cabernet Sauce, and Garlic Mashed Potatoes with Roasted Onion

From Richard Hughes of Pelican Club, New Orleans, LA

Serves 4

For meat and potato lovers: This recipe makes a fine steak fabulous by crowning it with an excellent mushroom and red wine sauce. And it makes good mashed potatoes great by adding roasted onion and garlic.

Filets Mignons
Four 8-ounce filets mignons
2 tablespoons butter
1 tablespoon chopped shallots
1 cup Shiitake mushrooms, stemmed
   and sliced
2 tablespoons bourbon
1/2 cup demi-glace (recipe follows)
1/2 cup Cabernet Sauvignon or
   other red wine
1/4 cup Madeira or dry sherry
2 tablespoons sweet butter
Salt and pepper to taste

Garlic Mashed Potatoes with Roasted Onion
1 onion unpeeled
2 garlic heads, outer papery husk removed
Olive oil
3 large white baking potatoes,
   peeled and cubed
6 tablespoons butter
1/2 cup milk, heated
Salt and pepper to taste

To make filets: Preheat the oven to 350°F. Brown the filets on all sides in 2 tablespoons of butter in a heavy, ovenproof sauté pan or skillet. Bake in oven for 8 to 10 minutes, or until medium rare. Set filets aside and keep warm. Transfer the filet pan to a burner on the top of the stove, add shallots and mushrooms to the pan, and sauté until shallots are translucent. Add the bourbon. Avert your face, ignite the bourbon with a long match, and shake the pan until the flames subside. Add the demi-glace and wines, and cook over medium heat to reduce until thickened, about 5 to 8 minutes. Stir in 2 tablespoons of butter, salt and pepper.

To make the mashed potatoes: Preheat the oven to 375°F. Rub the onion and garlic with olive oil and roast for about 30 minutes, or until slightly browned and softened. In a large saucepan, boil the potatoes in salted water to cover until tender, about 20 minutes. Peel the onion and purée it in a blender or food processor. Slice the garlic heads in half crosswise and squeeze out the garlic cloves; combine with the onion purée. Mash the potatoes with the onion-garlic mixture until soft. Add the butter, hot milk, salt and pepper.

To serve: Pour the sauce over the filets and serve the warm mashed potatoes alongside.

Demi-Glace Sauce

Makes about 1 to 1-1/2 quarts

5 pounds cut veal marrow bones
2 cups peeled and diced carrots
2 cups diced onions
2 cups diced celery
2 tablespoons tomato paste
2 bottles Cabernet Sauvignon or other red wine
1 bottle Madeira wine or dry sherry
1 gallon water
8 garlic cloves
1 fresh thyme sprig
3 bay leaves

Place the bones in a large baking pan and roast bones in a 400°F oven until brown, about 30 to 40 minutes. Add the carrots, onions, and celery, and roast for 20 minutes more. Add the tomato paste, stir and continue roasting for 10 minutes. Place on the stove top, pour in the wines and cook over medium heat, stirring to scrape, up the brown bits from the bottom of the pan. Place in a heavy stockpot, add the water, garlic, thyme, and bay leaves, and simmer for 24 hours. Strain through a fine-meshed sieve, and cook over medium heat to reduce to the consistency of heavy cream. Unused sauce may be frozen for later use. ∎

Summer Steak

From Mark Hollger of Santa Fe Restaurant, New Orleans, LA

Serves 2

And now for something completely different: Steak is topped with Stilton cheese, a brandy cream sauce, and a warm compote of fresh mixed fruit. The accompanying baked sweet potato is garnished with raisins, pumpkin seeds, and nuts. Somehow it all works beautifully together.

Two 8-ounce tenderloin steaks
Salt and pepper to taste
2 tablespoons clarified margarine
  (see Techniques) or oil
Two 2-ounce slices Stilton cheese

Brandy-Cream Sauce
2 tablespoons brandy
1/2 cup heavy (whipping) cream
1/2 cup demi-glace (recipe on this page)
  or brown gravy (see Techniques).

Fresh Fruit Compote
2 tablespoons butter
1 tablespoon honey
1 tablespoon poppy seed
Pinch of paprika
Juice of 1 lime
2 cups mixed sliced fruit such as
  pineapple, strawberries, kiwis, grapefruit,
  oranges, papaya, and mango, and/or
  whole raspberries.

Sprinkle the steaks on both sides with salt and pepper. In a large sauté pan or skillet over medium heat, heat the clarified margarine or oil, and cook the steaks for 5 minutes on one side. (Turn the steaks over and top each with a slice of Stilton cheese. Cook another 5 minutes, pour in the brandy, and remove the steaks to a warm platter. Add the cream and gravy to the pan and cook for about 3 to 4 minutes to reduce. Keep warm.

Filets Mignons with Shiitake Mushrooms and Cabernet Sauce, and Garlic Mashed Potatoes with Roasted Onion, Richard Hughes, Pelican Club

To make the compote: In a medium saucepan, melt the butter and add the honey, poppy seed, paprika, and lime juice. Add the fruit and stir gently until just heated through.

To serve: pour the cream sauce over the steaks and the fruit compote over that. Serve with baked sweet potatoes. (Recipe follows).

Baked Sweet Potatoes

Serves 2

2 small sweet potatoes
1 tablespoon raisins
2 tablespoons chopped nuts
2 tablespoons pumpkin seeds
2 pats of butter

Preheat the oven to 350°F and bake the sweet potatoes until tender, about 1 hour. Slice down the middle and sprinkle with the raisins, nuts, pumpkin seeds, and a pat of butter. Serve warm. ∎

Armand Jonté
Armand's, Waveland, Mississippi

What's a chef from Waveland, Mississippi, doing in a book about Lousiana chefs? Because he's Louisiana born and bred, and one of its best chefs who just slipped over the border a hop, skip and a jump. So many customers from New Orleans have found their way to his restaurant's door that there's talk of annexing Waveland, a community about fifty-five miles from New Orleans on the Gulf of Mexico where many New Orleanians keep summer homes.

Jonté was born in New Orleans and grew up there attending local schools, finishing with Tulane University. He began in the restaurant business—the way many accomplished chefs begin—by washing dishes. He answered a blind ad in the newspaper for a person "to learn Creole cooking." In answering the ad, he hit the apprentice jackpot. It was for Commander's Palace, and he apprenticed there from the late seventies to the early eighties.

After Commander's he opened the restaurant and the dining room at the Columns hotel. His year and a half there brought his talents to the attention of locals and he was hired by Gautreau's Restaurant to be its chef. Six and one-half years later, Jonté's reputation had blossomed and the good reviews and good news of his brand of new Louisiana cookery started coming in from both local and national press.

In 1990, Jonté moved to Waveland, where he worked as executive chef of the Bay-Waveland Yacht Club. And in July of 1992, he celebrated his own independence day—by opening Armand's.

His featured recipes in this book show his range, from appetizer Eggplant Eloise, to entrée Tournedos Louis Armstrong, to dessert Coffee Toffee Pie. His entrée combines shrimp and beef tenderloin. Instead of the traditional fried bread rounds that usually accompany beef tournedos, Jonté uses a crisp corn pancake.

Tournedos Louis Armstrong

From Armand Jonté from Armand's, Waveland, MS

Serves 2

Here is yet another creative variation on the "surf-and-turf" theme: shrimp and tournedos. Chef Armand Jonté's suggestion of placing the corn pancake on top of the tournedo not only keeps pancake crisp, it makes for an interesting presentation.

Corn Pancakes
1 ear corn, shucked
1 egg
3/4 cup all-purpose flour
3/4 cup corn flour
3/4 cup heavy (whipping) cream
Pinch of salt
Pinch of baking powder
Pinch of cayenne
1 tablespoon sugar
1 green onion, chopped
1/2 cup diced red and green bell peppers

3 to 4 tablespoons clarified butter
   (see Techniques)

Tournedos
Two (4 to 4-1/2 ounces) beef tournedos
Salt and cracked black pepper to taste
1/3 cup olive oil
2 large shrimp, peeled and butterflied
   (see Techniques)

Crème de Cassis Sauce
1 tablespoon butter
3 shallots, diced
1/3 cup Crème de Cassis
1/2 cup beef demi-glace (see recipe on page 81, or Techniques)
1 to 2 tablespoons butter

To make the pancakes: Cut kernels from the corn. Blanch in boiling salted water for 3 minutes. Remove with slotted spoon reserving water. In a blender or food processor, combine all the ingredients except the corn and clarified butter. Process until well blended. Stir in the corn and thin with some of the reserved water if necessary.

In a large sauté pan or skillet, heat the clarified butter, and cook the pancakes, using 1/4 cup batter for each, for 2 to 3 minutes, or until golden brown. Set aside and keep warm.

To make to tournedos: Rub tournedos with salt and pepper. In a large sauté pan or skillet heat the oil over medium heat and sauté the tournedos for about 2 to 3 minutes on each side for medium rare. Transfer to warm plates. In the same skillet, sauté the shrimp for 1-1/2 minutes, or until pink and opaque; set aside.

To make the sauce: In a medium sauté pan or skillet, melt the butter and sauté the shallots for 1-1/2 minutes. Remove from heat. Add the cassis, heat, avert your face, and light the mixture with a long match, shaking the pan until the flames subside. Add the demi-glace. Simmer for 2 to 2-1/2 minutes, or until reduced by one third. Swirl in the butter and strain through a fine-meshed sieve.

To serve: Pool sauce on each plate. Place one tournedo on the sauce in each plate, top with a pancake, a little more sauce, and a shrimp.■

Tournedos Louis Armstrong, Armand Jonté, Armand's

Osso Bucco, Bob Roth, The Steak Knife

Osso Bucco

*From Bob Roth, The Steak Knife,
New Orleans, LA*

Osso bucco, braised veal shank, is an Italian dish traditionally served with risotto. This is a fine dish to make a one day ahead and reheat before serving.

4 bacon slices, chopped
1 pound onions, cut into large dice
3 carrots, peeled and cut into 1/2-inch pieces
1 garlic clove, minced
2 tablespoons tomato paste
1 tablespoon flour
4 cups dry red wine
4 cups chicken stock or broth
4 cups beef stock or broth
2 tablespoons brandy
2 teaspoons cornstarch
1 tablespoon butter

Salt and pepper to taste
1 tablespoon oil
4 center-cut veal shanks, 2 inches thick

In a large casserole, cook the bacon until crisp and remove the bacon. Sauté the onions, carrots, and garlic in the fat until browned, about 10 minutes. Add the tomato paste and cook over low heat, stirring occasionally, for 5 minutes. Stir in the flour and cook over low heat, stirring constantly, for 5 minutes. Add the red wine, and cook over low heat for 30 minutes, or until reduced to half. Stir constantly near the end of the cooking time. Add stocks or broth and simmer for 45 minutes. Remove from heat and strain through a fine-meshed sieve. Mix the brandy and cornstarch together. Add to the sauce, stirring until thickened and smooth. Stir in the butter.

Preheat the oven to 375°F. Season and oil the veal shanks. Place the shanks in an ovenproof casserole and bake for 15 to 20 minutes, or until lightly browned. Add to the sauce and cook, partially covered, over low heat for 2 hours, or until fork tender. ∎

BOB ROTH
The Steak Knife, New Orleans

Bob Roth (Robert Roth, Jr.) first stepped into the kitchens of The Steak Knife in 1972. Except for a break to attend and graduate from the Culinary Institute of America in Hyde Park, New York, he hasn't stepped out since.

The Steak Knife restaurant was founded in 1971 by Bob's father, Robert Roth, Sr., and his partner Ernest L. Masson. In 1986, Robert Sr. and his son Guy Roth bought out Masson. With the passing of their father Robert in 1988, brothers Bob and Guy took over the restaurant. They were joined by their mother, Doris, and their sister, Susan, making The Steak Knife a full-fledged family effort.

Although Guy is a hotel-restaurant school graduate and took continuing education culinary classes at the Culinary Institute of America, and everybody in the family pinch-hits with ease, Bob Roth is the guy in the white hat, the chef de cuisine.

His food, in keeping with the name and spirit of The Steak Knife, is very straightforward—deceptively so. The heartiness of the fare is a thin disguise for a very creative chef. For example, among appetizers such as Crab Meat au Gratin, Fried Onion Rings, and Shrimp Rémoulade, is something called Tidbit in the Oven: assorted cheeses and seasonings melted over French bread slices.

Roth's menu has a sense of humor. Categories include From the Patch (potatoes), From the Garden (vegetables), From the Sea, From the Steer, From the Calf, From the Lamb, and From the Fowl.

Chef Roth's featured entrée, Osso Bucco, needless to say, comes directly From the Calf. It's a great one-dish meal, and a good representative of The Steak Knife food at its hearty best. His featured appetizer recipe, Soft-shell Crawfish and Creole Mustard Sauce, shows another facet of his talent, as does his dessert, Chocolate Mousse Cake with Strawberry Sauce.

WILLIAM S. VALENTINE
Windsor Court Hotel, New Orleans

"Billy" Valentine, as he is known to fellow chefs, has packed a lot of variety and more than fifteen years of cooking experience into his career. He started working in restaurants before attending Johnson & Wales University in Providence, Rhode Island. In 1982, he graduated with highest honors and a culinary degree. By 1983, he was working at the Royal Orleans Hotel, New Orleans, as broiler, sauté cook, *saucier/garde-manger, garde-manger,* and assistant in the pastry shop. Special duties included operating a new French rotisserie system in the dining room of the hotel's dinner restaurant, The Rib Room.

From the hotel, Valentine moved to Andrea's Northern Italian Restaurant in Metairie, Louisiana, where he worked closely with executive chef Andrea Apuzzo. His next culinary stop: Gautreau's restaurant in New Orleans where, as night sous-chef, he worked with then-chef Armand Jonté planning the menu, which changed daily. The eclectic menu at Gautreau's included Oriental, Indian, Italian, French, Creole, Cajun, and Nouvelle Cuisine dishes.

During this time, Valentine was also sous-chef and consultant to Clancy's restaurant in New Orleans, which specializd in mesquite-smoked foods.

In 1987, he relocated to East Hampton, New York, where, for a year, he was executive chef of a new American restaurant. The following year found him at Sagamore Omni Classic Resort in Boston Landing, New York, as executive sous-chef of this high-volume, four-star, four-diamond property with a banquet capacity of eighteen hundred.

When Great Chefs went to tape him, they found him at Windsor Court Hotel, where he has been since 1988, working under the direct supervision of Executive Chef Kevin Graham. Valentine has a hand in creating the constantly changing menus, and his exuberant cooking style can be seen in his entrée recipe for Grilled Veal Chops with Caponata in this chapter.

Grilled Veal Chops with Caponata

From Billy Valentine of the Windsor Court Hotel, New Orleans, LA

Serves 4

Caponata is a Sicilian relish and chef Billy Valentine's version is good enough to eat with a spoon, although here it is served with nicely-seasoned veal chops. For convenience, make the caponata a day or two ahead and store it, covered, in the refrigerator.

2 tablespoons crushed garlic
1/2 teaspoon crushed fresh rosemary
1/2 teaspoon freshly ground black pepper
1/2 teaspoon salt
4 veal chops
Caponata recipe follows)

In a small bowl, blend the garlic, rosemary, pepper, and salt into a paste. Rub the paste into the veal chops and let them sit at room temperature for 2 hours.

Sear the veal over hot coals for 3 to 4 minutes per side. Move them closer to the edge of the grill and cook for 2 minutes on each side or until medium rare. (The chops may also be roasted in a preheated 350°F oven for 10 to 15 minutes.)

To serve: Place a chop on each of four warm serving plates. Serve with caponata and garlic bread.

Caponata

Makes about 3 cups

1/2 cup olive oil
4 tomatoes, peeled, seeded, and chopped (see Techniques)
1/2 yellow onion, minced
1 tablespoon minced garlic
Pinch of dried basil
Pinch of dried oregano
1 large eggplant, peeled and finely chopped
4 tablespoons salt plus more to taste
5 celery stalks, trimmed and finely chopped
1 cup green olives, drained, pitted, and finely chopped
1 cup pine nuts, toasted (see Techniques)
1/3 cup red wine vinegar
1/3 cup sugar
1/3 cup water
Freshly ground black pepper to taste

Heat 1/4 cup of the oil in a heavy saucepan over high heat. Add the tomatoes, onion, garlic, and herbs. Lower the heat and sauté for 15 to 20 minutes. Remove from heat and set aside. Sprinkle the eggplant with the 4 tablespoons salt, toss, and let sit at room temperature for 20 minutes.

Fill a small pot with water, bring to a boil, and add the celery; blanch for 2 to 3 minutes. Remove and rinse under cold running water. Drain and pat dry. Drain the olives and pat dry. Stir the celery and olives into the tomato mixture.

Thoroughly rinse the salt from the eggplant under cold running water. Drain on paper towels. Heat the remaining 1/4 cup oil in a medium sauté pan or skillet over high heat. Add the eggplant and sauté for 2 minutes, or until tender. Stir the pine nuts into the eggplant. Remove the mixture from the heat and set aside to cool. Combine the eggplant mixture with the tomato mixture.

In a small saucepan over medium heat, combine the vinegar, sugar, and water. Cook for 3 minutes, or until the sugar dissolves. Remove from heat and set aside to cool.

Stir the vinegar-sugar mixture into the vegetable mixture a bit at a time, until the desired consistency is reached. The caponata should remain thick. Adjust the seasoning with salt and pepper and refrigerate until ready to use. This will keep for up to 1 week. ▪

Veal Chops with Roasted New Potatoes and Escarole

From Haley Gabel of Ristorante Bacco, New Orleans, LA

Serves 4

If you don't have a ribbed skillet or stovetop grill to give these chops grill marks, just sear them in a regular skillet. This combination of veal chops with a rich, savory sauce, roasted new potatoes, and quickly cooked escarole is an elegant dish for fall and winter.

Roasted New Potatoes
1 tablespoon olive oil
2 garlic cloves, minced
3 new red potatoes, quartered
Salt and pepper to taste

4 veal chops
Olive oil for coating
Salt and pepper to taste
4 sprigs fresh sage

Sauce
1 tablespoon butter
1 tablespoon minced chicken livers
Pinch of dried red pepper flakes
2 tablespoons balsamic vinegar
2 teaspoons chopped fresh sage
3/4 cup reduced veal stock or chicken stock
Pinch of salt

Escarole
2 tablespoons olive oil
2 tablespoons butter
1 teaspoon minced garlic
1/2 teaspoon dried red pepper flakes
1 cup packed escarole leaves
Salt to taste

To roast the potatoes: Preheat the oven to 400°F. In a large ovenproof sauté pan or skillet heat the olive oil with the garlic. Add the potatoes, salt, and pepper, and toss to coat the potatoes well. Bake for 25 minutes, or until potatoes are tender.

Meanwhile, coat each chop with oil and season on both sides with salt and pepper. Heat a ribbed skillet until very hot, or use a stovetop grill. Place sage sprigs on the grill. Place each chop over a sage sprig and sear the chops for a minute or so on each side to make grill marks. Place in a large ovenproof skillet and bake for about 8 minutes for medium rare.

To make the sauce: Melt the butter in a medium sauté pan and sauté the chicken livers and red pepper for about 2 minutes. Pour in the balsamic vinegar and stir over medium heat; scrape browned bits on the bottom of the pan. Add the sage and stock. Cook for about 4 to 5 minutes over medium heat to reduce. Season with salt.

To make the escarole: In a medium sauté pan or skillet, heat the olive oil and butter with the garlic and crushed red pepper. Add the escarole and toss until wilted. Add salt to taste.

To serve: Divide the escarole among four plates. Place a chop on each bed of escarole. Pour the sauce over the chops and serve with potato quarters. ▪

Veal Chops with Roasted New Potatoes and Escarole, Haley Gabel, Ristorante Bacco

Michael Uddo
G&E Courtyard Grill, New Orleans

Michael Uddo, a native of New Orleans and grandson of Italian immigrants, named his restaurant in honor of his grandparents Guiseppe and Eleanora. Their portraits hang in the restaurant, a tribute to the journey in 1907 that brought them from Palermo, Sicily, to New Orleans. In New Orleans, after years of hard work and more than their share of adversity, Guiseppe and Eleanora established a small mom-and-pop grocery store and, as the demand for quality Italian foodstuffs grew, founded Progresso Quality Foods. Guiseppe always set great store on family dinners because, he said, "You never grow old at the dinner table."

His grandson, Michael, graduated from the Cordon Bleu in London. While in London, Uddo worked as sous-chef at the renowned Joe Allen's Restaurant and as executive sous-chef at the New Orleans Jazz Club.

When he returned to New Orleans, Uddo became executive chef at Bouliny restaurant and, in the fall of 1992, he opened his G&E Courtyard Grill. The public swarmed it and the critics raved: "among the year's best new dining establishments for its uninhibited cuisine and charming atmosphere," wrote *Gambit's* Urbane Gourmet. G&E was featured in *USA Today, Gourmet, Bon Appétit,* and *Food & Wine.* Local food critic Tom Fitzmorris gave it four stars, and it was included in *Travel Holiday's* Good Dining, Good Value awards.

"We do ethnic peasant cuisine with humble ingredients—things you'd get in small trattorias in Italy," says Uddo. And, since he was born in New Orleans, his menu also offers Louisiana specialties such as Muffuletta Salad, Panéed Free-range Veal, Eggs Benedict and Louisiana Soft-shell Crab.

Uddo grows his own herbs organically in the courtyard garden, and his emphasis on fresh ingredients and unprocessed foods is evident in the menu: dishes are made with fresh ricotta, aged pancetta, homemade goat cheese, fresh spinach, fresh basil, baby red chard and radicchio, homemade mozzarella. "Freshness and simplicity are not just common terms used to describe great cooking, they are goals chefs work a lifetime to reach," says Uddo.

Like his grandfather before him, Uddo sets great store in home cooking and the family dinner. "People need to sit down together and laugh and converse." His advice to the home cook, "It's simple. Relax and enjoy."

Veal Tenderloin Crusted with Fresh Herbs and Black Pepper

From Michael Uddo of G&E Courtyard Grill, New Orleans, LA

Serves 4

If you are a fan of steak au poivre, you'll be an instant convert to chef Michael Uddo's veal dish, which is coated with a mixture of minced herbs, coarsely ground black pepper and Dijon mustard. Chef Uddo serves his veal tenderloin with Smoked Tomato and Shiitake Mushroom Risotto (recipe follows).

2 tablespoons minced fresh dill
2 tablespoons minced fresh parsley
2 tablespoons minced fresh rosemary
1-1/2 tablespoons minced chives
1/4 cup coarsely ground black pepper
1/4 cup Dijon mustard
2 tablespoons dry white wine
Salt to taste

One 12-ounce veal tenderloin, trimmed
2 tablespoons olive oil
Port wine demi-glace (recipe follows)

To make the herb crust: In a small bowl, combine all of the herbs and the pepper. In a separate cup, stir the mustard and wine together until well blended. Set aside.

To make the veal: Preheat the oven to 450°F. Lightly salt the veal tenderloin. Heat oil to very hot in a large ovenproof skillet and brown the veal on all sides. Bake for about 20 minutes for medium rare. Remove the meat from the skillet. With a small spoon, coat the veal thoroughly with the mustard mixture, then coat it heavily all over with the herb mixture. Place back into the skillet and bake for 1-1/2 mintues. Do not brown the herbs.

To serve: Remove the tenderloin from the oven and slice. Place on four serving plates, drizzle with port wine demi-glace, and serve.

Port Wine Demi-Glace

Makes about 2 quarts

5 pounds veal or duck bones
1 large white onion
5 gallons water
1-1/2 bottle port wine
5 fresh rosemary sprigs
1/4 cup sugar

Place the bones, onion, and water in a large pot. Simmer over low heat for 10 hours. Strain. Let sit for 1 hour; skim off the fat with a large spoon. Cook over medium heat for 1 hour. Add the wine, rosemary, and sugar. Cook 1 hour. Strain. Cook again to reduce to a light syrupy consistency, about 45 minutes. Freeze any leftover demi-glace for later use.

Smoked Tomato and Shiitake Mushroom Risotto

From Michael Uddo of G&E Courtyard Grill, New Orleans, LA

Serves 4

Not only are there dozens of traditional Italian risottos, but Louisiana chefs are adding their own recipes to the repertoire. Chef Michael Uddo's version uses smoked tomatoes, shiitake mushrooms, and fresh herbs.

3 tablespoons olive oil
1 cup minced onion
2 tablespoons minced shallots
2 cups Arborio rice
1/2 cup dry white wine
6-1/2 cups hot chicken stock
1/2 tablespoon salt
1/3 cup butter
2 smoked tomatoes, chopped (recipe
   follows)

8 shiitake mushrooms, thinly sliced
3 tablespoons minced fresh chives
3 tablespoons minced fresh parsley
Salt and pepper to taste

In a medium casserole, heat the olive oil and sauté the onion and shallots until golden, about 4 to 5 minutes. Add the rice to the shallots and stir to coat with oil. Cook the rice to toast (a light golden color) for about 5 to 6 minutes. Add the wine, stir well and then add 1/2 cup of the hot chicken stock and 1/2 tablespoon salt. Cook, stirring constantly, until all liquid is absorbed. Continue to add hot stock in small batches (just enough to completely moisten rice) and cook until each successive batch of the hot stock has been absorbed.

In a medium sauté pan over medium heat, melt butter. Add the tomatoes and mushrooms, and cook for 2 minutes. Add the tomatoes and mushrooms to the cooked rice. Cook, stirring contantly, for 3 minutes. Add the chives and parsley and season with salt and pepper.

Smoked tomatoes

2 medium ripe tomatoes
1 tablespoon olive oil

Brush the tomatoes with the olive oil. Place on a charcoal grill with medium hot coals topped with wood chips. Smoke with top closed for 15 to 20 minutes or until tomatoes are soft and slightly charred.∎

Crawfish-stuffed Loin of Lamb with Wild Mushroom Sauce, Kim Kringlie, The Dakota

Crawfish-stuffed Loin of Lamb with Wild Mushroom Sauce

From Kim Kringlie of The Dakota, Covington, LA

Serves 4

A highly seasoned crawfish stuffing is flavorful enough to complement but not compete with the assertive flavor of lamb. The stuffed lamb medallions make an elegant-looking entrée whose taste lives up to its looks.

Crawfish Stuffing
8 ounces crawfish tail meat
2 teaspoons minced garlic
2 tablespoons chopped red bell peppers
2 tablespoons chopped green onions
1/4 cup dry white wine
1 teaspoon basil
Salt, white pepper, and cayenne pepper
1/2 cup fresh bread crumbs

Four 8-ounce lamb loins
2 tablespoons olive oil 1 tablespoon minced garlic
1 teaspoon minced fresh basil
1 teaspoon minced fresh thyme
1 teaspoon minced fresh oregano
1 teaspoon cracked black pepper
1/2 cup wild mushrooms
1/4 cup red wine
1 cup demi-glace (see recipe on page 81, or Techniques)

To make stuffing: Preheat the oven to 400°F. Chop the crawfish tails and place them in a medium bowl with the garlic, peppers, green onions, white wine and basil. Season with salt, white pepper, and cayenne. Add the bread crumbs and mix thoroughly.

With a boning knife, make an insertion in each end of each lamb loin. Using your fingers, hollow out each loin and stuff with the crawfish stuffing. Rub the lamb with olive oil, garlic, herbs, and spices. Place in a ovenproof skillet and bake for 20 minutes. Remove the loins from the skillet. Add wild mushrooms and red wine and cook, stirring over medium heat, scraping up the browned juices from the bottom of the pan. Add the demi-glace and simmer for 2 minutes.

To serve: Slice the lamb into medallions and arrange on plates. Serve with the warm sauce. ∎

KIM KRINGLIE
The Dakota, Covington

The Dakota in Covington, Louisiana, is a far cry from the state for which it is named. But the name is chef Kim Kringlie's way of paying tribute to his roots in Grand Forks, North Dakota, a small town near the Canadian border. He and partner Ken LaCour, a Covington native who has been in the food business for sixteen years, opened in October 1990, choosing the name, design, and decor to suggest the nature of their restaurant. The Dakota uses Louisiana products and is based on Creole tradition, but its menu reflects broader tastes, interpreting freely from American regional, French and other cuisines.

Kringlie worked in restaurants from the age of fifteen; however he began his first serious apprenticeship at Jackson Hole, Wyoming, under Austrian chef Peter Leitner, who moved him to the executive sous-chef position.

When the Cajun-Creole craze swept the land, Kringlie moved to Baton Rouge where he operated the kitchen at Juban's restaurant, adding his own creative flair. To refine his understanding of Louisiana's products and seasonings, he worked with noted Lousiana chef John Folse, traveling with him to the Soviet Union to help open the first American restaurant there and to create dishes for the participants in the 1988 Presidential Summit in Moscow.

Back home in Louisiana, he returned to Juban's, where he began a winning streak of culinary honors and awards. Among his numerous awards are: 1989 Chef of the Year (Baton Rouge Culinary Federation); Best of Show awards (Acadiana Classic, Lafayette, and Baton Rouge Culinary Classic), and Louisiana's Best Seafood Chef, 1990.

Kringlie's entrée, Crawfish-stuffed Loin of Lamb with Wild Mushroom Sauce, is a showstopping main course from The Dakota's menu showing the chef's versatility. It is one of his many versions of rack of lamb, which is prepared differently each day. His featured dessert recipe in this book is Chocolate Coconut with Vanilla English Cream, and his appetizer is Beer-fried Asparagus with Crab Meat and Crawfish Sauce in Creole Mustard-Honey Butter.

Loin of Lamb with Provençal Tian

From John Neal of Peristyle,
New Orleans, LA

Serves 4

Tian is both the name of a utensil and the name of a finished dish. A tian is an earthenware gratin dish from Provence used for baking layered foods such as potatoes or eggplant and tomatoes. In this recipe the onion-tomato-zucchini tian may be baked in one large gratin dish or four small ones. In either case, the vegetables serve as a centerpiece for the lamb and its garlicky sauce with a touch of anchovy.

Provençal Tian
2 small white onions, chopped
2 tablespoons garlic oil
4 Roma (pear) tomatoes halved lengthwise, then cut into thin crosswise slices
2 zucchini halved lengthwise then cut into thin crosswise slices
2 tablespoons chopped fresh rosemary
Salt and pepper to taste
Olive oil for drizzling

Four 5-ounce lamb loins
Salt and pepper to taste
2 tablespoons minced fresh thyme
1/4 cup peanut oil

Garlic Sauce
1/4 cup garlic vinegar
2 tablespoons pureed roasted garlic (see Techniques)
2 tablespoons minced fresh thyme
1 cup dry white wine
2-1/2 cups demi-glace (see recipe on page 81, or Techniques) or reduced veal or beef stock or broth
1 tablespoon anchovy paste
1 tablespoon butter
Dash of lemon juice
Salt and pepper to taste

To make the tian: Preheat the oven to 375°F. Place a layer of onions on the bottom of four 4-ounce or one 6-ounce gratin dish. Alternate layers of tomatoes and zucchini. Season with rosemary, salt, and pepper, then drizzle the tops with olive oil. Cover with aluminum foil and bake for 20 minutes or until vegetables are set.

Meanwhile season the lamb with salt, pepper, and thyme. In a large sauté pan or skillet, heat the peanut oil and sear the lamb on both sides for a total of about two minutes. Bake at 375°F for 15 minutes for medium rare.

To make the garlic sauce: Combine the garlic vinegar, roasted garlic, thyme, and white wine in a medium saucepan. Cook over medium heat until reduced by two-thirds, about 5 minutes. Add the demi-glace, stock, or broth, and cook again to reduce by two-thirds or until thickened, about 4 to 5 minutes. Whisk in the anchovy paste, butter, and lemon juice and salt and pepper to taste.

To serve: Carefully unmold the tian or tians and place in the center of a hot platter or each of four plates. Slice the lamb and fan the slices around the tian or tians. Nap with garlic sauce. ∎

Marinated Roast Lamb and Vegetable Couscous

From Susan Spicer of Bayona,
New Orleans, LA

Serves 4 to 6

Chef Susan Spicer of Bayona restaurant in New Orleans draws on the Middle East for inspiration for this dish. Marinated lamb is roasted, sliced, and served over couscous, a North African staple of steamed semolina along with a spicy and savory vegetable stew, and a hot sauce to spoon over it all.

Marinade
2 tablespoons honey
2 tablespoons water
3 tablespoons olive oil
2 teaspoons minced garlic
1/2 teaspoon ground fennel seed
1/2 teaspoon ground cumin
1/2 teaspoon ground cinnamon
1/2 teaspoon chili paste
Salt and pepper to taste

One 2- to-3-pound boneless lamb, leg or shoulder

Vegetable Stew
Parsley and cilantro sprigs
1 stick cinnamon
2 tablespoons olive oil
1 chopped onion
1 small green bell pepper, seeded, deribbed, and diced
1 small red bell pepper, seeded, deribbed, and diced
2 tomatoes, peeled, seeded, and diced (see page Techniques)
6 cups vegetable broth or lamb broth
Pinch of saffron
1 carrot, peeled and diced
1 zucchini, diced
1 turnip, diced
1 cup cooked butternut or acorn squash, diced and peeled
1/2 cup cooked chick peas

Marinated Roast Lamb and Vegetable Couscous, Susan Spicer, Bayona

Couscous

1/2 pound (1/2 box) couscous
1 cup boiling water
2 tablespoons olive oil or butter or a
   combination of the two
2 tablespoons minced fresh parsley
2 tablespoons minced fresh cilantro
1/2 bunch green onions, thinly sliced
Salt and pepper to taste

To make the marinade: Whisk all of the ingredients together. Pour into a deep non-aluminum container, cover, add the lamb, and refrigerate overnight. Remove the lamb from the refrigerator 45 minutes before cooking.

Preheat the oven to 400°F, place the lamb in an ovenproof casserole, place in oven, and reduce the temperature to 300°F. Cook for about 30 to 45 minutes, or until medium rare.

To make the vegetable stew: Tie several parsley and cilantro sprigs to a cinnamon stick with white cotton string; set aside. In a large, heavy saucepan, heat the olive oil over medium heat and sauté the onion and peppers for 4 to 5 minutes, or until soft. Add the diced tomatoes, then the broth, saffron, and cinnamon-herb bundle. Bring to a boil, then reduce to a simmer. Add all the remaining vegetables and simmer for 20 minutes, or until vegetables are tender; keep warm.

To make the couscous: Add the couscous to the boiling water. Stir, cover, and set aside for 5 to 10 minutes. Uncover, stir to break up any lumps, and stir in the olive oil and/or butter, herbs and green onions. Season with salt and pepper. Keep warm.

Hot Sauce

Makes about 1 cup

1 cup vegetable or meat broth
1 teaspoon chili paste
1 teaspoon fresh lemon juice
1/2 teaspoon minced garlic
1/2 teaspoon ground cumin
1 tablespoon olive oil
1 teaspoon chopped fresh parsley
1 teaspoon chopped fresh cilantro

   Mix all the ingredients together.

To serve: Center each plate with couscous. Overlap three slices of lamb on one side of the couscous, and fill the remaining space with vegetable sauce. ▪

SUSAN SPICER
Bayona, New Orleans

"I use an eclectic mixture of ingredients and styles, but it all makes sense. My taste is the filter. And I have a good grasp of what's agreeable to my customers," says Susan Spicer, chef-proprietor of Bayona, discussing her menu that ranges from Boudin Noir with Apples and Onions to Crawfish Curry with Chutney and Lime Pickle.

Spicer served a three-year apprenticeship in New Orleans at the Louis XVI restaurant and, in the summer of 1982, apprenticed under chef Roland Durand at the Hotel Sofitel in Paris. "That was a turning point in my career. It gave me a real solid sense of where I was and a chance to compare myself to other professionals."

Spicer returned from France to become the executive chef at Savoir Faire restaurant in New Orleans where she cooked for celebrities such as Clint Eastwood. In 1985, after three years at Savoir Faire, she took a *Wanderjahr* and traveled extensively through Europe and California.

In 1986, as chef, Spicer opened the Bistro at Maison de Ville, and in 1990, as owner, she opened Bayona.

Spicer started receiving media acclaim in 1989—and the good reviews keep coming in. In 1989, she was featured in *Time* and *Esquire* magazines, and *Food & Wine* named her as one of its Ten Best New Chefs. Gault-Millau named Bayona among its Top 40 Places to Dine in the U.S., and she was honored at the James Beard Foundation Rising Star Dinner in 1991, and again as the Best Southeast Chef in 1993.

Spicer says that she has never found being a woman a drawback to advancement and fair treatment in the culinary field. And her kitchen is balanced between men and women staffers. She believes that in American cuisine, "trends develop through products as they become available." Some of her favorite flavors include citrus zest, soy sauce, Indonesian sweet soy sauce ("I lived in Holland as a kid"), curry pastes, lemon verbena and chives. And she finds birds—quail, pheasant, duck, chicken, turkey—among the most versatile products to work with. One of Spicer's entrées in this book, Marinated Roast Lamb and Vegetable Couscous, shows another dimension of her style as she translates flavors and textures of the Middle East for her menu—and our kitchens. Her other featured recipes are Grilled Shrimp with Coriander Sauce, and Black Bean Cakes (appetizer), and Crêpes with Walnut-Cream Cheese Filling (dessert).

Rack of Lamb with Apricot Sauce

From Hubert Sandot of L 'Economie, New Orleans, LA

Serves 4

As mentioned elsewhere in this chapter, one of the food trends of the nineties is the use of fruit in sauces for seafood, poultry, and meat. Here rack of lamb is enhanced by a piquant apricot sauce.

Apricot Sauce
16 dried apricots
4 cups chicken broth
3 teaspoons cornstarch
4 tablespoons butter
1/2 onion, minced
2 minced garlic cloves
1/2 cup apricot preserves
1 tablespoon honey

Four 8- to 12-ounce lamb racks, trimmed
3 tablespoons butter at room temperature
2 tablespoons minced fresh thyme
Coarsely ground pepper to taste
4 large garlic cloves, minced

To make the apricot sauce: In a bowl, soak the apricots in 2 cups of the chicken broth for 2 hours. Remove the apricots and dissolve the cornstarch thoroughly in the broth. In a medium, heavy saucepan, melt the butter over medium heat and sauté the onion and garlic until tender, about 3 minutes. Add the cornstarch mixture; cook and stir for 3 to 4 minutes. Add the rest of the broth, apricot purée, apricots, and honey. Simmer over low heat for 8 to 10 minutes, or until thickened. Keep warm.

Preheat the broiler. Dry the lamb racks with paper towels, then rub the meat (but not the bones) with butter. Sprinkle evenly with the thyme, pepper and garlic. Cover the bones with aluminum foil so as not to burn them. Broil racks, bone-side up, 3 inches from heat in the broiler for 10 minutes, then turn racks and broil them for 5 more minutes. Remove the lamb racks from the broiler, remove the foil, and serve the racks with apricot sauce poured over them. ∎

Chili-rubbed Pork Tenderloin with Savory Wild Mushroom Bread Pudding

From André Begnaud of Emeril's, New Orleans, LA

Serves 4

Chef André Begnaud of Emeril's puts a new twist on bread pudding; A savory mix of cream, eggs, bread, mushrooms, and seasonings, to serve alongside a pork entrée with a Southwestern accent.

Red Chili Paint
1 tablespoon olive oil
2 tablespoons minced onion
1/4 teaspoon minced garlic
1/8 teaspoon dried oregano
1/2 teaspoon ground cumin
1 tablespoon flour
4 tablespoons ground red chili pepper
1-1/4 cups water
1/4 teaspoon salt

2 pork tenderloins trimmed of any fat
1 teaspoon ground coriander
1/4 cup brandy
2 cups brown stock or chicken stock
 (see Techniques)
1 tablespoon molasses
1 tablespoon minced fresh cilantro
Salt and pepper to taste
2 tablespoons whole butter

To make the chili paint: In a medium saucepan over medium heat, heat the oil, and sauté onion and garlic until translucent, about 3 minutes. Stir in the oregano, cumin, and flour, and cook until golden brown, about 3 minutes. Add the chili, stirring constantly. Lower heat and add the water slowly, stirring constantly. Simmer 2 to 3 minutes, stirring. Add salt and remove from heat. Place all but 1/2 cup into a squeeze bottle.

Spread 1/4 cup of the chili paint over each tenderloin and let marinate at room temperature for 1 hour. Preheat the oven to 450°F. Heat a medium sauté pan or skillet over medium heat, and sear the tenderloins on all sides. Pour in the brandy and stir to scrape up the browned juices on the bottom of the pan. Avert your face, light the brandy with a long match and shake the pan until the flames subside. Add the stock or broth and the molasses, and bake for 4 to 5 minutes. Remove the tenderloins from the pan and set aside. Return the pan to medium heat and cook for several minutes until the sauce is slightly thickened. Add cilantro, salt, pepper and butter. Strain through a fine-meshed sieve and keep warm.

To Serve: Slice the tenderloins diagonally and arrange on each of four warmed plates. Place a large spoonful of bread pudding beside the tenderloin slices. With the squeeze bottle, squeeze the chili paint over the meat and pudding in a abstract design. ∎

Chile-rubbed Pork Tenderloin With Savory Wild Mushroom Bread Pudding, André Begnaud, Emeril's

Wild Mushroom Bread Pudding

From Andre Begnaud of Emeril's,
New Orleans, LA

Makes 4

1-1/2 cups heavy (whipping) cream
1/4 ounce dried mushrooms
1/2 tablespoon olive oil
1/2 small onion, cut into small slices
1/2 tablespoon minced shallots
1/2 teaspoon minced garlic
3 ounces fresh wild mushrooms, sliced
1 tablespoon molasses
3 beaten eggs
1/2 teaspoon Creole seasoning
Tabasco sauce to taste
Worcestershire sauce, to taste
Salt and pepper to taste
2 cups diced bread
2 tablespoons grated Parmesan Reggiano
   cheese

Preheat the oven to 350°F. Bring the cream and dried mushrooms to a boil in a heavy saucepan. Remove from pan and let cool. In a sauté pan or skillet over medium heat, sauté the onion, shallots, and garlic until the onion is slightly caramelized, about 3 to 4 minutes. Add the fresh mushrooms and cook until tender, about 3 to 4 minutes. Add the molasses and seasoning. Let cool.

Strain the cream through a fine-meshed sieve into the egg mixture. Season the mixture with Creole seasoning, Tabasco, Worcestershire, salt and pepper. Add the bread to the egg-cream mixture and let soak for 5 to 8 minutes. Stir in the mushroom mixture and season. Fill four 4-ounce buttered molds and top with cheese. Cover with aluminum foil and bake for 18 to 20 minutes. Remove the foil, and bake an additional 2 minutes to brown.

Let sit for 1 to 2 minutes, then unmold. Serve warm. ▪

ANDRÉ BEGNAUD
Emeril's, New Orleans

André Begnaud is a native Louisianian, born in Lafayette, a hundred miles north of New Orleans. He is Cajun on his mother's side and French ("my father came direct from France") on his father's side. Where Begnaud grew up, in the Acadian area, the cooking was "very rustic, more pot-cookery—no real restaurant food," he says, "but everyone cooked."

Before entering the restaurant field, he was a performing musician and owned a firm that represented fine artists. During one of his trips to Los Angeles to orchestrate an artist's gallery opening that involved catered food, "Somewhere in the desert my car blew up. By the time I reached L.A., my money was pretty much gone. The caterer I booked wouldn't do the event for the money I had—so I did it myself. I'd been cooking all my life."

Begnaud was still a young man in 1985 when he had a "sudden change of life," jumped on his motorcycle and moved to New Orleans to apply for culinary school. (He graduated in 1988 from Delgado Community College in New Orleans on the dean's list with a culinary arts degree.) The versatile Begnaud landed a job in a hospital, where he prepared regular meals for patients, staff, and doctors, and modified patient diets. From there he went to Jonathan, a Restaurant, in New Orleans as cook, and in 1986 he met and studied under Emeril Lagasse at Commander's Palace. Begnaud next went to Lagasse's alma mater, Johnson & Wales University, in Providence, R.I., and graduated with highest academic honors in 1989. While in Rhode Island, he was the lead cook at Al Forno Restaurant in Providence. Back in New Orleans, he worked at Mr. B's Bistro and in 1990 joined Lagasse at Emeril's.

Given his diverse background, it should come as no surprise that Begnaud's cooking style ranges beyond Cajun and Creole. He has a special affinity for Southwestern cooking, as seen in his featured entrée recipe for Chili-rubbed Pork Tenderloin with Savory Wild Mushroom Bread Pudding. The recipe is straightforward and quick to cook—and even quicker to eat. As Begnaud says, "After all, the best review is a clean plate."

Braised Pork Tenderloin with Sautéed Apples, Celery Julienne, and Louisiana Sweet Potato Pancakes

From Dennis Hutley of The Versailles Restaurant, New Orleans, LA

Serves 6

This company dish is time-consuming, but the end justifies the means. Take the chef's suggestion and try celeriac (celery root) in place of celery.

Marinade
1 cup sliced peeled carrot
2/3 cup sliced onion
1/3 cup sliced celery or celeriac
1 cup soy sauce
2/3 cup dry white wine
1/2 cup salad oil
4 cloves garlic, crushed
5 fresh thyme sprigs or 1/2 tablespoon dried thyme

Six 6-ounce pork tenderloin fillets, trimmed

Quick Brown Sauce
1 10-ounce can low-salt beef broth
1/4 cup water
1/4 cup port
1/4 cup plus 1 tablespoon Burgundy
2 teaspoons arrowroot
1/3 cup olive oil
1 cup dry white wine
1-1/2 tablespoon Dijon mustard
1 teaspoon chopped shallots
1 teaspoon minced garlic
1 cup Quick Brown Sauce
Dash of vinegar
Few drops of hot pepper sauce
2 tablespoons butter
Salt and white pepper to taste

Sautéed Celery
2 tablespoons butter
2-1/2 cups julienned celery or peeled celeriac
1/2 teaspoon minced shallots
Salt and white pepper to taste
1 tablespoon minced fresh parsley

Sautéed Apples
3 tablespoons butter
2 large firm apples, cored and cut into 1/2-inch slices
Salt and white pepper to taste
1 tablespoon apple cider vinegar

Louisiana Sweet Potato Pancakes (recipe follows)

Fresh thyme sprigs for garnish
1 cup shredded carrots for garnish

To make marinade: In a 3 quart non-aluminum container, combine all of the ingredients. Add the pork, cover, and marinate in the refrigerator for at least 24 hours, turning the pork at least twice.

To make the sauce: In a medium sauce pan over high heat, combine the broth, water, port, and 1/4 cup Burgundy. Bring to a boil and reduce heat to medium. Dissolve the arrowroot in 2 teaspoons of Burgundy, and stir into the sauce to thicken. Simmer for 1 minute and remove from the heat. Makes 2 cups.

Preheat the oven to 400° F. Drain the fillets. In a large ovenproof sauté pan or skillet, heat the oil to smoking and brown the fillets on both sides. Remove to a plate, and pour off excess oil, and add the white wine, mustard, shallots, and garlic, mixing well to dissolve the mustard. Add 1 cup brown sauce, vinegar, and hot pepper sauce; mix well. Return the pork to the sauce along with any juice that has accumulated. Bake for about 8 to 10 minutes, or until slightly firm to the touch. Remove pork from skillet, place on a warm plate, and keep warm. Return sauce to heat and cook until slightly thickened, about 4 to 5 minutes. Stir in butter and adjust seasoning. While the pork is cooking, make the sautéed celery and apples.

To make the sautéed celery: In a large sauté pan or skillet, melt the butter and sauté the celery for 4 to 5 minutes or until crisp-tender. Add the shallots, salt, and pepper, and cook for 5 to 6 minutes or until tender. Add the parsley, toss, and keep warm.

To make the sautéed apples: In medium sauté pan or skillet, melt the butter and sauté the apples for 4 to 5 minutes, or until soft. Add salt and pepper, then vinegar; toss well and keep warm.

To serve: On each of six heated plates, place sautéed celery in upper right quarter, and fan the apple slices in a shingled fashion in the upper left quarter. Slice each pork fillet into four diagonal slices. Fan the pork slices on the left side of the plate. Place a sweet potato pancake on the right side of the plate. Spoon the sauce onto the left side of the plate and the pork, garnish with a sprig or two of fresh thyme, and shredded carrot.

Louisiana Sweet Potato Pancakes

Makes 6

1 large egg, lightly beaten
1 large Louisiana or yam sweet potato, peeled and coarsely grated
1 tablespoon flour
1/2 teaspoon ground nutmeg
Salt and white pepper to taste
2 tablespoon minced fresh parsley
2 tablespoons oil

In a medium bowl, combine all the ingredients except for the oil. Heat the oil in a large sauté pan or skillet, drop the mixture by spoonfuls to make silver-dollar sized pancakes, and cook gently over medium high heat until browned around the edges, about 3 to 4 minutes. Flip each cake over and cook another 2 to 3 minutes or until browned. Remove to paper towels to drain. Serve warm with pork or steak. ■

Tenderloin of Pork St. John, Garnished with Sweet Potato Rosette

From Tom Weaver of Christian's Restaurant, New Orleans, LA

Serves 4

Almost any tenderloin of meat is made more interesting by a stuffing that adds visual interest as well as flavor variety. Here pork tenderloin becomes a succulent treat with the addition of an andouille-apple stuffing.

Sweet Potato Rosette
1 large sweet potato
1 tablespoon brown sugar
2 tablespoons butter
1/4 teaspoon salt
3 tablespoons heavy (whipping) cream
2 egg yolks

Andouille-Apple Stuffing
1/4 cup olive oil
1 cup finely diced onions
1/2 cup finely diced bell pepper
1/4 cup finely diced celery
12 ounces andouille sausage, removed from casings and coarsely ground

2 Granny Smith Apples, peeled, cored, and minced

1 teaspoon minced garlic

1/2 teaspoon salt

1/4 teaspoon black pepper

1-1/2 cups stale French bread cubes, 3/4 cup (1-1/2 sticks) butter

1/2 cup port wine

1/2 cup dry white wine

1-1/2 pounds pork tenderloins, trimmed, and sprinkled with water

To make the rosette: Preheat oven to 350°F. Bake potato for 30 minutes, or until center is soft. Let cool. Peel and dice the potato. In a small mixing bowl, combine the potato and other ingredients and mash until smooth. Put the mixture into a pastry bag fitted with a 1/2-inch tip and pipe onto buttered wax paper in rosettes measuring 1-1/2 inch in diameter. With a spatula, transfer rosettes to a lightly greased baking sheet and bake at 350°F for 8 minutes, or until firm. Keep warm.

To make the stuffing: Preheat the oven to 350°F. In a large sauté pan or skillet over medium heat, heat the oil and sauté the onions, bell pepper, and celery until the onions are translucent, about 3 minutes. Add the andouille, apples, garlic, salt, and pepper. Cook for about 5 minutes. Add the bread and mix well. Set aside to cool.

Preheat the oven to 350°F. Cut the pork tenderloins into 6-ounce portions, each about 4 inches long. Using a sharp boning knife, make an insertion in each end of each tenderloin. Using your fingers, hollow out each loin and stuff with the Andouille-Apple Stuffing.

Heat 1/2 cup (1 stick) of the butter in a large ovenproof sauté pan or skillet, and brown tenderloins on all sides. Remove the meat from the pan, pour in the port and white wine, and cook and stir over medium heat to scrape up the browned bits on the bottom. Return the meat to the pan, cover, and bake for about 15 minutes for medium rare.

To serve: Cut each portion of meat into 3/8-inch thick slices; set aside and keep warm. Strain the pan liquid through a fine-meshed sieve into a medium saucepan. Cook over medium heat for several minutes to reduce by half, and swirl in the remaining 4 tablespoons of butter. Divide tenderloin slices among four plates and ladle the sauce over them. Garnish with sweet potato rosettes. ∎

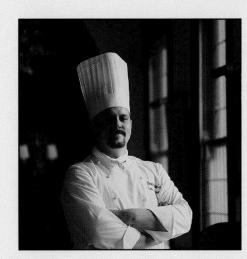

TOM WEAVER
Christian's Restaurant, New Orleans

Tom Weaver, executive chef at Christian's, was born and has lived all his life in St. Rose, Louisiana. Today he is raising his family there, and he is very proud of it. As far as he is concerned, there could be no better preparation for being a chef.

"I was always in the kitchen with my mother. I believe I was ten when I began to prepare various dishes myself—mostly breakfast. But it wasn't long after that that I learned to prepare dishes such as jambalaya, beans, and shrimp Creole."

His background, so rich in food, led him to pursue a culinary career. He graduated with honors from Delgado Community College in New Orleans with a culinary arts degree. During his apprenticeship he worked with chef George Rhode at George IV, chef John Folse at the Brass Lantern, and chef Roland Huet at Christian's, where Weaver is now executive chef. The cuisine at Christian's—a restaurant retrofitted into a former church—is a blend of Creole and classical French. "It's real New Orleans," says Weaver.

He characterizes his generation of young Louisiana chefs as under constant pressure to change and reform. "We just couldn't come on in and inherit the reputation of the chefs who preceded us," he says. "It's important that we take regional cooking to different levels, but the most important factor, as far as I am concerned, is to keep the identity of New Orleans cuisine what it's been for the past century." Among the characteristics of that food are good-quality ingredients, especially those locally produced.

And he has firm opinions about cross-cultural and cross-regional cookery. "I don't think we should vary into other regional foods. People come to New Orleans to eat our regional food. And there is a seasonal rhythm to cooking. To this day, I don't do pâtés until fall." Weaver's entrée in this book, Tenderloin of Pork St. John, Garnished with Sweet Potato Rosette, he considers a fall dish. (No one will know, or tell, if you cook it out of season.) His featured appetizer, Crawfish and Angel Hair Pasta Beignets, is an innovative update of a traditional beignet. And his other featured entrée, Grouper Iberville, might easily become a year-round favorite.

Grilled Baby Wild Boar T-Bone

From Patti Constantin of Constantin's, New Orleans, LA

Boar is leaner and drier than domestic pork, and also more flavorful. Because of its dryness, special care must be taken not to overcook it. Moistness is preserved in this recipe by spreading a garlic-mustard paste on the boar before grilling. Wild baby boar may be purchased from Broken Arrow Ranch in Texas. The accompanying peach-pineapple condiment is a contemporary version of the classic pairing of fruit and game.

Garlic-Herb Mustard Paste
6 roasted garlic cloves
1/2 teaspoon minced thyme
1/2 teaspoon minced sage
1/2 tablespoon minced parsley
1 tablespoon olive oil
1/2 cup stone-ground mustard
Freshly ground black pepper to taste

Eight 1-inch-thick baby wild boar T-bone steaks
Peach and Pineapple Condiment (recipe follows)

To make Paste: Press the garlic pulp out of the roasted garlic cloves and mix it with all the other ingredients.

Spread the paste over the T-bones and marinate at room temperature for 45 minutes. Grill boar over hot coals for 8 minutes on each side for medium rare.

Peach and Pineapple Condiment

Makes about 2 cups
1 tablespoon butter
6 small yellow onions or pearl onions
1/2 cup dry sherry
Leaves from 2 fresh rosemary sprigs
2 cups boar, veal, pork, or chicken stock (see Techniques)
3 peaches, peeled, pitted, and halved
1 pineapple, peeled, cored, and cut into small wedges
Freshly ground pepper and salt to taste

In a large saucepan over medium heat, melt the butter and cook and stir the onion until caramelized, about 5 to 6 minutes. Remove the onions and set aside. Pour in the sherry and cook and stir over medium heat to scrape up the browned bits on the bottom of the pan. Add rosemary and stock to the pan and cook over medium heat to reduce to a glaze, about 4 to 5 minutes. Add peaches, pineapple, onions, pepper, and salt. Cook for 2 to 3 minutes, or until the fruit is heated through. ▪

To serve: Place two T-bones on each plate, and serve the condiment alongside.

Venison and Smoked Scallops Bernhard

From Bernhard Gotz of Fillets , New Orleans, LA

Serves 2

Chef Bernhard Gotz of Fillets in New Orleans combines venison with a wild mushroom sauce with hickory-smoked scallops in a sauce made with cream and saffron. This is a dish to serve at an elegant dinner party, flanked by a simple first course and a make-ahead dessert.

Venison and Smoked Scallops Bernhard, Bernhard Gotz, Fillets

Smoked Scallops
Juice of 1 lemon
Pinch of ground ginger
1/4 teaspoon soy sauce
1 tablespoon sesame oil
1/2 cups hickory chips
6 sea scallops
3 dashes Louisiana Gold or other hot pepper sauce

Four 3-ounce pieces venison loin, well trimmed
2 tablespoons peanut oil
Pinch of salt
Pinch <u>each</u> of black and white pepper

Chanterelle Sauce
3 ounces bacon, finely diced
2 shallots, minced
2 tablespoons gin
1/2 cup dry red wine
1 cup Venison Sauce (recipe follows)
1 teaspoon green peppercorns
Salt and pepper to taste
3 ounce chanterelle mushrooms, sliced
4 tablespoons butter at room temperature

Tasso-Saffron Sauce
2 teaspoons oil
2 shallots, minced
1/2 cup Riesling or other fruity white wine
1/4 teaspoon saffron threads, crushed
1 cup heavy (whipping) cream
2 teaspoons diced tasso ham
3 tablespoons butter at room temperature
Salt and pepper to taste

To make the smoked scallops: Mix the first 5 ingredients together, pour into a non-aluminum container, add the scallops, and marinate at room temperature for 1 hour. Meanwhile, soak the hickory chips in water to cover. Preheat the oven to 350°F. Drain the chips and sprinkle over hot coals. Grill the scallops for 2 or 3 minutes on each side in the covered grill. Bake for no more than 5 minutes, or until just opaque throughout and tender to the touch. Keep warm.

To make the venison: Season the venison with salt and pepper and let sit for 20 to 30 minutes. In a large sauté pan or skillet, heat the oil and brown the veal on both sides.

To make the chanterelle sauce: In a medium sauté pan or skillet, cook the bacon until crisp. Sauté the shallots in the bacon fat until translucent, about 3 minutes. Pour in the gin and red wine and cook over medium heat, stirring, for 2 or 3 minutes. Add the venison sauce, peppercorns, salt, and pepper. Strain the sauce through a fine-meshed sieve. Return to the pan, add the mushrooms, and whisk in the butter.

To make the tasso-saffron sauce: In a medium sauce pan, heat the oil and sauté the shallots until translucent, about 3 minutes. Pour in the wine, add the saffron, and cook over medium heat for several minutes to reduce slightly. Add the cream and tasso; simmer until reduced by half. Strain the sauce through a fine-meshed sieve and return to the pan. Whisk in the butter.

To serve: Place 2 slices of venison in a pool of chanterelle sauce and 3 scallops in a pool of tasso-saffron sauce on each plate.

Venison Sauce

Makes 4 cups

1/2 cup bacon fat or oil
5 pounds venison bones, cut into chunks
1 pound onions, coarsely chopped
3 garlic cloves, crushed
1 pound carrots, peeled and coarsely chopped
2 pounds ham scraps
1 pound leeks, cut into 1/4-inch pieces
1/2 cup tomato paste
2 cups burgundy wine
Bouquet Garni
8 cups water
4 tablespoons brown roux (see Techniques)
Salt and pepper to taste

Bouquet Garni
3 bay leaves
1 tablespoon juniper berries
1 sprig fresh thyme
1 sprig fresh sage
1 tablespoon peppercorns
1 dozen parsley sprigs

In a large Dutch oven or heavy pot, heat the bacon fat and sauté the venison bones with the onions, garlic, carrots, ham scraps and leeks until all are well browned. Add the tomato paste and red wine and cook over medium heat to reduce by one third, about 10 to 12 minutes. Make a bouquet garni by tying the bay leaves, juniper berries, thyme, sage, and peppercorns in a square of cheesecloth with a cotton string. Add the water and bouquet garni to the pot and simmer for 3 to 4 hours, or until reduced by half. Add salt and pepper to the pot and strain the liquid through a fine-meshed sieve lined with cheesecloth. Add the liquid to the roux, stirring constantly over medium heat until the mixture begins to thicken. Simmer until smooth. Add salt and pepper to taste. Place leftover sauce in an airtight container and freeze. ∎

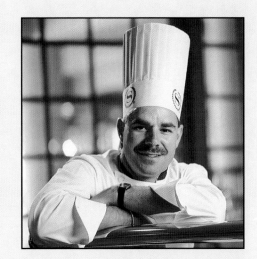

BERNHARD GOTZ
Fillet's, New Orleans

Executive chefs at well-known hotels are a special breed. Not only are they responsible for creating and executing the menu of a restaurant such as Fillet's in the Sheraton New Orleans, but they are also responsible for all the rest of the hotel's multifaceted food operations: room service, banquets, off-premise catering, and other hotel restaurants (in Gotz's case at the Sheraton, four in all).

Gotz joined the Sheraton New Orleans in 1987, and since that time has headed a team of fifty including eight sous-chefs. Like many European-trained chefs who apprentice in their early teens, he is still young but has been a chef for twenty-four years. He completed his culinary schooling and apprenticeship at the Gasthaus Adler in his native Germany and first joined ITT Sheraton in 1980, holding executive chef positions in several U.S. hotels.

Despite his impressive credentials, Gotz is down to earth, approachable, and known for his sense of humor. He is an active supporter of and participant in the American Culinary Federation's local culinary apprenticeship program at Delgado Community College. Great chefs of the future no doubt will regale their apprentices with lessons they learned while working under Gotz.

In 1988, Gotz received his Certified Executive Chef certification from the American Culinary Federation and has been its New Orleans chapter president twice. He was also named Chef of the Year twice by the New Orleans ACF Chapter, the first chef ever to receive this honor twice. He is an award-winning ice carver and an active competitor in professional culinary salons. And Gotz has been recognized by the American Heart Association and various local hospitals for his lectures on healthful cooking and his original heart-healthy recipes.

Gotz's three recipes in this book range in difficulty from his Chocolate-dipped Poached Pears (a delightfully easy to make but elegant dessert), to Sautéed Oysters with Sweet Potatoes (also easy if you choose not to pipe the sweet potatoes from a pastry tube), to his challenging Venison and Smoked Scallops Bernhard. This entrée is more than worth the effort and one that would win, hands down, any Most-Likely-to-Impress-Company contest.

Sweet Finales: Desserts

When it comes to dessert, logic loses, appetite wins. Study after study of consumption patterns reveals that our sweet tooth can neither be fooled nor denied. For example, according to several recent surveys, consumption of reduced- and non-fat desserts and artificially sweetened soft drinks is up; so is consumption of ice cream and cookies. And chefs have long been familiar with the dessert-reward phenomenon: customers who order broiled skinless chicken breast or broiled fish without sauce, and salad with dressing on the side, then proceed to order and consume the richest dessert the menu has to offer.

There is one change, however, in our relationship to desserts, and chefs are partly to blame. Our sweet tooth has become more educated and discriminating. And if, when it comes to dessert, we are going to sacrifice sensible nutrition (and we are), then it is all the more important that every calorie be worth the sacrifice. Over the years, desserts have become better and better—better tasting, better looking and offered in greater variety. Chefs and pastry chefs have researched regional favorites, reviving and updating. Louisiana's new garde chefs, for example, have done so much with (and to) old-fashioned bread pudding that they have turned this once-homey dessert duckling into a beautiful swan that any fine restaurant would be proud to feature—and one that would make a grand finale to dinner at home. One example in the recipes that follow is Dick Brennan's White Chocolate Bread Pudding, dripping with a white chocolate sauce (it's the most-requested recipe by customers at Palace Café in New Orleans). Then there is the traditional Acadian Bread Pudding, rich with eggs, milk, butter and fragrant with nutmeg and cinnamon, re-created by Patrick Mould of Hub City Diner in Lafayette. He tops it with a scoop of rich, creamy Roasted Pecan Rum Sauce. Lastly, Frank Brigtsen of Brigtsen's Restaurant, New Orleans, creates a Banana Bread Pudding with raisins, bananas and roasted pecans. But his sauce is an inspired takeoff of that flambéed favorite, Bananas Foster.

Another regional favorite dessert, strawberry shortcake, has been taken on a voyage of discovery by John Caluda of The Coffee Cottage, New Orleans. He replaces traditional biscuits with rosemary scones, plain strawberries with mixed berries, and tops the dessert with Grand Marnier-flavored whipped cream. The combination is outstanding. So is Gerard Maras' rendition of Sour Cream Pound Cake with Lemon Crème Sauce for Mr. B's, New Orleans.

Today's chefs have searched the world's cuisines for appealing confections. In the recipes that follow, you will find European desserts Americanized. Among them are John Caluda's Apple Strudel (Coffee Cottage, Metairie), Emeril Lagasse's Three-berry Tart with Vanilla Cream (Emeril's, New Orleans), André Poirot's Gratin of Berries with Sweet Marsala Sabayon (Begue's, New Orleans), Susan Spicer's Crêpes with Walnut-cream Cheese Filling (Bayona, New Orleans), and Fernando Saracchi's Crespella di Ricotta con Salsa al Caramello—ricotta-filled crêpes with caramel sauce—(Ristorante Bacco, New Orleans), and Michael Uddo's Pear Tarte Tatin (G&E Courtyard Grill, New Orleans).

Last, but certainly not the least of their sweet feats, today's chefs have created their own desserts, many of which bear no resemblance to traditional regional or European recipes. One shining example is Asian Napoleon by Mike Fennelly of Mike's on the Avenue, New Orleans. Instead of the traditional puff pastry used in French dessert Napoleons, Fennelly uses fried wonton wrappers dusted with confectioners' sugar as layers between lemon pastry cream, and pools the plate with fresh raspberry coulis. Kevin Graham of the Windsor Court Hotel, New Orleans, bakes a harlequin mask cookie to grace chocolate mousse, and Kim Kringlie of The Dakota, Covington, forms a chocolate coconut shell—with the help of a balloon—then fills it with coconut cream.

A few of the desserts that follow require above-average pastry skills, but can be simplified with suggested recipe shortcuts. Most desserts in this chapter are easy to make; many can be made in advance. And all fulfill that essential requirement for today's dessert: They are eminently worth making and worth eating.

Chocolate-laced Praline Shells, with Berries and Amaretto Cream, Andrea Tritico, Bella Luna

Summer Fruit Soup, John Neal, Peristyle

Summer Fruit Soup

*From John Neal of Peristyle,
New Orleans, LA*

Serves 4

Chef John Neal's dessert is a cross
between English summer pudding, a
molded dessert of bread and fresh berries,
and Scandinavian fruit soup, cooked fruit
purée served hot or cold. Neal's recipe has
the bread of summer pudding and the
simplicity of fruit soup. The prunes help
to thicken the soup and to flavor the wine.

1 bottle hearty red wine
1 cup sugar, plus sugar to taste
2 tablespoons ground cinnamon
2 tablespoons pure vanilla extract
1 cup pitted prunes
1 cup heavy (whipping) cream
Sugar to taste
4 slices dense white French or Italian
    bread, crust removed
Fresh berries for garnish.

Combine the wine, the 1 cup sugar,
cinnamon, vanilla, and prunes in a large
non-aluminum saucepan and simmer over
low heat for 1 hour. Cover and let sit
overnight. In a deep, small bowl, beat the
cream until soft peaks form. Stir in sugar
to taste. Place a slice of bread in the center
of each of 4 shallow-rimmed soup bowls.
Ladle the prunes and syrup over the
bread. Dollop the bread with whipped
cream. Garnish with fresh berries.
Serve cold. ∎

Chocolate-dipped Poached Pears

From Bernhard Gotz of Fillets,
New Orleans, LA

Serves 4

Poached pears are a timeless treat. They are also a time-saver for the busy cook because they may be poached a day or two in advance, covered, and refrigerated until time to serve. These are partially coated with chocolate and served with a sauce of vanilla yogurt spiked with citrus zest.

4 Bartlett or Bosc pears
1 orange
4 cups cranberry juice
1 cup dry red wine
1 cinnamon stick
2 whole cloves
1/4 cup Armagnac or cognac
1 tablespoon chocolate, chopped
1 cup (8 ounces) vanilla yogurt
1-1/2 tablespoon honey
Grated zest from 1/2 orange
Grated zest of 1/2 lime

Peel the pears, leaving the stem intact. Cut off the top and bottom of the orange down to the flesh, cut the peel from the sides down to the flesh, and cut out the orange segments from the membranes. Reserve half of the slices for another use. In a large saucepan over medium-high heat, bring the cranberry juice and wine to a boil. Add the pears, cinnamon, orange slices, and cloves. Reduce heat, cover, and simmer for 25 to 30 minutes, or until almost tender, turning the pears often. Remove from heat, add the Armagnac or cognac, and let cool in liquid. Remove pears, drain, and chill well before coating.

Pat the surface of each pear dry with paper towels. In a double boiler over barely simmering water, melt the chocolate, stirring until smooth; let cool slightly. Dip one end of each pear into chocolate. Allow to drip dry. In a small bowl, blend the yogurt, honey, and zests. Spoon the yogurt onto each of four dessert plates. Decorate the plate with the leftover melted chocolate. Place a pear in the center of each plate.■

JOHN NEAL
Peristyle, New Orleans

John Neal, chef-proprietor of Peristyle restaurant in New Orleans, came by his career as chef-restaurateur through force of habit: eating well. "My interest in cooking began because I had a mother who, like a lot of mothers of a certain era, cooked everything for us and didn't want us in the kitchen while she was doing so. When I moved away from home, I found that not only could I not prepare the meals I enjoyed; I didn't have the skills to prepare anything. Boiling frozen vegetables was a complete mystery."

With his first paycheck, Neal bought a set of pots and pans and half a dozen cookbooks and set out to solve this mystery. By the time he was living in New York, he rather obviously had some cooking clues. "Many years later, while living in New York City, I became the 'official' cook for a group of friends with whom I shared a summer house.

"When the time came—at the age of 25—to ask myself, 'What do I want to do with the rest of my life?', the answer was that cooking for others was what I enjoyed most." So Neal took the culinary curriculum at New York City Technical College.

His subsequent job experience is impressive. He worked at L'Hotel Rip-Alta in Plaisance-du-Gens, France; Harry's Bar in Venice, Italy; Mr. B's, and the Bistro at Maison de Ville, both in New Orleans. While he was executive chef at the Bistro at Maison de Ville, it was named the Number One restaurant in the "Haute New Orleans" category by the 1991 Zagat Survey, and was included in the Top 10 restaurants for 1991 by the *Times-Picayune*.

Neal's style of cooking ranges widely, and his genius lies in transforming culinary standards into fresh new dishes. His featured dessert, Summer Fruit Soup, combines the best of Scandinavian fruit soup with an English summer pudding. And it is guaranteed to satisfy anyone for whom the fruit sauce is the best part of any dessert.

JOHN CALUDA
Coffee Cottage, Metairie

"This is what I always wanted to do," says John Caluda, chef-proprietor of the Coffee Cottage on Metairie Road, "open up a pastry shop in my old neighborhood—one that would make fresh pastries daily for people who would appreciate them."

Caluda, a Culinary Institute of America (Hyde Park, New York) graduate, is a pastry natural. "One of the first things I ever made was chocolate eclairs when I was about 10 years old."

His professional experience ranges from being the chief steward-baker for a crew of 300 on an oil rig the size of a football field in the Gulf of Mexico, to being executive pasty chef at the Royal Orleans Hotel in New Orleans. When he was baking on the oil rig his reputation spread, and people would take a helicopter to the rig to pick up pastries and fly back with them to the other rigs in the vicinity.

Caluda also opened and operated the World's Fair Beignet Cafe at the World's Fair in New Orleans, 1984. He was the pastry cook and baker at Hotel Iberville, and the executive chef at Flagons Wine Bar, both in New Orleans. He opened and operated two Italian bistro-style restaurants called Sweet Basil's, one in New Orleans and one in Panama City Beach, Florida.

After two years in Florida and the birth of their first child, Caluda and his wife decided to move back home to Louisiana. "I always like this little spot on Metairie Road and had looked at it before, so when it became available I decided to take it and open the Coffee Cottage. Part of the charm of this place is atmosphere as well as food. It's like a counter coffee shop, open 7:30 a.m. to 11 at night. And we serve breakfast, lunch and dinner. I'd rather have nice, down-home cooking than a beautifully presented plate all the time."

His customers must agree, because after the Great Chefs television shoot, he enlarged the kitchen to three times its original size. When people ask how come his pastries are so light and flaky, he says, "There's no secret to it. I use fresh ingredients—and they were just made an hour ago."

Fresh Fruit Strip

From John Caluda of Coffee Cottage, Metairie, LA

Serves 6

Chef John Caluda has a pastry chef's love of embellishment, but don't be daunted by his recipe. Although it has a number of elements—pastry cream, a puff pastry shell, a layer of sliced fruits, an apricot glaze, and two sauces—each of them is simple to make, and the result is spectacular.

Pastry Cream
1-1/2 sheets gelatin, or 1 teaspoon granulated gelatin and 2 tablespoons of milk
2 cups milk
1/2 cup sugar
4 egg yolks
2 tablespoons cornstarch
2 tablespoons butter

Fruit Strip
1 sheet thawed frozen puff pastry
1 egg, beaten
1 tablespoon seedless raspberry jam
2 cups heavy (whipping) cream
1 tablespoon Amaretto or Grand Marnier, or other orange liqueur
Fresh raspberries, blackberries, sliced hulled strawberries, or mango slices
1 cup apricot jam
1 cup simple syrup (see "Food and Drink")

White chocolate sauce
1/2 cup heavy (whipping) cream
8 ounces chopped white chocolate
1 tablespoon Grand Marnier or other orange-flavored liqueur.

Fruit sauce
2 cups peeled, diced seasonal fruit
Sugar to taste

1/2 pound chopped bittersweet chocolate
Vanilla ice cream for serving

To make the pastry cream: Soak the sheet gelatin in cold water to cover. Or, if using granules, place 2 tablespoons of the cold milk in a cup and stir in the gelatin; set aside.

Combine 2 cups milk and 1/4 cup of the sugar in a medium sauté pan and bring to a boil over medium heat. Meanwhile, in a medium bowl, whisk together the egg yolks and 1/4 cup of the sugar until a ribbon forms on the surface of the mixture when the whisk is lifted. Gradually whisk half of the hot milk into the yolk mixture. Add the yolk mixture back to the milk in pan, stirring constantly over low heat until the mixture is thickened and starts to boil. Remove from heat. Drain the gelatin sheets if using. Add the gelatin sheets or the gelatin-milk mixture, the cornstarch, and the butter to the custard; whisk to combine. Let cool completely, preferably overnight.

To make the fruit strips: Preheat the oven to 350°F. Line a baking sheet with baking parchment or grease it. Cut the puff pastry sheet in half to make 2 strips 3 to 4 inches wide and 10 or 11 inches long. Cut two 1/2-inch strips from one of the strips. Brush the edges of the remaining four strips with beaten egg. Place a 1/2-inch strip on each edge of the 4-inch strip and press down lightly. Prick the center of the strip with a fork to keep it from rising too much. Place on the prepared pan and let sit for 15 minutes. Brush the 1/2-inch strips with beaten egg and place a piece of baking parchment on top, letting it stick to the egg wash. Bake for 5 to 10 minutes or until the pastry starts to brown. Remove the paper from the top of the pastry, reduce the oven temperature to 325°F, and bake for 15 more minutes, or until puffed and golden. (You may have to straighten the sides of the pastry with the edge of a knife.) Let cool on a wire rack. Spread the center of the pastry with the raspberry jam.

In a deep, medium bowl, beat the heavy cream, until stiff peaks form. Whisk the pastry cream until smooth (if it is lumpy, pass it through a fine-meshed sieve). Flavor with Amaretto or Grand Marnier, and fold in the whipped cream until blended.

Using a pastry bag with a 1/2-inch plain tip, pipe the custard over the jam in the center of the strip. Decorate with fresh fruit. Combine the apricot jam and simple syrup in a medium saucepan and cook over medium heat to reduce by one third, about 4 to 5 minutes. Brush the hot glaze evenly over the fruit. Chill the fruit strip for 30 minutes. Cut into 6 portions.

To make white chocolate sauce: In a double boiler over barely simmering water, melt the chocolate, stirring until smooth. Remove from heat and mix in the heavy cream and Grand Marnier.

To make fruit sauce: Purée the diced fruit in a food processor or food mill. Strain the puré through a fine-meshed sieve. Add sugar to taste.

To serve: In a double boiler over barely simmering water, melt the bittersweet chocolate. Cover half of each of six plates with white chocolate sauce and the other half with the fruit sauce. Decorate with the melted dark chocolate. Place the slice of fruit strip on the other side of the plate. ∎

Fresh Fruit Strip, John Caluda, Coffee Cottage

Apple Strudel

From John Caluda of Coffee Cottage, Metairie, LA

Serves 8 to 10

Chef John Caluda has added some special touches to his apple strudel, such as the brown butter used to brush the pastry, giving it extra flavor and a head start on browning. If you don't have time to make your own strudel dough, use fresh or thawed frozen filo.

Strudel Dough
2-1/2 cups bread flour
1 teaspoon salt
1 cup warm water (105° to 115°)
2 tablespoons oil

Apple Filling
1 cup brandy
1/2 cup raisins
2 cups (4 sticks) unsalted butter
10 apples
Juice of 1 lemon
2 tablespoons oil

1-1/2 cups granulated sugar
1/4 cup packed brown sugar
1/2 cup honey
1 cup heavy (whipping) cream
1/2 teaspoon ground cinnamon
1 cup dried white bread crumbs or cake crumbs
1 teaspoon vanilla
1/2 cup finely chopped nuts
1 egg, beaten

Fruit Sauce
2 cups peeled, diced seasonal fruit
Sugar to taste

Sifted powdered sugar for dusting
Vanilla ice cream for serving

To make the strudel: Place flour and salt into a heavy-duty mixer. Add the warm water and beat with a dough hook for 10 to 12 minutes. Form the dough into a ball, rub lightly with oil, and cover with plastic wrap. Let sit at room temperature for 15 to 30 minutes.

Meanwhile, warm the brandy in a small saucepan and add the raisins; set aside. In a medium saucepan, melt 1-1/2 cups of the butter and cook over low heat until the butter turns a light brown; set aside. Peel and core the apples and slice them 1/4 inch thick. Place the apples in a large bowl with lemon juice. Strain the raisins and reserve both the raisins and the brandy.

Heat a large sauté pan or skillet and add the oil and remaining 1/2 cup butter. Cook over medium high heat until the mixture sizzles and starts to turn brown. Add three-fourths of the apples and sauté for 3 minutes. Add the sugars and honey. Stir over medium heat until the liquid from the apples evaporates and begins to caramelize. Be careful not to burn. Add the reserved brandy and heat. Avert your face, light the brandy with a long match, and shake the pan until the flames subside. Add the heavy cream, cinnamon, vanilla, and raisins to the pan and cook over medium heat until thick, about 3 to 4 minutes. Add the reserved apples. Drain in a sieve, reserving the liquid. Let the apples cool.

Preheat the oven to 350°F. Lay a tablecloth on a table at least 24 inches by 24 inches. Dust with flour. Roll out the dough with a rolling pin to a small rectangle. If the dough feels tough, cover it with plastic and let rest for 15 more minutes, then proceed. Start pulling the sides of the dough in opposite directions from each other, working all areas of the dough. When the dough starts to get very thin, slip the backs of your hands underneath the dough. Stretch the dough until it is thin enough to see through and hangs several feet over the edge of the table. Trim off the thick edges and brush the dough with the cooled brown butter. Sprinkle with the bread or cake crumbs and nuts.

Spread the apple mixture on the top third of the dough. Use the tablecloth to roll the strudel up like a jelly roll, first brushing any dough that was hanging with butter, crumbs, and nuts. Seal the ends and place on a baking sheet. Brush with butter and let sit for 10 minutes. Brush with beaten egg and bake for 20 to 30 minutes, or until golden. Let cool.

Apple-raspberry Crisp, Randy Barlow, Kelsey's

To make the fruit sauce: Purée the diced fruit in a food processor or food mill. Strain the puré through a fine-meshed sieve. Add sugar to taste.

To serve: Slice the strudel on an angle and dust with powdered sugar. Serve with fruit sauce and vanilla ice cream. ▪

Apple-raspberry Crisp

From Randy Barlow of Kelsey's, Gretna, LA

Serves 6

America is famous for its fruit crisps: fruit and sugar topped with streusel and baked until the fruit forms its own irresistible sauce and the streusel is golden brown and crisp. Here chef Randy Barlow combines apples and raspberries for an exceptional flavor.

4 Golden Delicious or Granny Smith
   apples, peeled, cored, and diced (about
   2 cups)
1 cup fresh or frozen raspberries
1-1/2 cups sugar
1/2 cup (1 stick) butter at room
   temperature
1/2 cup (1 stick) margarine at room
   temperature
1 cup all-purpose flour
Ice cream or whipped cream for serving

Preheat the oven to 350°F. In a medium bowl, mix together the apples, raspberries, and 1/2 cup of the sugar. Spread evenly in a greased 10-inch cake pan. In a medium bowl, knead together the butter, margarine, remaining 1 cup sugar, and flour until crumbly. Sprinkle over the fruit. Bake for 30 minutes, or until golden brown. Serve warm with ice cream or whipped cream. ▪

RANDY BARLOW
Kelsey's, New Orleans

Randy Barlow, chef-proprietor of Kelsey's on New Orleans' West Bank, was born and raised in Ruston, Louisiana., which is the home, he says, of "unbelievable peaches! My mother use to make a dessert cobbler with them. Now when I can get them, I won't put them in dessert—I just eat them." His featured dessert, Apple-raspberry Crisp, evokes the flavors and textures of his mother's specialty but with his own signature touches. "If I tried to take it off the menu, I'd get hung." (Although he uses only fresh raspberries, he counsels the home cook to use frozen raspberries in this particular recipe when fresh are too expensive or out of season.)

Barlow is a chef, by education and training, who became an accomplished pastry chef from necessity. "Many of the places I worked were restaurants—unlike large hotels—that were too small to afford and hire a professional pastry chef, so I learned to do desserts." After attending the University of Southwest Louisiana, he received a culinary degree from Delgado University in New Orleans. Thereafter he worked with chef Gerard Crozier at Crozier's, chef Willy Coln at Willy Coln's Restaurant, and chef Paul Prudhomme at K-Paul's Louisiana Kitchen.

Barlow opened Kelsey's (named after his nine-year-old daughter) in 1991. Customers—he has a large local following—and critical acclaim came his way almost immediately. He was at the top of local food critic Gene Bourg's list of restuarants Where the Tourists Don't Go.

He finds it hard to label his style of cooking. He can and does make all the traditional Louisiana dishes from jambalaya to panéed rabbit. But he also is at home with European classics, which find their way onto is menu, such as wiener schnitzel, braised veal shanks and pasta with a putanesca sauce. On the other hand he can just as easily broil fish and create a mango salso to accompany it. "I try to take the best of what I have seen and use it to create my own ideas."

Barlow is a working chef, "And that means I spend my time in the kitchen, not parading around the dining room. When customers want to see me, I often invite them into the kitchen. I have a couple of customers who like to cook and they spend some time with me in there." Not that he's complaining: "This is the only thing I know how to do. I consider myself lucky to have this god-given talent."

Rosemary Scones with Fresh Berries and Grand Marnier Cream, John Caluda, Coffee Cottage

Rosemary Scones with Fresh Berries and Grand Marnier Cream

From John Caluda of Coffee Cottage, Metairie, LA

Serves: 8 to 10

This glorified strawberry shortcake is made with raisin scones, fragrant with fresh rosemary, filled with fresh berries and topped with Grand Marnier-flavored whipped cream.

Scones
2-1/2 cups all-purpose flour
2 teaspoons baking powder
1/4 cup sugar, plus sugar for sprinkling
3/4 teaspoon salt
1/3 cup cold unsalted butter, cut into small pieces
4 eggs
1 tablespoon milk
1 egg yolk
3/4 cup heavy (whipping) cream

3 tablespoons chopped fresh rosemary
3/4 cup golden raisins
2 tablespoons milk

Fruit
8 cups fresh blackberries, raspberries, or sliced hulled strawberries
1-1/2 cup sugar
Juice of 1/2 lemon
2 tablespoons brandy
1 teaspoon pure vanilla extract

Grand Marnier Cream
2 cups heavy (whipping) cream
1/2 cup sugar
2 tablespoons Grand Marnier or other orange liqueur

Sifted powdered sugar for dusting

To make scones: Preheat the oven to 350° F. Line baking sheets with baking parchment, or grease. Combine the flour, baking powder, the 1/4 cup sugar, and the salt in a medium bowl. Cut in the butter with a pastry cutter or your fingers until the mixture is the texture of coarse cornmeal. In another bowl, beat together 2 of the eggs, the egg yolk, the cream, and the rosemary. Add the raisins to the dry ingredients. Add the liquid ingredients to the dry ingredients and stir just until combined.

Using a medium ice cream scoop place 1/4 cup scoops of batter 2 inches apart on the prepared baking sheets. In a small bowl, beat together the remaining 2 eggs and the milk. Using a pastry brush, brush the dough with this mixture. Sprinkle lightly with sugar and let sit for 10 minutes. Bake for 10 to 12 minutes, or until lightly browned. Transfer to wire racks.

To make the fruit: Combine all of the ingredients in a large bowl. Remove 2 cups of the fruit and purée in a blender or food processor. Return the purée to the fruit.

To make the cream: In a deep, medium bowl, beat the cream until thick. Add the sugar, then the liqueur. Beat until soft peaks form.

To Serve: Split each warm scone horizontally. Place the bottom of each scone on a dessert plate and place a heaping spoonful of berries and juice on top of the scone. Place a generous spoonful of Grand Marnier cream on the top of the berries. Place the top of the scone on top of the cream and dust with powdered sugar. ∎

Asian Napoleon

From Mike Fennelly of Mike's on the Avenue, New Orleans, LA

Serves 8

Chef Michael Fennelly substitutes wonton wrappers for puff pastry and turns the classic French Napoleon into a lighthearted dessert for the contemporary cook.

2 eggs
2 egg yolks
1/2 cup plus 2 tablespoons granulated sugar
6 tablespoons plus 1 teaspoon fresh lemon juice
2 teaspoons grated lemon zest
1/2 cup (1 stick) cold unsalted butter, cut into 1-inch pieces
1 cup cold heavy (whipping) cream
4 cups fresh raspberries

6 cups peanut oil for deep-frying

24 square wonton wrappers (about 8 ounces)

Lemon or orange zest, cut into thin strips, for garnish

1/2 cup sifted powdered sugar

In a double boiler, whisk together the eggs and egg yolks. Whisk in 1/2 cup of the granulated sugar, 6 tablespoons of the lemon juice, and the lemon zest. Add the butter pieces all at once and place over simmering water. Cook, stirring constantly, until the mixture begins to thicken, about 4 to 5 minutes. Do not boil. Remove from heat and pour through a fine-meshed sieve into a bowl. Cover

with plastic wrap and refrigerate until chilled. In a deep medium bowl, whip the cream until soft peaks form. Fold the chilled lemon mixture into the cream. Cover and refrigerate.

Combine the berries, the remaining 2 tablespoons granulated sugar, and the remaining 1 teaspoon lemon juice in a blender or food processor. Process until smooth. Pass through a fine-meshed sieve to remove the seeds. Cover and refrigerate until ready to serve.

In a large heavy pot or deep-fryer, heat the oil to 375°F, or until a bit of wonton wrapper turns brown within seconds of being dropped into the oil. Separate the wrappers and drop them into the oil

several at a time, frying them until they are golden brown, about 3 to 4 minutes. Remove with a slotted utensil to paper towels to drain. Repeat with the remaining wrappers. When the wrappers are cool, break them into smaller pieces and dust with powdered sugar.

To serve: Napoleons, ladle a pool of the raspberry sauce onto each serving plate. Forming 4 layers in all, alternate broken wontons and spoonfuls of lemon cream, ending with the cream. Garnish with citrus zest, dust with powered sugar and serve immediately. ∎

Asian Napoleon, Michael Fennelly, Mike's on the Avenue

Three-berry Tart with Vanilla Cream

From Emeril Lagasse of Emeril's and NOLA, New Orleans, LA

Makes one 8-inch tart, serves 6

Too much of a good thing is never enough when berries are in season. Chef Emeril Lagasse combines berries and puff pastry to make a contemporary deep-dish berry tart.

Tart

1 thawed frozen sheet puff pastry
2 tablespoons butter at room temperature
2 teaspoons sugar
1/2 teaspoon ground nutmeg
1/2 teaspoon ground cinnamon
1-1/4 cup fresh blackberries
1-1/2 cup fresh blueberries
2 cups strawberries, hulled and halved
Powdered unsweetened cocoa and sifted powdered sugar for garnish
Vanilla Cream (recipe follows)
Fresh mint sprigs for garnish

Preheat the oven to 375°F. Press puff pastry into an 8-inch tart pan with a removable bottom; trim off excess. Prick the pastry on the sides and bottom with a fork. Spread 1 tablespoon of the butter over the pastry. Sprinkle with 1 teaspoon of the sugar, 1/4 teaspoon of the nutmeg, and 1/4 teaspoon of the cinnamon. Arrange the berries in the tart. Dot the remaining 1 tablespoon of the butter onto the berries. Sprinkle with the remaining 1 teaspoon sugar, 1/4 teaspoon nutmeg, and 1/4 teaspoon cinnamon. Bake for 20 to 25 minutes, or until golden brown. Let the tart cool slightly on a wire rack and remove from the pan. Cut into wedges and serve. Sprinkle the rim of each dessert plate with powdered cocoa and powdered sugar. Ladle vanilla cream over the tart and garnish with fresh mint.

Three-berry Tart with Vanilla Cream, Emeril Lagasse, Emeril's and NOLA

Vanilla Cream

Makes about 2 cups

2 cups heavy (whipping) cream
1/2 cup sugar
1 vanilla bean, split lengthwise
3 tablespoons Grand Marnier or other orange liqueur
3 egg yolks, beaten

Place the cream and sugar in a medium saucepan. Scrape the inside of the bean with a knife and add the bean and pulp to the mixture. Bring to a boil over medium-high heat, reduce heat, and simmer for 4 to 5 minutes. Add the Grand Marnier and egg yolks, stir, and cook for 1 minute. Remove from heat and strain through a fine-meshed sieve. Serve hot. ∎

Acadian Bread Pudding

From Patrick Mould of Hub City Diner, Lafayette, LA

Serves 6

Chef Patrick Mould of Hub City Diner in Lafayette, Louisiana, has given his bread pudding a pedigree. The Acadians were French immigrants who, driven from Canada by the British, settled in Louisiana. Their descendants are today's Louisiana Cajuns. This very traditional bread pudding has a *lagniappe*: Roasted Pecan Rum Sauce, meltingly delicious when scooped over bread pudding hot from the oven—and just as good served cold.

Roasted Pecan Rum Sauce

Serves 6, about 5 tablespoons per serving

1/2 cup pecan halves
2 cups heavy (whipping) cream
4 tablespoons sugar
4 tablespoons light rum
2 tablespoons cornstarch
1 tablespoons water
1 teaspoon orange zest

6 cups cubed French bread
4 eggs
1-1/2 cup sugar
1/2 teaspoon ground nutmeg
1 teaspoon ground cinnamon
3-1/2 cups milk
1/2 cup (1 stick) unsalted butter, melted

Preheat oven to 350°F. Place the pecans on a baking sheet and roast the pecans for 5 minutes. In a heavy saucepan over medium heat, cook the cream for

3 minutes. Add the sugar and rum. Whisk the mixture until the sugar is dissolved. Combine the cornstarch and water and stir until the cornstarch is dissolved. Add this mixture to the cream, and stir for 2 to 3 minutes or until the mixture is thickened. Stir in the orange zest and pecans.

Place the French bread in a greased 8- by-12-inch greased baking dish. With a mixer, beat the eggs and sugar on high speed for 3 to 4 minutes. Add the nutmeg and the cinnamon, and beat in the milk, then the butter, on low speed. Pour the milk-egg mixture over the French bread. Let sit for 1 hour and 30 minutes.

Preheat the oven to 350°F. Bake for 20 minutes, then lower temperature to 300°F and bake for an additional 20 minutes or until puffy and brown. Serve with Roasted Pecan Rum Sauce. ▪

Banana Bread Pudding with Banana Rum Sauce and Whipped Cream

From Frank Brigtsen of Brigtsen's Restaurant, New Orleans, LA

Serves 12

Chef Frank Brigtsen's recipe is a wonderful cross between bread pudding and Bananas Foster, New Orleans' famous flaming banana and ice cream dessert.

6 cups bite-sized pieces of day-old French
   bread
3 large eggs
3 cups milk
2/3 cup plus 1 tablespoon sugar
2 large very ripe bananas
1 tablespoon ground cinnamon
1/4 teaspoon ground nutmeg
3/4 teaspoon pure vanilla extract
1/2 cup seedless raisins
1/2 cup roasted pecans (see Techniques)
3 tablespoons unsalted butter
3/4 cup heavy (whipping) cream

Banana Rum Sauce

Makes 1-1/2 cups

2/3 cup unsalted butter, at room
   temperature
1/2 cup packed light brown sugar

Banana Bread Pudding with Banana Rum Sauce and Whipped Cream, Frank Brigtsen, Brigtsen's

6 large ripe bananas, quartered
1 teaspoon ground cinnamon
1/4 teaspoon ground nutmeg
3 tablespoons dark rum
2 tablespoons banana liqueur (optional)
1/2 teaspoon pure vanilla extract

Preheat the oven to 300°F. Put the French bread pieces into a 9- by-12- by-2-inch baking pan and set aside. In a blender or food processor, blend the eggs, milk, 2/3 cup of the sugar, the bananas, cinnamon, nutmeg, and 1/2 teaspoon of the vanilla until smooth. Pour this mixture over the French bread pieces. Fold in the raisins and pecans and let the mixture set for 20 minutes. Top with small pieces of the butter.

Cover the pudding with aluminum foil and place the pan into a larger pan. Add warm water to a depth of 1 inch in the larger pan. Bake for 1 hour. Remove the foil and bake uncovered for 15 minutes or until set.

In a deep, medium bowl, whisk the cream just until it begins to thicken. Add the remaining 1 tablespoon sugar and 1/4 teaspoon vanilla. Continue whisking until soft peaks form. Cover and chill.

To make the sauce: Heat a large sauté pan or skillet over low heat. Add the butter, sugar, bananas, cinnamon, and nutmeg. Moving the skillet back and forth, cook until the butter and sugar become creamy and the bananas begin to soften, about 1 minute. Remove the skillet from heat and add the rum and optional liqueur. Return the pan to heat. Tilt the pan, avert your face, and light the liquid with a long match. Shake the skillet until the flames subside. Add the vanilla, remove from heat, and keep warm. ▪

To Serve: Place a large scoop of bread pudding in the middle of each serving plate or bowl. Place 2 slices of banana on each plate and top with about 3 tablespoons of sauce. Spoon the whipped cream over the bread pudding and serve immediately. ▪

White Chocolate Bread Pudding

*From Dick Brennan, Jr., of Palace Café,
New Orleans, LA*

Serves 8 to 10

Chef Dick Brennan says that this is the
most-requested recipe at Palace Café in
New Orleans: a rich bread pudding
flavored with white chocolate and topped
with a warm white chocolate sauce.

3 cups heavy (whipping) cream
10 ounces white chocolate, chopped
1 cup milk
1/2 cup sugar
2 eggs
8 egg yolks
1 loaf French bread, cut into 1/4-inch-
　thick slices
2 tablespoons chocolate shavings for
　garnish

Preheat the oven to 275°F. In a medium
saucepan, heat the cream but do not boil.
Remove from heat, add the white
chocolate, and stir until melted and
smooth. In a double boiler over barely
simmering water, beat the milk, sugar,
eggs, and egg yolks together, and heat
until warm. Blend the egg mixture into
the cream and chocolate mixture.

Place the bread slices in a baking pan.
Pour half of the chocolate mixture over
the bread. Let sit for 30 minutes, then
pour in the rest of the chocolate mixture.
Cover it with aluminum foil and bake 1
hour. Remove the foil and bake for 15
minutes or until golden brown.

To serve: Spoon the pudding hot out of
pan, top with warm sauce, and garnish
with chocolate shavings. Or, let cool to
room temperature for about 45 minutes,
loosen sides, and invert pan to unmold.
Cut into squares. Top each serving with
warm sauce and sprinkle with chocolate
shavings.

White Chocolate Bread Pudding, Dick Brennan, Jr., Palace Café

White Chocolate Sauce

Serves 8 to 10

8 ounces white chocolate, chopped
1/3 cup heavy (whipping) cream

In a double boiler over barely simmering
water, melt the chocolate, stirring until
smooth. Remove from heat and mix in
the heavy cream. Keep warm. To store, let
cool slightly and store in airtight jar in the
refrigerator. Melt over barely simmering
water and stir until smooth.∎

Creole Cream Cheese Cheesecake

From Jamie Shannon of Commander's Palace, New Orleans, LA

Makes one 10-inch cheesecake, serves 10 to 12

Creole cream cheese is lower in fat than Philadelphia-style cream cheese and resembles fine-curd cottage cheese, farmer's cheese, or ricotta in texture. Ricotta may be substituted for Creole cream cheese in this recipe. The combination of cheeses gives the cake a very special texture.

Crust
5 cups graham crackers
1 cup (2 sticks) butter, melted
1 cup sugar

Filling
2 pounds cream cheese at room temperature
1 cup sugar
2 eggs, beaten
1-1/2 cups Creole cream cheese or ricotta cheese

Sour Cream Topping
1 cup sour cream
3 tablespoons sugar

To make the crust: Preheat the oven to 225°F. Break up the graham crackers and grind them into a fine meal in a blender or a food processor. In a large bowl, blend together the crumbs, butter, and sugar. Press into the bottom and sides of a 10-inch springform pan.

To make the filling: In a food processor or with a mixer blend the regular cream cheese and sugar until completely smooth. Combine the eggs and Creole cream cheese, and add to the cream cheese mixture. Combine thoroughly. Pour into the crust and bake for about 2 hours, or until the cake is set and a cake tester inserted in the center comes out clean. Chill the cake for at least 2 hours before unmolding and serving.

To make the topping: In a small bowl whisk the sour cream and sugar together until the sugar has dissolved. Spread the topping over the cheesecake, being careful not to pull crumbs from the edge of the crust onto the topping. ▪

Creole Cream Cheese Cheesecake, Jamie Shannon, Commander's Palace

Chocolate Mousse Cheesecake

From Robert Krol of Crozier's, Metairie, LA

Serves 8

Here's a chocolate cream cheesecake topped with a chocolate mousse. Are we chocoholics in heaven yet? For variations, try using chocolate cookies in place of vanilla wafers in the crust and sweet baking chocolate in the chocolate mousse.

Crust
15 vanilla wafers
2 tablespoons sugar
1 tablespoon unsweetened powdered cocoa
2 tablespoons butter, softened

Filling
6 ounces semisweet chocolate, chopped
4 tablespoons butter
20 ounces cream cheese at room temperature
2 eggs
3 egg yolks
1 cup sugar
1 teaspoon pure vanilla extract

Chocolate Mousse Topping
6 ounces semisweet chocolate, chopped
1 tablespoon rum
2-1/3 cup heavy (whipping) cream
1/2 cup sugar

To make the crust: Preheat the oven to 350°F. Grind all of the ingredients in a blender until fine. Oil a 10-inch cheesecake pan. Press the crust onto the bottom of the pan.

To make the filling: In a double boiler over barely simmering water, melt the chocolate and butter, stirring until smooth. Mix the chocolate mixture with all the remaining ingredients in a blender or food processor until well blended. Pour over the crust. Bake for 35 minutes, or until set. Let cool completely.

To make the topping: In a double boiler over barely simmering water, melt the chocolate with the rum and 1/3 cup of the cream, stirring until smooth; set aside to cool. In a deep, medium bowl, whip the remaining 2 cups cream until stiff peaks form. Fold in the sugar and the chocolate mixture. Cover and chill. Pipe the mousse onto the cheesecake with a pastry bag. Chill for 2 hours. ∎

Chocolate Mousse with Harlequin Cookie Mask

From Kevin Graham of the Windsor Court Hotel, New Orleans, LA

Take yourself to Mardi Gras with chef Kevin Graham's Harlequin Cookie Mask. It makes a spectacular dessert presentation. You may, of course, prefer to serve his superb chocolate mousse out of costume--simply presented in an elegant glass container such as a cognac, Champagne or parfait glass. Top with sweetened whipped cream and a few strategically placed raspberries.

Chocolate Mousse

1 pound semisweet chocolate, broken into
   pieces
4 large eggs, separated
1/3 cup water
1/3 cup dark rum
1/3 cup granulated sugar
3 cups heavy (whipping) cream, whipped
   into peaks

Slowly melt the chocolate in the top half of a double boiler over simmering water. Place the egg yolks in a bowl, then whisk in 1/3 cup water and the dark rum. When thoroughly blended, stir in the melted chocolate.

Chocolate Mousse Cheesecake, Robert Krol, Crozier's

Beat 4 egg whites until foamy. Add 1/3 cup sugar and continue to beat until stiff peaks form. Beat the egg whites until stiff. Fold the beaten egg whites into the chocolate mixture, then fold in the whipped cream. Spoon into serving glasses and chill.

Harlequin Mask
1/2 cup all-purpose flour
1/2 cup confectioners' sugar
Pinch cinnamon
1/2 teaspoon pure vanilla extract
4 egg whites
Heavy cream, if needed
1 teaspoon unsweetened cocoa powder
Vegetable oil spray

Trace a mask shape, about 7 inches long, onto a piece of cardboard, making sure that you allow a border. Cut the shape out, leaving a mask stencil with straight edges and a 2-inch border all around. Cut around the eyes, leaving them attached to the upper edge of the stencil by a thin strip of cardboard.

Sift the flour and confectioners' sugar together into a large bowl. With an electric mixer on low speed, add the cinnamon and vanilla, then the egg whites, one by one, mixing well to make a paste. Let the mixture sit in the bowl for 45 minutes at room temperature. (If the paste is still thick after 45 minutes, thin with a small amount of heavy cream.) Mix 2 tablespoons of the paste with the cocoa and place in a pastry bag with a narrow tip. Set aside.

Preheat the oven to 375°F. Cover a baking sheet with parchment paper and spray lightly with vegetable oil spray. Lay the mask stencil on top of the greased paper. Using a spatula, spread a thin layer of paste over the mask. Lift up the stencil and repeat to make twelve masks in all. Using the pastry bag, pipe a thin band of chocolate paste 1/2 inch wide along the edge of each mask. Draw a toothpick through the chocolate band using an up-and-down motion to create a decorative effect resembling feathers. Place in the preheated oven and bake for 10 minutes, or until the dough begins to turn golden. Remove from the oven and immediately peel each mask, one at a time, off the paper. Place a large round canister on its side and wrap the masks around the

canister to give them a curved shape. Let cool on the canister before handling. The masks can be stored in an airtight container for up to 8 hours.

To serve: Prop each mask against a tall champagne or martini glass filled with Chocolate Mousse. ∎

Chocolate Mousse Cake with Strawberry Sauce

From Bob Roth of The Steak Knife, New Orleans, LA

Serves 8

The easy-to-put-together chocolate mousse cake may be made a day in advance and frozen, then assembled just before serving.

Chocolate mousse
8 ounces chocolate chips
1/2 tablespoon butter
4 cups heavy (whipping) cream
4 cups sugar
1 tablespoon brandy
1 tablespoon Tia Maria or other coffee liqueur
1 tablespoon Grand Marnier or other orange liqueur
3 eggs, separated

Sponge Cake
8 eggs
2 tablespoons cornstarch
1 cup sugar
1-1/4 cup all-purpose flour
5 tablespoons butter, melted and at room temperature
1 teaspoon pure vanilla extract

Strawberry Sauce
4 cups fresh strawberries, hulled
1 tablespoon strawberry liqueur (optional)
3 tablespoons honey
1/2 cup dry white wine

1 cup heavy (whipping) cream
1 tablespoon Grand Marnier or other orange liqueur
1 pint fresh strawberries for garnish

To make the chocolate mousse: In a double boiler over barely simmering water, melt the chocolate and butter, stirring until smooth. Sit aside to cool slightly. In a deep large bowl, whip cream

until soft peaks form. Add the sugar, then add the brandy and liqueurs. Blend thoroughly. Mix a small amount of the whipped cream into the melted chocolate, then fold that mixture back into the whipped cream. In a double boiler over barely simmering water, whisk the egg yolks for 2 minutes; set aside. In a large bowl, beat the egg whites until soft peaks form. Fold the egg yolks, then the beaten whites into the chocolate whipped cream until smooth and blended. Cover and refrigerate.

To make the cake: Preheat the oven to 350°F. Grease and dust with flour a 4- by 12-inch pan. In a double boiler over barely simmering water mix together the eggs and sugar and beat until thickened and smooth, about 4 to 5 minutes. Set aside. Sift the cornstarch, sugar, and flour together and fold into the egg mixture. Fold the butter and vanilla extract into the batter. Pour into prepared pan. Bake for 30 to 40 minutes or until cake springs back when pressed. Let cool.

Cut the cooled cake into 6 slices to fit a loaf pan. Line a cake pan with the slices of sponge cake. Ladle in the chilled chocolate mousse until the pan is full. Cover mousse with slices of sponge cake. Cover with plastic wrap and freeze.

To make the sauce: Purée the berries in a blender or food processor. Strain through a fine-meshed sieve. In a medium saucepan heat the purée over low heat and stir in the remaining ingredients. Let cool, then cover and refrigerate.

To make the flavored whipped cream: In small deep bowl whip the cream until soft peaks form. Add orange liqueur. Cover and refrigerate.

To Serve: Warm a large knife in hot water and cut the mousse cake into 8-inch slices. Ladle strawberry sauce onto each of eight serving plates. Place a slice of frozen mousse on the sauce. Place in the refrigerator until semi-soft. Top with flavored whipped cream, garnish with strawberries and serve. ∎

JOYCE BANISTER
Bistro la Tour, New Orleans

Joyce Banister, pastry chef at Bistro la Tour, is a good example of a somewhat common culinary conundrum. That is, almost all pastry chefs can fill in for chefs, but not all chefs can step into the pastry chef's shoes. Pastry chefs are specialists. Theirs is a more mathematical discipline where measurements must be exact, and a dessert may well rise--or fall--on the difference between one teaspoon or two.

Banister's education reveals an aptitude for art, shared by many in her field. She graduated from the University of New Hampshire, Durham, N.H., with a bachelor of arts degree. Then she attended the New England Culinary Institute in Montpelier, Vermont, graduating with an associate degree in culinary arts.

Her first job was combination pastry cook and line cook at a twenty-five room, family-owned inn in Vermont. She was responsible not only for pastries but for breakfast and lunch.

Two years after she moved to New Hampshire to be head baker and pastry assistant at La Boulangerie Cafe and Bakery, a retail bakery where everything was made from scratch, including hand-rolled pastas. At La Boulangerie, Banister assisted with the production of wedding cakes as well.

Her wedding cake proficiency came in handy when, after moving to New Orleans, she landed a job as assistant pastry chef at the prestigious Windsor Court Hotel, the site of elegant wedding receptions.

After almost two years at the Windsor Court, she moved to Bistro la Tour as pastry chef. Her responsibilities include all dessert design and chocolate work, pastry, and the nitty-gritty of purchasing, staff supervision and inventory and cost control. And, true to form, she often works the sauté station.

Chocolate Coconut with Vanilla English Cream

From Kim Kringlie of The Dakota, Covington, LA

Serves 4

Chef Kim Kringlie recipe is a lesson in trompe l'oeil. He dips mylar balloons into chocolate halfway up, refrigerates them to harden the chocolate, and then pops the balloons. Voilà! a hollow chocolate half sphere ready to fill with cream cheese-coconut cream filling. Once the cream freezes, a melon baller is used to hollow out the center to resemble the interior of a coconut half. This chocolate molding technique can be used with other fillings such as chocolate mousse, ice cream, and fresh berries drizzled with sabayon.

8 ounces milk chocolate, chopped
1/4 cup macadamia nuts, finely chopped
8 ounces cream cheese at room temperature
1 cup sifted powdered sugar
1/4 cup coconut cream
1 cup heavy (whipping) cream
1/4 cup shredded coconut
English Cream (recipe follows)

Blow up Mylar balloons to a 2-1/2-inch diameter; set aside.

In a double boiler over barely simmering water, melt the chocolate. Add the macadamia nuts. Dip each balloon halfway into the chocolate and refrigerate on a tray until chocolate is firm.

In a large bowl, beat the cream cheese, sugar, and coconut cream until smooth. In a deep, medium bowl, whip the heavy cream until stiff peaks form. Fold the whipped cream into the cream cheese mixture and add the shredded coconut.

Pop the balloons and remove them from the chocolate shells. Fill the chocolate shells to the top with the filling. Place in the freezer until firm. Using a melon baller, hollow out the middle of the shell to resemble a coconut half. Serve with English cream.

English Cream

Makes two cups

3/4 cup heavy (whipping) cream
1/2 cup milk
4 egg yolks
1/2 cup sugar
2 tablespoons pure vanilla extract

In a medium saucepan, heat the heavy cream and milk. In a medium bowl, beat the egg yolks and sugar until pale in color. Gradually beat in the hot milk and cream. Return to the saucepan and cook over medium heat, stirring constantly, until the mixture coats the back of a spoon. Add the vanilla and strain through fine-meshed sieve. ■

Chocolate Pâté

From Joyce Banister of Bistro la Tour, New Orleans, LA

Serves 8

Delightfully decadent describes chef Joyce Banister's Chocolate Pâté, especially when it is served, as Banister suggests, with a small glass of a nice, full-bodied, Cabernet Sauvignon.

2 pounds bittersweet chocolate, preferably Callebaut, chopped, plus 1/2 pound, chopped
1-1/2 cups (3 sticks) sweet butter, cut into 1-inch pieces
1/2 cup Chambord (raspberry liqueur)
1 cup water
4 egg yolks, beaten

Line a small loaf pan with plastic wrap to form a mold.

In a double boiler over barely simmering water, melt 2 pounds of the chocolate, and butter with the Chambord and water, stirring until smooth. Set aside and let cool slightly.

Whisk the egg yolks into the chocolate mixture. Strain though a fine-meshed sieve into the mold, cover, and chill.

To serve: Melt the remaining 1/2 pound of chocolate in a double boiler over barely simmering water, stirring until smooth.

Dip a large knife into hot water and cut the pâté into 1-inch slices. Decorate each serving plate with swirls of melted chocolate. Place a slice of pâté on each plate and serve. ■

Chocolate Pâté, Joyce Banister, Bristro la Tour

Terrine of White Chocolate and Praline, with Coconut Tile Cookies and Caramel Sauce, Dennis Hutley, The Versailles Restaurant

Terrine of White Chocolate and Praline, with Coconut Tile Cookies and Caramel Sauce

From Dennis Hutley of The Versailles Restaurant, New Orleans, LA

Serves 6

Crisp, shaped tile cookies provide a contrast in texture to the pecan-studded white chocolate terrine.

Terrine of White Chocolate and Praline
6 ounces white chocolate, chopped
4 tablespoons unsalted butter
2 teaspoons plain gelatin
1/4 cup praline or other nut liqueur or brandy, chilled
3/4 cup heavy (whipping) cream
1/2 cup chopped pecans, blanched almonds, or peeled hazelnuts (see Techniques)

Caramel Sauce
1/4 cup sugar
1 tablespoon unsalted butter
1/2 cup heavy (whipping) cream

Coconut Tile cookies (recipe follows)

1/2 cup heavy (whipping) cream
Fresh mint sprigs candied flowers or fruit, and unsweetened cocoa powder for garnish

To make the terrine: In a double boiler over barely simmering water, melt the chocolate and butter, stirring until smooth. Sprinkle the gelatin over the liqueur in a small cup and set aside. In a small saucepan over medium heat, bring 1/4 cup cream to a boil, and stir it gradually into the chocolate mixture. Add the gelatin-liqueur mixture, then the pecan pieces; mix well. Refrigerate until chilled, stirring occasionally. In a small, deep bowl, beat the remaining 1/2 cup cream until stiff peaks form; fold into chocolate mixture. Line a 4-cup mold with plastic wrap, pour in the terrine mixture, and chill for at least 2 to 3 hours.

To make the sauce: Place sugar in a small skillet or saucepan over medium-low heat. When sugar starts to turn color around the edges, begin to shake and swirl pan to uniformly brown the sugar. When it becomes thoroughly golden brown, add the butter and mix well. Then stir in the cream gradually, being very careful of the resulting steam from the saucepan. Remove from heat, transfer to a clean container, and let cool.

To serve: In a medium bowl, whip 1/2 cup heavy cream until stiff peaks form. Stand a cookie upright in the top center of each of 6 chilled plates. Unmold and unwrap the terrine and cut it into 12 even slices. Place 2 slices on the left side of each cookie and spoon about 2 tablespoons caramel sauce onto the left side of plate. Using a pastry bag fitted with a fluted tip, pipe a mound of freshly whipped cream next to the cookie. Garnish with mint sprigs, candied violets or rose petals, or candied fruit, and dust the border of the plates with cocoa powder from sugar shaker.

Coconut Tile Cookies

Makes 6

1 egg
1/4 cup shredded coconut
1/4 cup sugar
1-1/2 teaspoon flour

Preheat oven at 375°F and place a large baking sheet in oven to preheat. In a small bowl, beat the egg and stir in the remaining ingredients. Remove the baking sheet from oven and coat well with shortening or spray with cooking oil. Stirring well each time, drop batter 4 to 5 inches apart on the pan. Bake for about 10 minutes, or until the outside edges are brown and the cookies are crisp-looking almost to the center. If the oven rack or baking sheet is not level, the wafers will run together. If this happens, about halfway through baking, cut the cookies apart with edge of a metal spatula. Leaving the pan in the oven with oven door open, remove one cookie with a metal spatula, transfer to a cool suface and roll into a cylinder; hold the shape in place for 15 to 20 seconds, then set aside. Repeat until the remaining wafers are shaped. Keep in an cool, dry place. ∎

Chocolate-laced Praline Shells with Berries and Amaretto Cream

From Andrea Tritico of Bella Luna, New Orleans, LA

Makes about 18 shells; serves 18

This make-ahead recipe can be assembled right before serving. Make the batter for the praline shells two days before serving, and make the shells themselves the day before. Coat the insides of the shells with chocolate. Fill the coated shells with fresh berries and top with amaretto cream just before serving.

1/2 cup (1 stick) butter
1-1/2 cups packed brown sugar
1 cup corn syrup
2 cups all-purpose flour

Amaretto Cream
2 cups sour cream
1/3 cup packed brown sugar
1/4 cup Amaretto liqueur

1 pound semisweet chocolate, chopped
2 cups fresh strawberries, hulled and quartered
2 cups fresh raspberries

In a large saucepan combine the butter, sugar, and corn syrup and bring to a boil over medium heat. Place the flour in a large bowl and pour in the hot mixture; stir until well mixed. Cover and chill overnight.

Preheat the oven to 350°F. Divide the batter into 1-1/2 tablespoon portions and roll into balls. Place the balls on a baking sheet lined with baking parchment, leaving at least 5 inches of space between each one. Bake until golden in the center and darker brown around the edges. Remove the entire parchment paper from the pan and place on a cool working surface. With one quick motion, turn the paper over, leaving the shells on the surface. Pick up the shells and one by one drape them over a teacup or custard cup. This entire process should be completed as quickly as possible. Let cool.

To make the Amaretto cream: Place all ingredients in a small bowl and mix until thoroughly blended; set aside.

When the shells have set and completely cooled, melt the chocolate in a double boiler over barely simmering water, stirring until smooth. Using a pastry brush, coat the inside

ANDREA TRITICO
Bella Luna, New Orleans

Andrea Tritico, Bella Luna's pastry chef, finds pastry fascinating because of its potential for creativity. Her backgrouund is in sculpture and painting, and she holds a degree in art from Loyola University, New Orleans.

Rather than academic culinary training, she completed a culinary apprenticeship through the local chapter of the American Culinary Federation. She was pastry cook at the Century Plaza Hotel in Los Angeles, and at the St. James Club in Hollywood. She relocated to Houston, Texas and worked as pastry chef at the Ritz-Carlton there for two years, before moving to New Orleans.

She calls her situation at Bella Luna, "a dream job. I have the freedom to create some fantasy desserts, and I spend a lot of time thinking about how a dessert will be best presented and best executed." For example, she does not make her crème brûlée on the range top, as in traditional, but bakes it in a water bath in the oven. "When baking it, it's a little more like a flan—that's a subtle difference—but I find the taste and texture better."

She gets rave reviews on Bella Luna's bread pudding. The secret? "So many bread puddings come out as solid as a rock. I use a lot less bread and increase the amount of custard. And I bake it in a mold that has been lined with caramelized sugar. It's like a sauce."

Some of her own menu favorites include a milk chocolate orange cream pie with meringue on top ("I love milk chocolate."); a key lime pie made with real key lime juice from Florida ("I can't take it off the menu"). and, of course, her featured dessert, Chocolate-laced Praline Shells. It's a make-ahead dessert, she says, and she suggests baking the cookie shells the day before, letting them cool and then coating with chocolate. The chocolate coated shells may be filled with fruit and Amaretto cream right before serving time. The shells also make edible bowls for ice cream.

of each shell with a thin layer of chocolate. Let sit for about 10 minutes or until hardened. Combine the strawberries and raspberries. Divide the berries among the shells and pour Amaretto cream over them. ∎

Crespella di Ricotta con Salsa al Caramello

From Fernando Saracchi of Ristorante Bacco, New Orleans, LA

Serves 4

The following recipe is the Italian version of a French dessert crêpe: A sweetened ricotta and goat cheese mixture spiked with orange, cinnamon, and chocolate, piped into a crêpe and served with caramel crème anglaise.

Filling
2 pounds plus 2 ounces fresh ricotta cheese
1/4 cup fresh mild white goat cheese
1/2 teaspoon ground cinnamon
1 cup sifted powdered sugar
1/2 cup finely chopped candied orange peel
2 ounces semisweet chocolate, shaved

Crêpe Batter
2 cups all-purpose flour
1/2 cup sifted powdered sugar
Pinch of salt
4 eggs, beaten
2 cups milk
4 tablespoons butter, melted

Butter for cooking crêpes
Caramel Crème Anglaise (recipe follows)

To make the filling: Press the ricotta through a fine-meshed sieve or whirl in a blender or a food processor until smooth. Beat in the goat cheese and cinnamon. Stir in the powdered sugar until smooth. Cover and refrigerate at least 2 hours or up to 24 hours.

To make the crêpe batter: Place the flour, sugar, and salt in a large bowl. Add the eggs. Gradually add the milk, whisking until all the ingredients are well blended. Stir in the melted butter, cover, and let rest in the refrigerator for at least 1 hour.

About 20 to 30 minutes before you plan to use it, take the filling out of the refrigerator, press through a fine-meshed sieve and stir in the candied orange peel and the shaved chocolate; set it aside at room temperature.

To make the crêpes: In an 8-inch nonstick pan, melt 1/2 teaspoon butter over medium-low heat, rotating the pan so that the bottom is evenly coated with butter. Pour about 3 tablespoons of batter into the center of the pan, quickly tilting the pan so that the batter covers the bottom evenly. Cook until the crêpe has set and turned a pale brown color on one side. Turn it with a spatula and brown it very lightly on the other side, then transfer it to a plate and place in a warm oven. Repeat until all of the crêpes are cooked, stacking them as you go. Scoop the filling into a pastry bag fitted with a 1/2-inch plain tip and pipe the filling down the center of each crêpe.
Or, spoon 2 to 3 tablespoons of filling down the center. Roll up the crêpes around the filling, overlapping the seam. Place two crêpes seam-side down on each of four warm dessert plates. Pour the Caramel Crème Anglaise over them and serve.

Caramel Crème Anglaise

Makes about 2 cups

8 egg yolks
2 cups plus 2 tablespoons sugar
2 cups milk
1 teaspoon fresh lemon juice
6 tablespoons water

In a large bowl beat the egg yolks and 1 cup plus 2 tablespoons of the sugar together until the yolks have entirely absorbed the sugar. In a medium saucepan bring the milk to a boil, then whisk it very gradually into the egg mixture. Pour back into the saucepan, place over low heat, and stir until the mixture has thickened enough to coat a spoon; do not boil. Strain through a fine-meshed sieve into a bowl. Set aside. Place the remaining 1 cup of sugar, the lemon juice, and 3 tablespoons of the water in a medium saucepan over low heat and cook until the mixture turns golden. Remove the pan from the heat and place it in a bowl of ice water until cool. Add the remaining 3 tablespoons of water and cook until the caramel is dissolved. Cool again in the bowl of ice water. Fold the caramel into the sauce. ∎

Crêpes with Walnut-Cream Cheese Filling

From Susan Spicer of Bayona, New Orleans, LA

Makes 18 crepes; serves 8 to 9

Sweet filled crêpes are a classic French dessert. Chef Susan Spicer shows how a Louisiana chef adds flavor. Her Basque aromatic mixture—an engaging blend of citrus, anise, almond, and spirits—is used in the crêpe batter, the crêpe filling, and the sauce.

Crêpes
3 eggs
1 cup all-purpose flour
3/4 cup milk
2 tablespoons melted butter
1-1/2 tablespoon sugar
1/2 teaspoon salt
3 tablespoons Basque Aromatic Mixture (recipe follows)
Oil for cooking crêpes

Filling
1/2 pound cream cheese at room temperature
1-1/2 tablespoons lavender honey or other aromatic honey
1/4 teaspoon grated orange zest
1/4 teaspoon grated lemon zest
1/2 cup walnuts, finely chopped
1/2 tablespoon Basque Aromatic Mixture (recipe follows)

Sauce
1 cup plus 3 tablespoons lavender or other aromatic honey
1/2 cup fresh orange juice
1 tablespoon Basque Aromatic Mixture (recipe follows)

Orange segments and grated orange zest for garnish
Powered sugar for garnish

To make the crêpes: In a medium bowl, beat the eggs and whisk in the flour 1/3 cup at a time. In a small saucepan, heat the milk, butter, sugar, and salt until the butter is melted and the sugar is dissolved. Whisk gradually into the egg-flour mixture until smooth. Add the aromatic mixture and strain through a fine-meshed sieve. Let sit for 30 minutes.
Heat a 6-inch nonstick skillet over medium high heat and swirl in 1/2 teaspoon cooking oil. When the pan is almost smoking, ladle in 2 tablespoons

Crêpes with Walnut-Cream Cheese Filling, Susan Spicer, Bayona

of batter, and quickly tilt and swirl the pan so that the batter coats the bottom of the pan. Cook over medium-high heat until crêpe is golden brown on one side, then loosen the edge and flip or turn the crêpe over for a few seconds to lightly cook the second side. Slide out onto a plate and place in a warm oven; continue with the rest of the batter, stacking the crêpes as they are cooked.

To make the filling: In a large bowl, beat together all of the ingredients until blended. Spread about 2 tablespoons of filling on lower half of each crêpe, fold over the top half, then fold in half again to make wedge shape.

To make the sauce: In a medium saucepan over low heat, warm all of the ingredients. Keep warm.

To serve: Place 2 crêpes on each of 8 warm plates and drizzle warm sauce over them. Garnish with orange segments, and zest, dust with powered sugar, and serve at once.

Basque Aromatic Mixture

Makes about 1-1/4 cup

1/4 cup orange flower water
1/4 cup anisette
1/4 cup dark rum
1/2 cup Armagnac or other brandy
1 teaspoon almond extract
2 strips lemon zest
2 strips orange zest

Place all of the ingredients in a jar, shake, and let stand for a least 1 hour. Cover tightly and store for 4 to 6 weeks. ∎

Crème Brûlée

From Randy Windham of the Bistro at Maison de Ville, New Orleans, LA

Serves 10

Crème brûlée with its hardened caramelized sugar crust capping the velvety smooth custard has been a favorite restaurant dessert for decades and is currently enjoying a new wave of popularity. Chef Randy Windham's version uses aromatic vanilla beans to flavor these rich treats.

1 quart heavy (whipping) cream
2 vanilla beans, split lengthwise
6 egg yolks
2/3 cup granulated sugar
5 tablespoons raw or brown sugar

Preheat the oven to 325°F. In a medium saucepan, scald the cream and vanilla beans over medium heat. Remove from heat.

In a large bowl, whisk the yolks and sugar together until thick and lemon-colored. Remove the vanilla beans from the cream. Slowly whisk the hot cream into the yolk mixture. Whisk until smooth. Strain through a fine-meshed sieve.

Fill ten 4-ounce soufflé dishes to 1/4 inch from the top. Place the cups in a baking pan and add 1 inch of warm water to the pan. Cover the cups with aluminum foil or a baking sheet. Bake for 30 to 45 minutes, or until set. Remove from the oven and cover each cup with plastic wrap. Chill for at least 8 hours.

ANN DUNBAR
NOLA, New Orleans

Although pastry chef Ann Dunbar has had no formal culinary training, she entered the restaurant field "Years ago, as a hostess, waitress and bartender. In 1983, I applied for a job in management at K-Paul's Louisiana Kitchen. My sister, Mary Sonnier, was already working there in the kitchen. But Chef Paul Prudhomme wanted me to cook instead —figuring it kind of ran in the family." Prudhomme was right, because Dunbar hasn't been out of the kitchen since. She worked with Prudhomme for five years, which she describes as "Really intense. I traveled all over the country with him for some unforgettable experiences." Among them was the huge benefit for the Children's Hospital Centennial in Pittsburgh in 1989. Dunbar's philanthropic bent still engages her in work for various charitable causes, such as the Battered Women's Shelter in New Orleans.

"Paul taught me to be very quality-minded, and to this day I'm very picky about ingredients, especially fruit. I like to get it in season."

After working at K-Paul's, Dunbar catered for a year and consulted for Al Copeland (creator of Popeyes' Chicken and Copeland's restaurant) developing some classic New Orleans sandwiches for his menus.

When she heard, in 1992, that Emeril Lagasse was opening NOLA, she wrote him a letter, and he hired her as pastry chef. In that capacity Dunbar supervises an assistant and three apprentices who, between them, make all the homemade breads, desserts, ice creams and sorbets for the busy French Quarter restaurant. The recipes are Dunbar's and range from French bread to sweet potato pecan rolls, herb and cheese biscuits, onion focaccia and banana or zucchini bread. Among customers' favorite desserts at NOLA is the Turtle Pie, the Coconut Pots de Crèmes with Coconut-almond Snaps (featured here), and the Lemon Icebox Pie, her grandmother's recipe with which she won a cooking contest when she was 11 years old.

When she's not cooking and baking, Dunbar is creating new recipes for tasting with Lagasse and NOLA's chefs. "We get together and taste and critique—it keeps me fresh. It's not like work—I really enjoy it. I've always been that way about cooking, all or nothing."

To serve: Preheat the broiler. Evenly spread the raw or brown sugar on top of custards. Place under the broiler, about 4 inches from the heat until the sugar is caramelized. Let the custards cool and the tops harden before serving.

Coconut Pots de Crèmes with Coconut-Almond Snaps

From Ann Dunbar of NOLA, New Orleans, LA

Serves 4

Pastry chef Ann Dunbar of NOLA tucks both toasted and untoasted coconut into her pots de crèmes and then accompanies them with coconut-almond cookies. Both recipes are fairly simple for the home cook. The pots de crèmes are simple baked custards, and the cookies are made with prepared puff pastry.

2 cups heavy (whipping) cream
1/4 cup sugar
4 egg yolks
1/2 teaspoon pure vanilla extract
3 tablespoons grated coconut
Coconut-Almond Snaps (recipe follows)

Preheat the oven to 300°F. In a medium saucepan over low heat, heat the cream to warm. In a medium bowl whisk together the sugar and egg yolks until thick and lemon-colored. Stir in the warm cream and vanilla. Strain mixture through a fine-meshed sieve.

Spread half of the coconut on a baking sheet and bake for about 15 minutes, or until toasted. Put 1 teaspoon of toasted coconut and 1 teaspoon of untoasted coconut in each of four 4-ounce ramekins. Place the ramekins in a baking dish. Skim the bubbles from the custard, then pour custard into the ramekins. Pour hot water into the baking dish to halfway up the sides of the ramekins. Cover with aluminum foil or a baking sheet. Bake for 45 to 50 minutes or until custards are set. Let cool for several hours before serving. Serve with coconut-almond snaps.

Coconut-Almond Snaps

Makes 16

1 sheet thawed frozen puff pastry
Granulated sugar for sprinkling
1 cup (2 sticks) unsalted butter at room
    temperature
1/2 cup grated coconut
1/2 cup (2 ounces) ground almonds

Place the puff pastry on a work surface
that has been sprinkled with sugar. Using
a pastry brush, spread 1/2 cup butter
evenly over the pastry. Then generously
sprinkle sugar over the buttered pastry.
Next lightly sprinkle coconut and ground
almonds over the pastry. Roll up jellyroll
style and sprinkle with sugar. Refrigerate
for 1 hour, then cut into 1/2-inch slices.
Place the slices 2 inches apart on a baking
sheet that has been lined with baking
parchment, or greased. Press each slice
with the palm of your hand to flatten,
then spread each slice with some of the
remaining butter, and sprinkle with sugar.
Refrigerate for 1 hour. Preheat the oven
to 375°F. Bake for 10 to 12 minutes, or
until snaps are golden brown. Turn the
cookie sheet halfway through baking to
ensure even browning. ∎

Gratin of Berries with Sweet Marsala Sabayon

*From André Poirot of Begue's,
New Orleans, LA*

Serves 1

This is one of those blissfully easy recipes
that goes from oven to table in the same
dish. A good thing it's easy, because its
table life, once served, is about two minutes
(or as fast as guests can gobble it up).

Sweet Marsala Sabayon
2 tablespoons sugar
1/4 cup sweet Marsala wine or sweet
    sherry, plus more for sprinkling
2 egg yolks

One 4-inch slice of sponge cake
1 white chocolate truffle (optional)
1/4 cup sliced fresh strawberries
1/4 cup fresh raspberries
1/4 cup fresh blueberries
1/4 cup fresh blackberries
Fresh mint sprigs for garnish
To make the sabayon: Preheat the

ANDRÉ POIROT
Begue's, New Orleans

André Poirot, executive chef of the Royal Sonesta hotel and chef de
cuisine of its gourmet restaurant, Begue's, was born in France. However,
he is a relative newcomer to New Orleans, arriving late in 1989.

He attended secondary school and culinary school in France, receiving
his culinary diploma in 1977. Thereafter he followed a traditional
European appreticeship, serving as a *commis* at the Ets Blanche restaurant
in Remiremont, France; and the Savoy Hotel in London.

His military duty was discharged at Pont St. Vincent, France, as a
chef mess officer, then he moved up the kitchen brigade ladder to *saucier*,
a position he held at Thomas de Quincey's restaurant in London for a year.

Poirot's next position was as chef at Le Caveau restaurant in Bordeaux,
a post he traded for sous-chef at Ets Cuny Traiteur also in Bordeaux.

From 1982 to 1983 he has head chef at Relais de Ballons in St.
Maurice-Moselle, France. When he moved to Strasbourg, to the
Campanile Hotel, he stepped out of the back of the house and into
the front as assistant manager—for a year. By the time he relocated to
Bermuda he was chefing it again at the Princess Hotel, as chef de cuisine
at Harley's restaurant and gourmet chef at the Tiara restaurant.

In 1989 Poirot made his move to New Orleans, a city where his
training in classical French cuisine brought new life to the menu at
Begue's. His cooking style is light and elegant, and his recipes in this
book are thoughtfully tailored for the nonprofessional cook. His appetizer
recipe, Artichoke and Hearts of Palm Salad, is made with a citrus
vinaigrette that has a ratio of equal parts oil to acid (in this case red wine
vinegar, fresh lemon and orange juices) rather than the standard two parts
oil to one part vinegar. Poirot's entrée, Scaloppine of Chicken with Stir-
fried Vegetables, uses a white wine-pasta sauce for chicken and tops
steamed potatoes with low-fat yogurt instead of butter or sour cream. His
featured dessert, Gratin of Berries with Sweet Marsala Sabayon, is one of
those perfect combinations that looks and tastes fabulous, but is easy to
prepare.

Coffee Toffee Pie, Armand Jonté, Armand's

Pour the melted ice cream on each of 4 dessert plates. Arrange the fig halves over the ice cream. In a small sauté pan or skillet, warm the Pernod and sprinkle in the pepper. Avert your face and light the Pernod with a long match, shaking the pan until the flames subside. Pour over the figs and serve at once.∎

Sour Cream Pound Cake With Lemon Crème Sauce

From Gerard Maras of Mr. B's, New Orleans, LA

Serves 8 to 10

The slight tang of sour cream balances the sweetness of this pound cake, and the lemon crème sauce is a perfect complement. Try serving this with fresh berries.

Sour Cream Pound Cake

2-1/2 cups sugar
1 cup (2 sticks) butter at room temperature
6 eggs, separated
1/4 teaspoon baking soda
1 cup (8 ounces) sour cream
3 cups sifted all-purpose flour
1 teaspoon pure vanilla extract
Pinch of salt

Preheat the oven to 300°F. Butter and flour a 10-inch bundt pan. In a large bowl, cream the sugar and butter together until fluffy. Beat in the yolks one at a time. Dissolve the soda in the sour cream. Add the flour to the butter-yolk mixture alternately with sour cream, beginning and ending with the flour. Stir in the vanilla. In a large bowl, beat egg whites with the salt until they hold stiff peaks. Stir one third of the beaten whites into batter to lighten it. Fold in the remaining whites. Pour the batter into the prepared pan and bake for 1 hour and 30 minutes.

Lemon Crème Sauce

10 egg yolks
1 cup sugar
4 cups heavy (whipping) cream
Juice of 6 to 7 lemons

In a medium saucepan, heat but do not boil the cream; set aside. In a double boiler, beat the yolks and sugar together. Gradually whisk in the heated cream. Cook over simmering water, stirring constantly, until custard thickens slightly.

broiler. Place the sugar, the 1/4 cup of Marsala or sherry, and egg yolks in a double boiler over barely simmering water; whisk until thickened and doubled in volume, about 3 to 4 minutes. Place the sponge cake in an ovenproof gratin dish, sprinkle with Marsala, or sherry, and place the optional truffle on the cake and the berries around it. Cover the fruit with the sabayon and place under the broiler 3 to 4 inches from the heat until golden brown, about 1 to 2 minutes. Decorate with mint sprigs and serve at once.∎

Figs in Vanilla Sauce, Flambéed with Pernod

From Hubert Sandot of L'Economie and Martinique, New Orleans, LA

Serves 4

Every so often a recipe is so brilliantly simple that we ask ourselves, "Now, why didn't I think of that?" Chef Hubert Sandot's recipe is an example: His dessert sauce is made by melting ice cream. But the genius is in pairing the vanilla sauce with ripe black figs and flambéed Pernod.

8 large fresh black figs, halved
1 cup good-quality vanilla ice cream, melted
1/4 cup Pernod
2 pinches of freshly ground pepper

Let cool to room temperature. Whisk in the lemon juice. Strain through a fine-meshed sieve.

To serve: slice the pound cake and serve with room-temperature lemon crème sauce. ∎

Coffee Toffee Pie

From Armand Jonté of Armand's, Waveland, MS

Makes one 8-inch pie; serves 8

Chef Armand Jonté's recipe is user-friendly because the chef builds in shortcuts for the home cook. The crust is made using packaged pie crust mix and is pressed into a pie pan rather than being rolled out. A rich coffee-chocolate custard is frozen in the crust, and the pie is topped with coffee-flavored whipped cream.

Pie Shell
5 ounces packaged pie crust mix
1/4 cup packed brown sugar
3/4 cup (3 ounces) chopped walnuts
1 ounce grated unsweetened chocolate
Water as indicated by packaged mix
1/8 teaspoon pure vanilla extract

Filling
1 ounce unsweetened chocolate, chopped
1/2 cup (1 stick) butter at room temperature
3/4 cup sugar
2 teaspoons instant coffee powder
2 eggs

Topping
2 cups heavy (whipping) cream
2 tablespoons instant coffee powder
1/2 cup sifted powdered sugar

To make the shell: Preheat the oven to 375°F. In a medium bowl, combine the pie crust mix, brown sugar, walnuts, and grated chocolate. Add the water and vanilla. Mix until well blended. Spread in a 8-inch pie pan and press firmly to line the bottom and sides. Bake for 15 minutes or until golden brown. Let cool. Refrigerate.

To make the filling: In a double boiler over barely simmering water, melt the chocolate, stirring until smooth; set aside to cool slightly. In a large bowl, cream the butter and sugar together, beating until fluffy. Blend in the chocolate and coffee.

Pear Tarte Tatin, Michael Uddo, G&E Courtyard Grill

Add 1 egg and beat for 5 minutes. Add the second egg and beat for 5 minutes. Pour into the crust, cover, and freeze overnight.

To make the topping: In a medium, deep bowl, combine the cream and coffee. Chill for 15 minutes. Beat until peaks form. Fold in the sugar. Place in a pastry bag and pipe over the top of the pie to cover it evenly. Cut the pie into wedges with a large knife, and serve. ∎

Pear Tarte Tatin

From Michael Uddo of G&E Courtyard Grill, New Orleans, LA

Makes one 12-inch tart; serves 8

This is a lovely version of one of the most famous French desserts, an upside-down apple tart created by the Tatin sisters of Orléans. Instead of the traditional pie crust dough, chef Michael Uddo substitutes puff pastry, and in place of apples, pears.

1/2 cup (1 stick) butter, cut into 1-inch pieces
2 tablespoons sugar
4 green d'Anjou pears, peeled, cored, and cut into slices
Juice of 1 lemon
1-1/2 teaspoons vanilla extract
1/4 teaspoon ground nutmeg
1/4 teaspoon ground cinnamon
1 sheet thawed frozen puff pastry

Preheat the oven to 350°F. Meanwhile, divide the butter pieces evenly over the bottom of a 12-inch cast iron skillet. Sprinkle evenly with sugar. Combine the pears, lemon juice, vanilla, nutmeg, and cinnamon in a medium bowl and toss the pears to coat them evenly. Arrange the pear slices in the skillet in an overlapping spiral with a rosette in the center. Cook over medium heat until the juices and sugar thicken and just begin to darken, about 20 minutes. Bake for 20 minutes.

Roll out the puff pastry to a thickness of 1/4 inch. Cut a 13-inch circle from the sheet of puff pastry. Cover the skillet with the circle of puff pastry, tucking in the edges. Poke a few air holes in the pastry. Raise the oven temperature to 400°F and bake for 15 to 20 minutes, or until the pastry is nicely browned. Let cool on a wire rack for 20 minutes. Place a serving plate on top of the skillet and carefully invert the tart. ∎

Deep Dish Mango Pie

From Mary Sonnier of Gabrielle, New Orleans, LA

The captivating flavor of mangos has made them the darling of chefs, who use them in salsas, chutneys, ice creams, sorbets, and crèmes brûlées. Chef Mary Sonnier's recipe for deep dish mango pie combines the exotic and the homespun.

Pie Crust
5 tablespoons butter
1 tablespoon margarine
1-1/2 cup all-purpose flour
2 tablespoons baking powder
1/2 teaspoon salt
1 egg
1 egg yolk
2 tablespoons warm water
3 tablespoons sugar

Filling
4 to 6 mangos
1/3 cup sugar
1/4 teaspoon ground cinnamon
Dash of salt
Zest of 1 orange
Zest of 1 lemon
2 tablespoons cornstarch
Juice of 1 lemon
Juice of 1 orange

4 tablespoons butter
1 teaspoon pure vanilla extract

1 egg, beaten
1 cup heavy (whipping) cream
Sugar to taste

To make the crust: In a small saucepan, melt the butter and margarine together; set aside. Sift the flour, baking powder, and salt together into a medium bowl. In a mixer with a whisk attachment, beat the eggs, water, and sugar together until foamy; gradually add the warm melted butter and beat until thick and creamy, about 1 minute. Change to a dough hook, add flour mixture, and mix and knead the dough until it forms a ball. (If the dough is too sticky, add a little flour) The kneading should take about 1 minute. Remove the dough from the bowl, cover with a towel and let rest.

To make the filling: Peel the mangos and cut the flesh from the pits. Cut the flesh into slices. You should have 2 cups of sliced mango. Squeeze pulp from seeds. In a blender or food processor, purée enough additional sliced mangos to make one cup purée when added to pulp from seeds. Place the mango purée, sugar, cinnamon, salt, and orange and lemon zest in a small saucepan over medium heat and bring to a slow simmer.

In a cup, dissolve the cornstarch in the lemon and orange juices. Stir this mixture into the purée, cooking and stirring constantly until the purée comes to a boil. Remove from heat and add the butter and vanilla. Set aside to cool.

Preheat oven to 300°F. On a lightly floured board, roll the dough out, and form it into a ball. Cut the dough into 2 pieces, one slightly larger than the other. Roll the larger section out and line an 8-inch round cake pan; trim the edge. Place 1 cup of mango slices on the pastry and top with half of the purée. Layer with the remaining mango slices, and top with the remaining purée. Roll out the second piece of dough and cut it into 1-inch strips. Place the strips on top of the pie, weaving them to form a lattice. Brush the lattice with the beaten egg. Bake for 45 minutes, turn the oven up to 350°F, and bake an additional 15 to 20 minutes, or until golden brown. Let cool slightly. Meanwhile, in a deep, medium bowl, beat the cream until soft peaks form; add sugar to taste. Spoon some of the cream over each serving of pie. ∎

Helter Skelter Parfait

From Shane Gorringe of Windsor Court Hotel, New Orleans, LA

Serves 6

The three flavors and colors of this layered sorbet parfait make a beautiful dessert. If making chocolate ornaments isn't your cup of tea, melt only 3 ounces of chocolate for the parfait mixture, and substitute chocolate curls or shaved chocolate for the lattices to be made from the remaining chocolate.

Parfait
8 egg yolks
1 cup sugar
1/4 cup water
3 ounces chopped bittersweet chocolate
6 cups heavy (whipping) cream
3 tablespoons Framboise liqueur
1/2 cup raspberries

Marinated Raspberries and Sauce
2 cups raspberries
3/4 cup crème de cacao
1/4 cup sugar

Chocolate Garnish
2 ounces semisweet chocolate

To make the parfait: Put the egg yolks in a medium mixing bowl. Place the sugar and water in a small saucepan, stir together,

Deep Dish Mango Pie, Mary Sonnier, Gabrielle

and bring to a boil over medium heat. When the sugar reaches 245°F or soft ball stage (a small amount dropped from a spoon into cold water will form a soft ball), pour it over the yolks while mixing at medium speed. When all the sugar is added, increase the speed to high. Continue whipping the mixture until the mixture is cool. Divide this mixture between two bowls, and set aside.

In a double boiler over barely simmering water, melt the chocolate, stirring until smooth; set aside.

In a large, deep bowl, beat the heavy cream until soft peaks form. Using first bowl of reserved egg-sugar mixture, fold in one half of the whipped cream, and 2 tablespoons of Framboise, into the mixture. Set aside. Using the second bowl of reserved mixture, fold in the remaining whipped cream, 1 tablespoon Framboise, and the melted chocolate into mixture. Pipe or spoon alternating layers of the two mixtures into each of six 6-ounce parfait glasses or tumblers, placing a few raspberries between each layer. Freeze for 8 to 10 hours.

To make the berries and sauce:
Combine the raspberries and crème de cacao and let sit at room temperature for 3 to 4 hours. Drain the crème de cacao from the berries into a small saucepan, reserving the berries for later. Add sugar to the crème de cacao, and bring to a boil over medium heat for 4 to 5 minutes. Let cool. Put the raspberries back into the sauce.

Unmold the parfaits by dipping them up to the rim in a pan of warm water for 5 to 10 seconds, and then turning them onto a plate. The parfaits should slide out; if not, return them to the warm water and turn them over again. Place the parfaits on a tray and return them to the freezer for 5 to 10 hours.

To make the chocolate garnish: Cut 6 strips of baking parchment about 14 inches long and 3 inches wide. Melt the semisweet chocolate in a double boiler over barely simmering water, and put it in a pastry bag fitted with a 1/4-inch tip. Pipe a chocolate lattice design the length of each strip. Before the chocolate sets, wrap a strip around each parfait. Freeze.

To serve: Unwrap the paper from the chocolate. (if the chocolate gets too soft, place the lattices in the freezer for a few minutes to reset). Garnish with berries and sauce. ∎

MARY SONNIER
Gabrielle, New Orleans

Mary Sonnier is chef and partner in Gabrielle, a restaurant she owns and operates with her husband Greg. They named their restaurant after their now five-year-old daughter. "My cooking interest began as child, when my dad taught me to make French toast at the age of five. As the oldest of six children, I would cook dinner often for my family—who love to eat!"

Sonnier's sister, Ann Dunbar, herself a pastry chef at NOLA restaurant in New Orleans, says "She always liked to cook—and she cooked everything. One of my earliest memories is of Mary preparing Chinese food, something nobody else was cooking, especially at home."

Mary started cooking professionally at K-Paul's Louisiana Kitchen in 1983. She was hired as an apprentice sausage-maker but soon went to work at every station in the restaurant from baker to sauté cook to purchaser.

She met her husband Greg at K-Paul's. They were married and left in 1988. In 1989, Garbrielle was born, and Mary opened her own small catering business. Four years later she and Greg opened their own restaurant.

Her desserts are half the reason people come to dine at Gabrielle—Greg's cuisine is the other. Mary's fruit shortcakes are a local legend: She bakes her own biscuits, splits, toasts, and butters them, piles them high with ripe seasonal fruits marinated in fruit purée, and crowns them with heavy cream, lightly whipped. A second desert for which she is famous is her signature Peppermint Patty, a dense flourless chocolate cake slice, served warm, topped with housemade peppermint ice cream, and drizzled with chocolate sauce.

A third menu favorite is featured here, Deep Dish Mango Pie.

SHANE GORRINGE
Windsor Court Hotel, New Orleans

A native of Surrey, England, pastry chef Shane Gorringe ("Rhymes with orange," he says) apprenticed at Sweet Vienna Patisserie, a renowned Austrian pastry shop south of London. Thereafter, he was assistant pastry chef at luxury hotels in England, Germany, Holland, Venezuela, and in the Middle East.

He has been about the business of making pastries since he was 16 years old. "After 20 years in this field, you learn that when you come to a new city, you don't assume that just because the desserts that you did at the previous location worked there, that they're going to work here." Because the Windsor Court caters to an international clientele, his desserts shy away from strictly regional favorites such as bread pudding. However, he finds that New Orleanians,, no matter how sophisticated, do have specific affinites—for chocolate, desserts with apples, sorbets, exotic fruits, and crème brûlée. He has contributed his share to local and visiting palates with a new specialties that have become hotel signatures such as Chocolate Breathlesss (chocolate meringue enveloped in a chocolate mousse), and Blueberry Cheesecake Crumble.

Since joining the Windsor Court, he has elevated the breads, pastries and desserts another notch, starting with the enlargement of the pastry shop, an expansion that doubled the size of his working space. As if to put a new spin on the adage that work fills the time allotted for it, Gorringe's works now fills the space allotted: He and his staff now produce all breads and baked goods, as well as pastries, ice creams, sorbets and pastries for the hotel, and scones for the hotel's famous afternoon tea.

Gorringe's advice to the nonprofessional cook who wants to recreate his featured dessert recipes, Twists of Sorbet and Helter Skelter Parfait, is to not be put off by the presentation. The sorbets may be scooped instead of sliced into tubes that fit into tuile cookie twists. He suggest scooping the sorbet hours ahead of serving and placing the scoops on a waxed-paper lined tray in the freezer. At serving time, place scoops in individualized serving dishes. For Helter Skelter Parfait, he suggests freezing the parfaits in glass serving dishes, then making simple chocolate decorations: Melt chocolate and spread in thin layer on parchment paper to harden. When hardened, break off in chunks, place on top of parfait and pipe or dribble on semisweet melted chocolate.

Twists of Sorbet

From Shane Gorringe of the Windsor Court Hotel, New Orleans, LA

Serves 8

Despite its beautiful and creative presentation, this recipe from pastry chef Shane Gorringe is a simple mango sorbet served with a tuile cookie and a blackberry sauce. If you prefer, scoop into serving dishes, drizzle with blackberry sauce, and serve with butter cookies.

Mango Sorbet
4 to 6 mangos
1/2 cup water
1/2 cup sugar

Hazelnut Tuiles
3 cups plus 3 tablespoons hazelnut flour
1 pound powdered sugar, sifted
1 cup plus 2 tablespoons all-purpose flour, sifted
3/4 cup plus 1 tablespoon butter, melted and warm
12 egg whites at room temperature

Powdered sugar for dusting
Blackberry Sauce (recipe follows)

To make the sorbet: Peel the mangos and cut the flesh from the pits with a sharp knife. Purée the mango slices in a blender or food processor. Combine the mango purée, water, and sugar in a small saucepan and bring to a boil. Chill the mixture, and freeze it in an ice cream maker according to the manufacturer's instructions. Fill a pastry bag fitted with a 1-inch plain tip with the sorbet. Pipe a 4-inch strip onto baking parchment or waxed paper approximately 1 inch from the end. Roll the sorbet tube up in the paper and freeze until very firm. Repeat until all of mixture is used.

To make the tuiles: Preheat the oven to 375°F. Grease and flour a baking sheet. Combine all ingredients in a mixing bowl with a mixer. Spread the batter on the tray in strips each 1-1/2 inches wide and 12 inches long. Bake for 15 to 20 minutes, or until slightly browned. Using a thick broom handle or a 1-inch diameter wooden dowel, wrap a warm strip around the handle or dowel to make a spiral. Repeat with the rest of the tuile strips.

Remove the sorbet from the freezer and slice into 4-inch-long sections. Slide one into each cookie spiral. Arrange on each of 8 plates and dust with powdered sugar. Garnish with blackberry sauce and serve immediately.

Blackberry Sauce

Makes about 4 cups

Zest and juice of 1 orange
Zest and juice of 1 lemon
1/4 cup Chambord (raspberry liqueur)
1/4 cup crème de cassis
2 tablespoons Pernod or other anise-flavored liqueur
1/2 cup sugar
2-1/2 cups fresh blackberries
1 vanilla bean, split lengthwise

Combine all of the ingredients except 1-1/2 cups of the blackberries and the vanilla bean in a medium saucepan. Scrape the pulp from the vanilla bean with a knife and add the pulp and the bean to the pan. Bring to a boil. Strain through a fine-meshed sieve. Add the remaining blackberries. ∎

Snappy's Polar Chip

From Patti Constantin of Constantin's, New Orleans, LA

Serves 12

Our fascination with double- and triple-decker sandwiches testifies to the kid in us all. Chef Patti Constantin translates this favorite sandwich form into dessert, a double-decker ice cream sandwich with scoops of ice cream layered between chocolate chip-oatmeal cookies. Try two kinds of ice cream, such as vanilla and chocolate, vanilla and butter-pecan, chocolate swirl and chocolate, rum-raisin and vanilla, coffee, and toffee.

Cookies
2 cups old-fashioned rolled oats
1 cup packed light brown sugar
1 cup granulated sugar
1 tablespoon flour
1 cup (2 sticks) butter, melted and cooled
2 eggs, beaten
1 teaspoon pure vanilla extract
1/4 cup mini chocolate chips

Chocolate Sauce
2 cups sugar
4 cups half and half
1 pound bittersweet or semisweet chocolate, chopped
1 pound unsweetened chocolate, chopped

1/2 cup heavy (whipping) cream
12 scoops ice cream of your choice

To make the cookies: Preheat the oven to 350°F. Line 2 baking sheets with aluminum foil. Combine the oats, brown sugar, white sugar, and flour in a large bowl. Stir in butter, then the eggs and vanilla. Stir in the chips and chill the mixture until firm. Divide the dough into 1-teaspoon portions and roll into balls. Place 2 inches apart on the prepared baking sheets. Bake for 15 minutes. Let cool and peel off of foil.

To make the sauce: Place the sugar and half-and-half in a large heavy saucepan. Heat but do not boil over medium-low heat. Add the chocolate and stir until the chocolate is melted and mixture is smooth.

To serve: In a small, deep bowl, beat the cream until soft peaks form. Layer a cookie with one scoop of ice cream, top with a cookie and a second scoop of ice cream. Spoon chocolate sauce over the layered cookies and ice cream. Top with whipped cream. ∎

Twists of Sorbet, Shane Gorringe, Windsor Court Hotel

Pecan Profiteroles with Vanilla Ice Cream, Chocolate Sauce, and Seasonal Fruit

From Daphne Macias of Pelican Club, New Orleans, LA

Makes 24 small profiteroles; serves 8, 3 profiteroles per serving

Chef Daphne Macias adds pecans and fresh fruit to a classic French dessert: Cream puffs filled with ice cream and topped with chocolate sauce.

Pâte à Choux
1/2 cup milk
1/2 cup water
1/2 cup (1 stick) butter
1 cup all-purpose flour
2 tablespoons sugar
4 eggs

Chocolate Sauce
2 cups heavy (whipping) cream
1 cup packed brown sugar
1 pound chocolate, chopped

Vanilla ice cream
2 tablespoons ground pecans
Mixed fresh blackberries, raspberries, and sliced hulled strawberries

To make the pâte a choux: Preheat oven to 400°F. Line 2 baking sheets with baking parchment. Place the milk, water, and butter in a medium saucepan and bring to a boil over medium-high heat. Add the flour and sugar all at once and stir the mixture until it forms a ball and comes away from the side of the pan, about 2 or 3 minutes. Add the eggs one at a time; stirring until each is blended. Remove from heat and let stand 5 minutes. Place the mixture in a pastry bag with a 1-inch plain tip. Pipe 24 portions

Pecan Profiteroles with Vanilla Ice Cream, Chocolate Sauce, and Seasonal Fruit, Daphne Macias, Pelican Club

2 inches apart on the prepared pans. Bake for 10 minutes, then reduce heat to 350°F and bake for 10 to 15 minutes, or until light brown.

To make the sauce: Combine the heavy cream and brown sugar in a medium saucepan. Bring to boil over medium-high heat and turn off the heat. Stir in the chocolate pieces until melted and blended; keep warm.

Using a 2-ounce ice cream scoop, make 24 scoops of ice cream and place them on a waxed, paper-lined tray. Place in the freezer.

To serve: Cut the profiteroles in half crosswise. Fill each with a scoop of ice cream and cover with the top. Serve 3 profiteroles per serving. Ladle 1 tablespoon chocolate sauce over each profiterole. Garnish with pecans and fresh fruit.∎

DAPHNE MACIAS
Pelican Club, New Orleans

When Daphne Macias does dessert at the Pelican Club, it tastes as good as it looks—and that's a tall order because, according to her, "proper presentation will enhance all foods."

Macias was just 26 when Great Chefs taped her in the kitchens of the Pelican Club preparing her interpretation of the classic French miniature cream puffs, Pecan Profiteroles with Vanilla Ice Cream, Chocolate Sauce, and Seasonal Fruit. At that time she had already logged 12 years working in the restaurant industry.

By the time Macias attended The Culinary Institute of America in Hyde Park, New York, she had already worked for four years as a cook in a New England restaurant-tavern, where she also tended bar, and at an Italian restaurant. While she was attending the Culinary Institute she worked at Charlie's Crab in Palm Beach, Fla., and at the Old Forge Spirits and Pub in New Jersey. After graduating from the Culinary Institute in 1987, she became head night line cook at Doral Saturnia International Spa Resort in Miami for two years. The Doral is known for its focus on light and healthful fare that is flavorful and beautifully presented.

Macias' next position was as line cook at Silverado Cafe in Davie, Florida, where she worked until relocating to New Orleans and joining the culinary crew at the Pelican Club.

When Macias makes the Pecan Profiteroles, she stuffs them with housemade ice cream; however, for the home cook, good quality commercial ice cream will fill the bill. She suggests garnishing with fruits at the peak of seasonal ripeness and flavor.

Menus For Entertaining

There are signs that—even in today's fast-paced world—home cooking is return-ing to favor. Television cooking shows are more numerous and more popular than ever, The major magazines devoted to food, wine and entertaining are being joined by newer magazines that target some specialized niche, such as light cooking, vegetarian cooking, and advanced techniques for serious cooks. And new cookbooks are being published every year, many written by professional chefs for the home cook.

However, home cooking has undergone a change from decades past when full-time homemakers prepared dinners—and sometimes breakfasts—daily. Today, cooking during the week necessarily tends to be quicker and simpler. Cooking for fun—and usually for company—lends itself to weekends. And just as we all go to restaurants as much for entertainment value as food, today's cooks often cook together, turning food preparation into part of the evening's entertainment.

Contrary to the adage that too many cooks spoil the broth, the more cooks the merrier, and the more dishes they can cook in the same period of time—provided they have learned *mis en place. Mis en place* is French for "to put in place," or to assemble in advance everything that will be needed for a recipe. It seems so basic; however, many cooks waste countless steps and minutes pulling out ingredients as needed while cook-ing. *Mis en place* is more than just assembling ingredients on a tray before cooking. It is also, according to Ferdinand Metz in *The New Professional Chef* (1991, Van Nostrand Reinhold, New York), "a state of mind. Someone who has truly grasped the concept is able to keep many tasks in mind simultaneously, weighing and assigning each its proper value and priority." For the home cook this means planning a menu in advance with an eye toward time and labor, reading the recipes through, making a list of ingredients, shopping, and cooking ahead where possible.

The following menus were created by Emeril Lagasse, chef-proprietor of Emeril's and NOLA in New Orleans. He has expertly balanced the courses with flavor, texture, color and progression in mind. Be sure to round out the menus with salads or simple vegetable courses, and starches when necessary, such as bread, rice pilaf, or oven-roast-ed potatoes. In menus where the entrée seems complex or labor-intensive, feel free to simplify by substituting a simple salad for the appetizer and an easy dessert for a more complicated one.

Note: Most of the recipes in this book serve from four to eight, allowing the home cook to double, halve, or count on leftovers depending on the number of invited guests. In several menus, chef Lagasse has proposed two or three appetizers, revealing his penchant for tantalizing first courses. (His own menus are loaded with them!) In such cases, choose two appetizers and prepare each to serve four.

Roast Duck with Hunter's Sauce,
Randy Barlow, Kelsey's

A Louisiana Thanksgiving Dinner

And now for something completely different to surprise and delight family and friends on what has been dubbed "turkey day." This Thanksgiving menu has no turkey, but it is a bona fide feast, starting with oysters and crab meat-topped eggplant, proceeding to roast duck with wild rice, and ending with a festive flaming banana bread pudding.

Appetizers: Oysters Gabie, page 40
            Pan-fried Eggplant with Crab Meat,
              Basil Hollandaise, and Creole Tomato Sauce, page 20
Entrée: Roast Duck with Hunter's Sauce, page 78
Dessert: Banana Bread Pudding with Banana Rum Sauce and Whipped Cream, page 111

Christmas Louisiana-Style

Christmas dinner is a family meal and one, I'm sure, that many professional chefs would like to see take place in the home. (That way they could have Christmas dinner at home as well.) But although traditional Christmas dinners are rich in food and spirit, they are often poor in imagination. The following dinner is packed with both from beginning to end.

Appetizers: Crawfish Spring Rolls with Three-chili Dipping Sauce, page 30
            Shrimp and Andouille Cheesecake with Creole Mustard-Tomato
              Coulis, page 32
Entrée: Chili-rubbed Pork Tenderloin with Savory Wild
              Mushroom Bread Pudding, page 94
Dessert: Pecan Profiteroles with Vanilla Ice Cream, Chocolate
              Sauce and Seasonal Fruit, page 130

New Year's Eve Gala Dinner

With this menu chef Lagasse proves he knows how to ring out the old and ring in the new. There are several opportunities for advance preparation in this menu, and many of the components for each course may be cooked ahead of time and finished or assembled right before serving. The rack of lamb—what a classic entrée!—is simply roasted and beautifully sauced.

Appetizers: Grilled Shrimp with Coriander Sauce, and Black Bean Cakes, page 36
            Potato Cake with Creamed Leeks and Escargots, page 23
Entrée: Rack of Lamb with Apricot Sauce, page 94
Dessert: Terrine of White Chocolate and Praline, with Coconut Tile
              Cookies and Caramel Sauce, page 118

New Year's Eve Buffet

Nothing is sweeter for a host than to create a great party spread and let people serve themselves while the host enjoys the party, too. Many of the dishes for this New Year's Eve buffet may be served at room temperature. For those dishes that need to be served hot like the bisque and the bouillabaisse, use a chafing dish or food warmer. Set up the dessert buffet separately and have the midnight bottles of Champagne ready to pop. Happy New Year!

Appetizers: Quail Salad with Pâté, Baby Greens, Roquefort Cheese,
            and Caramelized Shallots with Sherry Vinaigrette, page 17
            Louisiana Corn and Crab Bisque, page 14
Entrées: Cajun Smothered Duck, page 79
            or Roast Leg of Duckling with Spring Leeks, and New Potatoes, page 76
            Tuna with Japanese Noodles and Soy Dipping Sauce, page 68
            Creole Bouillabaisse, page 50
Desserts: Apple Strudel, page 106
            Chocolate-laced Praline Shells with Berries and Amaretto Cream, page 119
            Crème Brûlée, page 121

Jazz Brunch

New Orleans is famous for its Jazz Brunch, created by Ella and Dick Brennan at Commander's Palace, where every Sunday the music plays, the wine and special cocktails flow, and spirits soar. You can recreate your own special brunch with the following menu, which begins and ends with cheesecake (as different as night and day). Don't forget to put some great jazz on the stereo and don't neglect the special New Orleans drink recipes in Chapter VI, "Food and Drink."

Crawfish Cakes with Lemon Butter Sauce, Dick Brennan, Jr., Palace Café, New orleans, LA

Appetizers: Crawfish Cakes with Lemon Butter Sauce, page 35
Shrimp and Andouille Cheesecake with Creole Mustard
   Tomato Coulis, page 32
Oyster and Eggplant Ravioli, page 27
Entrées: Painted Pasta Ribbons with Louisiana Soft-shell Crab,
   and Roasted Poblano-Ginger Beurre Blanc, page 52
Louisiana Crab and Vegetable Hash with Vanilla
   Bean Sabayon, page 69
Tournedos Louis Armstrong, page 82
Dessert: Creole Cream Cheese Cheesecake with Caramel Sauce, page 113

A Cocktail Party

When some folk throw a cocktail party, the menu is salted nuts, or cheese and olives. When Chef Lagasse throws a cocktail party, he likes to feed his guests. This buffet offers nibbles and tastes for everyone and doesn't neglect those with a sweet tooth. You can omit the vegetable accompaniments in the Grouper Iberville if you prefer and cut the fillets into bite-size chunks, which will hold their shape in the Creole Sauce. Slice the dessert Pear Tarte Tatin into thinner wedges than you would for a regular dinner party. The NOLA Vegetable Terrine may be sliced, the slices halved, and presented on a large platter. The same arrangement will be nice for the fried asparagus and the goat's cheese in filo. Pass the platters, and serve the rest buffet style with lots of napkins, small plates and flatware for frequent tasting. We guarantee that you'll be remembered for this cocktail spread!

Beer-fried Asparagus with Crab Meat and Crawfish in
   Creole Mustard-Honey Butter, page 18
NOLA Vegetable Terrine, page 23
Goat Cheese in Filo Provençal, page 35
Maw Maw's Chicken Stew, page 73
Grouper Iberville, page 54
Pear Tarte Tatin, page 125

A Vegetarian Dinner

Chef Lagasse says that the requests for non-meat courses is on the rise at Emeril's and NOLA in New Orleans. Here he proposes his vegetarian dinner menu; however, these vegetarians do eat dairy products. (Simply omit the prosciutto from one risotto recipe, and cook with half-water, half-white wine in place of the chicken stock.)
These vegetarians are lucky indeed—they get two desserts!

Appetizers: Artichoke and Hearts of Palm Salad, page 15
Asparagus with Tomato Basil-Coulis, page 17
Entrée: Risotto Mille e Una Notte, page 53
or Smoked Tomato and Shiitake Mushroom Risotto, page 89
Desserts: Sour Cream Pound Cake with Lemon Crème Sauce, page 124
Rosemary Scones with Fresh Berries and Grand Marnier
   Cream, page 108

An Informal Sit-down Dinner

Ever get the urge just to have a bunch of your favorite people over for fun, without formality and too much fuss? Here's the perfect menu.

Be sure to have lots of French bread on hand for the barbecued shrimp (along with napkins for fingers and bowls for shrimp shells). Some bottles of Dixie beer wouldn't hurt either. The chicken roulade entrée is complete on one plate with vegetables and stuffing. Feel free to use seasonal vegetables of your choice; no need to rob the cradle for baby vegetables. You could also offer guests an alternative of salmon, which is quickly cooked to order. And for dessert, do double chocolate; but do omit all the frills and garnishes on the chocolate desserts. Serve the mousse simply in a parfait glass without its mask, but offer a plate of your local bakery's best butter cookies. And serve the chocolate pâté on a white plate with a sliced, fanned ripe strawberry and a dollop of whipped cream.

Appetizer:	New Orleans Barbecued Shrimp, page 39
Entrées:	Chicken Roulades with Andouille and Cornbread Stuffing, Baby Vegetables, and Roasted Garlic Sauce, page 70
	Caramelized Salmon, with Mirliton Slaw, page 57
Desserts:	Chocolate Pâté, page 117
	Chocolate Mousse with Harlequin Cookie Mask, 114

Louisiana Lovers' Supper

Louisiana men and women share the French reputation for being amorous. Is it true? Try this menu on Valentine's day—or for that matter any other day of the year—and see.

Appetizers:	Sea Scallops with Roasted Red Pepper Sauce, page 43
	Sautéed Oysters with Sweet Potatoes, page 42
Entrée:	Sautéed Duck Breast with Gingered Fig Sauce, Braised Fennel, and Celeriac-Potato Timbale, page 74
Desserts:	Chocolate Mousse Cake with Strawberry Sauce, page 115
	Three-berry Tart with Vanilla Cream, 110

A Dinner to Cook with Friends

With everybody working long and hard today, it's increasingly popular to have friends over to cook and, of course, eat. Chef Lagasse says that on his day off he and his wife Tari do exactly that. So stock the larder, invite your friends and cook up a good old time with the following menu. If your kitchen is small, choose just one of the entrées. And if you want to be a good egg you can make the cookies and the Coconut Pots de Crèmes in advance. Also the Caponata. And don't expect everyone to wait until they sit down to eat the quesadillas. Ten-to-one they'll be gone as soon as they're plated.

Appetizer:	Pecan Wood-smoked Shrimp Quesadillas, page 31
Entrées:	Grilled Cornish Hen with Voodoo Barbecue Sauce, page 74
	or Grilled Baby Wild Boar T-Bones, page 98
	or Grilled Veal Chops with Caponata, page 84
Dessert:	Asian Napoleon, page 108,
	or Coconut Pots de Crèmes, page 122

Coconut Pots de Crèmes with Coconut-Almond Snaps, Ann Dunbar, NOLA

Food and Drink

by Daniel R. Mann

During the last ten years we have experienced a wine revolution in this country, not so much in the making of wines as in the acceptance of and demand for them. We are more at ease with the language used to describe wines and with what wine represents. The experience of combining wine with food has reached a similar plateau.

Several factors contributed to our present appreciation of food and wine as a total experience, not the least of which was the explosion of new culinary trends in the seventies and eighties: New restaurants popped up like mushrooms, the Culinary Institute of America became famous for the quality of its education and chef-graduates, and dining out became both a way of doing business and a style of entertaining. We no longer went out just to eat. The eighties and nineties have introduced us to a variety of global culinary influences: Asian and other ethnic cuisines, a new palette of spices, a larder of exotic ingredients. This high intensity of taste and food presentation have led us into higher expectations and greater knowledge of wines.

A mere twenty years ago, ninety percent of American wines were generic Chardonnay. Chardonnay has been the great bridge to wines in America. Of course, Americans traveling to Europe, where they experienced a general acceptance and wide variety of wines, helped speed the process. But twenty years ago, red wine was still too complex. Wine needed to be cold and pale, hence the proliferation of Chardonnay. Then in the early eighties, there was a boom of boutique wineries that concentrated heavily on Chardonnays. No longer generic wines, Chardonnays became complex, big, fat, buttery, and oaky. Wineries worked to achieve that style in the eighties.

Robert Mondavi deserves a lot of credit for introducing Americans to good red wines at a tolerable price. Sometime in the early eighties he made a Cabernet Sauvignon that was well made without being horribly expensive. Next, he made a reserve, which let us know that different qualities and levels exist in wine. Mondavi was instrumental in making the American public comfortable with the next step in wines. Other wineries began their own production and releases of red wines, mostly Cabernets. And just as Chardonnay had been a bridge, now Cabernets became a bridge to the acceptance and appreciation of red wines in America. After the Cabernets, Pinot Noirs became more visible. And, as Americans started to become familiar enough with grape varieties, varietals became part of dinner-table conversation. This all happened in a very short time. Also in the eighties, people wanted to have a little wine cellar of their own, and today almost everyone has some bottles of wine at home.

By the time the nineties arrived, we felt comfortable with the taste, use, and general terminology of wines, and we knew the names of most of the varietals. Wineries began to make more white varietals, such as Sauvignon Blanc, Fumé Blanc, and the Cabernets (just like the Chardonnays before them) entered their second phase. Every winemaker wanted to make the "great" Cabernet. But in the beginning Cabernets were 100 percent Cabernet, a wine that requires aging, a wine that is not ready to drink. The public, however, wanted to buy wine and drink it, not buy wine and store it. Our impatience (a pronounced national character trait) led to the bottling of a more readily drinkable red varietal, Merlot. Merlot is a wine that allows us to demonstrate a certain level of expertise and yet is instantly enjoyable.

After that, many vineyards saw a new way to market Cabernet grapes by blending Cabernet with Merlot and Cabernet Franc grapes, producing a wine that has longevity and drinkability without sacrificing quality. The majority of today's Caberenets are Merlot blends. Today, of course, we produce numerous wines of national and international repute. And these have made Americans confident with what is wine.

When it comes to matching food and wine there are some general principles, of course, but the goal is for the two to complement each other. We need to focus on the dominant ingredient in the food and complement it with wines that will be able to complement the strongest flavor note but not overpower the more delicate flavors of a dish. Wine offers the same wide range of consistency and flavors as food, and the real gift lies in making each one better with the proper combination.

Every city has good retail wine houses with wonderful selections and great service personnel who are willing to help you. Let them know what you want to spend, the nature of your menu, and ask for some recommendations. You will find that your palate will change as your knowledge increases.

In choosing the wines to match the specific recipes in this cookbook, there is no exact science for the perfect choice. One tries to complement the ingredients of the recipe with the flavors and aromas most pleasing to the individual. Acidity, tannins, maturity, and balance are some of the characteristics I look for in my recommendations.

I believe that with today's extraordinary level of wine making, hundreds of choices could be selected for each dish.

Our list at Windsor Court has almost six hundred selections from around the world, making only an humble representation from the tens of thousands available. Individual likings as they relate to origins play a great role in matching wine and food. Do you prefer Burgundies to Bordeaux, whites over reds, dislike tannins in wine? Are you interested in experiencing new trends and tastes from Australia, Chile, the United States?

I found myself asking these questions above all others: Which country to select from? What grape variety would be good? Which age could be important? How soft or tannic should the wine be? And, will you enjoy my tastes and choices? Difficulties and decisions notwithstanding, I have made some quick choices for wine matches with some of the appetizers, entrées and desserts created by Louisiana chefs. The first few are accompanied by comments to show the process that went into making the wine selections.

DANIEL R. MANN
Manager
Windsor Court Hotel, New Orleans

Daniel R. Mann says he is as comfortable in a hotel as he is at home, "because I never saw the difference." His international career began in a family hotel in Wiesbaden, Germany, where he worked both front and back of the house: kitchen, pastry, front desk and reservations. In Europe his career took him to some of the world's most prestigious restaurants and hotels. He received his education in both Germany and Switzerland and speaks fluent English, German and French.

Prior to joining the Windsor Court in 1993, Mann was associated with other American luxury properties including the Four Seasons Hotel in Philadelphia; The Pierre Hotel, New York; Hotel Du Pont, Wilmington, Delaware, the Fairmont Hotel, New Orleans, and the Ritz-Carlton, Cleveland, Ohio.

Despite his classical European food-and-wine training, he is enthusiastic about American foods and wines. He has personally selected recipes from *the Louisana's new Garde* to match with wines. We think you will find his recommendations, which follow, both instructive and exciting.

APPETIZERS

Pan-fried Eggplant Topped with Crab Meat, Basil Hollandaise, and Creole Tomato Sauce:

When reading this recipe I first thought of Italy—the eggplant, basil, and tomato. This made me want to experience a refreshing yet not too complex white wine from Italy.

1990 Greco di Tufo, Masterberardino (Campania)

Quail Salad with Pâté, Baby Greens, Roquefort Cheese, and Caramelized Shallots and Sherry Vinaigrette:

This appetizer has a variety of game, cheeses, and other spices as well as the challenge of a vinaigrette. I reach straight for the Pinot Noir, in this case a relatively new addition to the United States.

1989 Domaine Drouhin, Pinot Noir, Joseph Drouhin

Clancy's Quail:

This dish is rich in flavor with a hint of sweetbreads. It is delicate, yet needs a wine that can stand up to the smoked quails while not overpowering the foie gras.

1990 Grgich Hills Chardonnay, Napa Valley

Grilled Shrimp with Coriander Sauce, and Black Bean Cakes:

This dish has a flair of the Southwest with its spices of cumin, coriander, and cilantro. Two Alsatian wines came to mind.

1985 Riesling, Brand, Zind-Humbrecht
1989 Gewürztraminer, Cuvee Theo, Domaine Weinbach

ENTRÉES

Filet Mignon with Shiitake Mushrooms and Cabernet Sauce, and Garlic Mashed Potatoes with Roasted Onion:

We need a soft yet big wine to stand up to this classic filet presentation.

1988 Chateau Cos d'Estournel, St.-Estèphe

Dover Sole Medusa:

This fish should allow for a choice of better wine. Because sole is a delicate, soft-flavored fish, we must be careful not to overwhelm it with oak or acids.

1989 Mersault-Charmes, Drouhin, Côte de Beaune

Garlic-crusted Trout with Sweet Pepper and Shrimp Sauce:

As the trout is crusted in spiced bread crumbs, then sautéed, a dry, full-bodied wine from California would suit it best.

1990 Sonoma-Cutrer, Les Pierres Vineyards, Chardonnay, Sonoma

Veal Chops with Roasted New Potatoes and Escarole:

This dish is prepared relatively lightly and should be paired wih a similarly light wine, with enough depth to match the veal.

1987 Acadia, Pinot Noir, Carneros

Crawfish-stuffed Loin of Lamb with Wild Mushroom Sauce
1982 Ridge Zinfandel, Geyserville!

Blackened Yellowfin Tuna with Roasted Vegetable Salsa, and Smoked Corn Sauce
1990 Pouilly-Fumé, Domaine Dagueneau

Tournedos Louis Armstrong
1987 Sassicaia, Tenuta San Guido, Marchese di Riccetti

Scaloppine of Chicken with Stir-fried Vegetables
1990 Matanzas Creek Chardonnay, Sonoma Valley

Grouper Iberville
1989 Chassagne-Montrachet, Latour, Côte de Beaune

Pan-roasted Snapper with Crab Meat, Roasted Garlic, and Sun-dried Tomato Butter
1989 Chablis Grand Cru, La Moutonne, Domaine A. Long-Depaquit

DESERTS

Terrine of White Chocolate and Praline, with Coconut Tile Cookies and Caramel Sauce
1989 Dolce, Far Niente, California Late Harvest Wine

Gratin of Berries with Sweet Marsala Sabayon
1992 Bonny Doon Muscat Canelli Vin de Glaciére, Santa Cruz Late-Harvest Wine

Créme Brûlée
1988 Chateau Suduiraut, Sauternes

Pecan Profiteroles with Vanilla Ice Cream, Chocolate Sauce and Seasonal Fruit
1990 Muscat de Beaumes de Venise, Domaine du Durban, Rhône

Three-berry Tart with Vanilla Cream
1983 Deidesheimer Herrgottsacker Riesling Eiswein, Wegeler-Deinhard

CLASSIC NEW ORLEANS COCKTAILS

Traditionally, New Orleans has been famous for its cocktails, and no book about Louisiana cookery would be complete without some classic cocktail recipes. These follow, courtesy Windsor Court's mixologist Tony Scott.

Note: All the cocktails below serve one. The standard bartender's jigger holds 1 ounce.

Cajun Bloody Mary

1-1/2 ounces vodka
3 ounces V-8 or tomato juice
1 dash steak sauce
1 dash Worcestershire sauce
1 teaspoon low-salt canned beef bouillon
1 teaspoon horseradish
2 dashes Tabasco or other hot pepper sauce
1/2 teaspoon black pepper
1/2 teaspoon celery salt

Combine all the ingredients in mixer and shake well. Serve over ice in an old-fashioned glass. Garnish with slice of lime and pickled okra or pickled green bean.

Mint Julep

1-1/2 ounces bourbon
6 fresh mint leaves
3 tablespoons simple syrup (recipe follows)

Combine simple syrup and mint leaves in bottom of an old-fashioned glass. Use a muddler (a bartender's tool that resembles a pestle) or a wooden pestle to crush leaves. Add ice cubes or crushed ice. Add the bourbon and stir.

Simple Syrup

1 cup sugar
2 cups water

In a medium saucepan, combine 1 cup sugar and 2 cups water. Bring to a boil, stirring. Reduce heat and simmer 5 to 10 minutes. Cool and store in a covered jar in the refrigerator.

Sazerac

Dash Herbsaint or Pernod
1-1/2 ounces rye whiskey
2 dashes Peychaud bitters
1 tablespoon simple syrup
1 lemon twist

Swirl a martini or Champagne glass with Herbsaint or Pernod, then pour out the excess. Pour the rye, bitters and simple syrup into a shaker with ice cubes. Shake well to mix. Strain the ingredients into glass. Garnish with a twist of lemon.

Mimosa

1 ounce fresh orange juice
4 ounces your favorite Champagne
Stir to combine. Pour into chilled Champagne glasses.

Brandy Milk Punch

1-1/2 ounces brandy
1 tablespoon Créme de Cacao
3 ounces half-and-half

Combine all of the ingredients in cocktail shaker half-filled with ice cubes and shake well. Strain and serve (with or without ice) in an old-fashioned glass.

Glossary:

Barely ten years ago, anyone writing a glossary of special ingredients for a Louisiana cookbook would have had a fairly simple task. There would be andouille, crab meat, crawfish, Creole tomatoes, Creole cream cheese, gumbo filé, mirliton, tasso—and perhaps a few additional local specialties such as Peychaud bitters.

How times—and Louisiana chefs—have changed. Today the world is their marketplace and their recipes combine ethnic and local ingredients in ways that were undreamed of a decade ago. The traditional larder of Louisiana ingredients has been enriched by exotic mushrooms, Asian spices, boutique lettuces, Southwestern chili peppers, Italian olive oil, and new ingredients are still being added.

This glossary lists and describes both traditional Louisiana foodstuffs and special ingredients called for in the recipes.

Helter Skelter Parfait, Shane Gorringe, Windsor Court Hotel

andouille sausage:
Spicy, smoked pork sausage, a Cajun specialty.

arborio rice:
Imported Italian rice with a short, fat grain and high starch content that makes it ideal for risotto.

arrowroot:
Made from a tropical tuber with the same name, arrowroot is used in cooking as a thickener. When cooked it is transparent and tasteless. It has twice the thickening power of flour.

celeriac (celery root):
Available September through May, celeriac is a brown, gnarled root prized for its flavor, which is more intense than celery. It should be placed in acidulated water after peeling to prevent discoloration. It can be eaten raw in salads, or braised, sautéed or boiled and puréed. Store, wrapped in plastic, in the refrigerator for seven to ten days.

chanterelle mushrooms:
Wild mushroom imported from France and also found in the East and Pacific Northwest coasts. Chanterelles are prized for their nutty, apricot-like flavor. Fresh chanterelles can be found in markets specializing in fine produce. Dried and canned chanterelles are also available.

couscous:
Couscous, a granular semolina, is to North African cuisine what rice is to Asian, and potatoes are to European, cuisines. It is traditionally cooked in the upper part of a couscoussière, over a stew of meat or vegetables. Traditional preparation, labor-intensive, requires a two-step steaming and rubbing process. Precooked couscous is widely available in supermarkets and markets specializing in Middle Eastern food.

crab meat:
The crab meat called for in the recipes in this book is lump crab meat from the blue crab. Lump meat distinguishes the large pieces of white body meat from flaked crab meat, or small pieces of dark and white body meat from the body and claws. Crab meat is sold fresh, frozen, pasteurized, and canned.

crawfish:
These fresh-water crustaceans resemble little lobsters and are sold fresh and frozen, whole and raw, or whole and cooked. Tails are also sold blanched and peeled, and blanched, peeled, and frozen.

creole cream cheese:
A Louisiana specialty that has the texture of very thick sour cream. Ricotta may be substituted.

creole mustard:
German settlers on Louisiana created this hot, spicy brown mustard enlivened with horseradish. It is available in some supermarkets.

creole tomatoes:
Grown in Louisiana in reclaimed Mississippi River Delta land where the soil has a higher salt content, these tomatoes are prized for their sweet flavor and firm texture. Because they are not widely available, substitute vine-ripened locally grown tomatoes.

creole holy trinity:
Green peppers, onions, and celery are called the holy trinity of Creole cuisine because they form the basis for so many dishes from jambalayas and gumbos to Creole sauces and seafood dishes.

filé powder:
Ground dried sassafras leaves used to thicken gumbos. It was originally used by the Native American Choctaws in Louisiana and adopted by Cajuns and Creoles. Add filé to the cooked dish after it is removed from the heat, because prolonged cooking makes it tough and stringy.

herbsaint:
A popular New Orleans licorice-flavored liqueur. Pernod may be substituted.

ketjap manis:
A sweet, thick, dark soy sauce from Indonesia used as both seasoning and condiment, often used with satay. It is available in Asian food markets.

mirliton (chayote):
Originally a staple of the Mayas and the Aztecs, this pear-shaped gourd with pale green furrowed skin is grown in the States in California, Florida and Louisiana. Widely available in supermarkets, mirliton may be stored, wrapped in plastic, in the refrigerator for up to 30 days. It can be boiled, sautéed, baked and stuffed, or used raw in salads.

oyster mushrooms:
The oyster mushroom is now widely cultivated. Shaped like a fan, it ranges in color from pale to dark brownish gray. It is prized for its mild flavor once cooked (tasted raw, it is peppery), and for its firm texture.

peychaud bitters:
Originally created by New Orleans apothecary Antoine Amadée Peychaud from a secret family recipe, this unique-tasting bitters is an ingredient in many Louisiana cocktails.

poblano peppers:
A dark green chili pepper, about three inches wide and five inches long, poblanos are widely available fresh in U.S. supermarkets, and are also sold canned. They are the chili used in chiles rellenos. In their dried form, they are known as ancho peppers.

porcini mushrooms (cèpes):
Crowned by culinary concensus as the king of mushrooms, porcinis (as they are known in Italy), are prized for their earthy, woodsy flavor and meaty texture. It is possible to find them fresh in fancy food markets in spring and fall; however, they are most widely available dried. Dried porcini should be soaked in hot water for about thirty minutes before using.

seafood seasoning:
Mixed, dried herbs and spices for seafood sold under several brand names and widely available in supermarkets.

shiitake mushrooms:
Although they originated in Japan and Korea, shiitake mushrooms are now cultivated in the United States. They have a meaty flavor and texture and average from three to six inches in diameter. Widely available year round both fresh and dried, the fresh ones tend to be expensive. They are most plentiful in spring and fall.

soba noodles:
Japanese buckwheat flour noodle available in Asian food markets.

soft-shell crabs:
When the crab sheds its old shell in order to grow, there is a period of a few days before the new shell hardens. Crabs are harvested during that time when the new shell is tissue thin and edible. The crab most commonly harvested for consumption as soft-shell crab in the United States is the blue crab.

somen:
Japanese eggless wheat noodles made from flour, salt and water. They are very white in color because of the absence of egg yolk.

tasso:
Highly spiced, heavily smoked ham, a Cajun specialty.

wild leeks (ramps):
A wild onion that grows from Maine to California. It is known for its strong flavor, a cross between onion and garlic, and can be found in specialty produce markets in spring and early summer.

Great Chefs®
the Louisiana new Garde

Book Production

Publisher	Great Chefs Publishing
Proprietors	GSI, Inc.
Editorial and Production Services	Mimi Luebbermann
Book Design	Larry Escudier Dwain Richard, Jr.
Writer *Recipe Development*	Nancy Ross Ryan with Chan Patterson
Photography	Eric Futran
Sales and Marketing	Charles Flood
Public Relations	Linda Anne Nix Brown & Whiting

Television Production

Presenter	Mary Lou Conroy
Narrator	Andres Calandria
Camera / Lighting	Dave Landry Paul Combel
Field Audio	Charles C. Sainz

Culinary Advisor	Chan Patterson
Post Production Audio	Andres Calandria
Assistant Editor	Maria D. Estevez
Editor	George Matulik
Graphics Design	Escudier & Richard
Computer Animation	Imagetech
Recording Studio	Ultrasonics
Public Relations	Brown & Whiting Linda Anne Nix
Official Hotel	Hotel Provincial New Orleans
Theme Music	Bela Fleck & The Flecktones
Original Music	CHARLIE BYRD TRIO Charlie Byrd Jeff Meyerriecks Rick Whitehead
Production Assistant	Angela Balius
Assistant to the *Exective Producer*	Cybil W. Curtis
Assistant Producer	Charles C. Sainz
Producer/Director/Writer	John Beyer
Executive Producer	John Shoup

INDEX

NOTES